HOW TO TALK SO PEOPLE LISTEN

The real key to job success

Sonya Hamlin

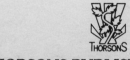

THORSONS

THORSONS PUBLISHING GROUP

First published 1988 by Harper and Row, New York.
This UK edition published 1989.

British Library Cataloguing in Publication Data

Hamlin, Sonya
How to talk so people listen.
1. Business firms. Management.
Communication, — Manuals
I. Title
658.4'5

ISBN 0-7225-1991-5

Published by Thorsons Publishers Limited,
Wellingborough, Northamptonshire NN8 2RQ

Typeset by Harper Phototypesetters Limited, Northampton
Printed in Great Britain by Mackays of Chatham, Kent

1 3 5 7 9 10 8 6 4 2

To my friends:

T.A.W.; C.H.; A.P.; J.N.; N.L.G.; M.D.A.;
E.A.C.; K.V.; I.M.; N.N.; H.S.

The ones who, unlike your family, don't have to let you in when you knock, but by voluntarily reaching for your hand tell you that you are indeed loved and supported.

Contents

1 • WHAT'S THE PROBLEM? Why we don't communicate well in the workplace   17

What this book is about   18
   How do I know?   19

Why we have such a hard time communicating   20
   Where it begins   21
   How it develops   22
   What we want   23

What motivates work   24
   Status   24
   Usefulness   25
   Affection/acceptance   25
   Money/security   26

Our public image   28
   What works, what doesn't and why   28
   What we already know   29

Basic work personalities   30
   Achievers   31
   Affiliators   32
   Influencers   32
   Using the work types   35
   A predominance of achievers   35

2 • THE BASICS OF COMMUNICATING: Why and how people listen 37

    Speaking and listening 37
        The one-sided nature of speaking 37
        Listening is work 38
        Motivation 38

    What makes people listen 39
        Self interest 39
        Who's speaking 41
        How they tell it 47

    The new techniques of telling 50
        Basic techniques of television communication 50
        Communication consequences of TV 52
        Implications for business communication 56

    Verbal vs. non-verbal communication 57
        How we communicate 57

    Common obstacles to communications 60
        How people feel about learning 60
        Language 62

3 • GETTING READY TO COMMUNICATE: Forethought for strategies 65

    Developing strategies 65
        What goes wrong and why 65
        Where we get stuck 68

    Forethought 69
        Who is your audience? 69
        What you know, what you need 70

    The forethought chart 73
        The basic idea 73
        The process 74
        Objective goals 75
        Emotional needs 78
        Probable expectations 84
        A chart for the summoned 91

    Forethought check-list 92
        Forethought for larger audiences 93

4 • STRUCTURING AND ORGANIZING BUSINESS ENCOUNTERS 95

Preparation 95
Choose and edit your goals 96

Scheduling the meeting 98
When to meet 98
Which day 101
Where to meet 102
To lunch or not to lunch 106
Breakfast meetings 107

Getting on the calendar 108
Techniques 108

5 • DESIGNING PRESENTATIONS: What captures attention and understanding 113

Guidelines for designing presentations 114
How we think 114
What we need so we understand and stay interested 115

Structuring a presentation 121
Outline form 121
Order of presentation 121
Checklist 126

Making messages visual 127
Why use visual reinforcement 127
What to show; what to tell 128
'Leave-behinds' 129

Designing visual materials 131
Basic guidelines 131
Techniques for using visual aids 135

6 • CLOSE ENCOUNTERS: One-to-one 137

Openers 137
Before you begin 138
Change gears 138
Warm-up 138
Small talk 139
Where to sit 141

Amenities 142
Body language 143

Substance 144
Up front: agenda, goals, time 144
Sharing the power 145
Motivation 147
Telling and explaining 147
Discussion 148

Special issues 150
Creative criticism 150
Getting at the truth 152
Handling anger — yours and his/hers 154

Closure 156
Recap and clarify 156
List next steps 157
Follow-up 157
End on a high note 157

Checklist 158

7 • PRESENTATIONS: How to make memorable
speeches 161

Understanding audiences 161
How audiences feel 161

Planning your presentation 164
Profile your audience 164
Why are they coming 166
Physical realities 168

Designing your presentation 170
Positioning the speech 170
Basic organization of a speech 172

Should you write it? 174
Written vs. oral speeches 174
The effect of written speeches on the audience 176
The effects on you, the speaker 176
For addicted speechwriters 177
For extemporizers 178

Making usable notes and outlines   178
   The basic process   179

Techniques for delivering memorable speeches   184
   Attention-getting openings   184
   Audience involvement   188
   Presenting subject matter   191
   Endings   194

Personal style   195
   Being yourself   195
   How you feel toward your audience   196
   Stage fright   197
   Getting started   199
   The lectern or podium   201

Speaking and language skills   202
   Making language clear   202
   Analogies   203
   Use words visually   203
   Emphasize   204
   The use of silence   204

A postscript   205
   The never-make-a-speech-without-it checklist   205

8 • THE ART OF BEING QUESTIONED: The audience or the boss vs. you   209

Basic principles of answering questions   209
   The questioning process   209
   Conditioning   210
   How we answer questions   210

The audience vs. you: answering audience questions   212
   Why answer questions?   212
   Preparation for Q & A   214

Answering techniques   217
   Getting started   217
   Handling questions   220
   Handling difficult questions and questioners   222
   Buying time   223
   Avoiding the question   224

Turning questions around   225
Cutting people off   226
Getting the audience on your side   226

Handling hostility   227
Why people get hostile   227
Techniques for handling hostility   229

The boss vs. you   233
The dynamics of power   233
How much room at the top?   233
Preparation   235

Basic techniques for answering   236
Answering informational questions   237
Answering critical questions   239
Role play and practice   242

9 • MEETINGS: Leading and participating effectively   245

What goes wrong and why   245
Factual issues   245
'Feeling' issues   247
Why meetings?   249
Comparison of what should be and what is   250

Basic personalities at meetings   251
Players in a group interaction   252
Interaction   255

Basic communication skills for meetings   256
Listening   256
Supporting   259
Disagreeing   262
Personal skills for leaders   263
Personal skills for meeting participants   266

Creating and leading effective meetings   269
Planning   269
Creating the agenda   270
Designing and implementing the meeting   272
Leadership techniques   273
Warm-ups   274
Openings   275

The body of the meeting   276
Assign visual charting   276
Closure   278

10 • THE LAST WORD

A personal note   281

Acknowledgements

Now that it's done, there's finally time to reflect on the process. No book ever grows full-bloom from the author's head. It has hands to help it along the way: phone calls for advice, critical notes written in margins by friends and colleagues, serious review by professionals and, most of all, the endless support of always available friends at the other end of those frantic, exhausted, end-of-my-tether calls for help.

Having already thanked my friends in the dedication, let me now turn to my professional colleagues. Thanks to the gifted business leader James D. Robinson III, chairman and chief executive officer of American Express and chairman of the New York City Partnership, who made room in his super-human schedule to read and criticize the chapters as they rolled out and feed back how they would fit the needs of business. Thanks also to James J. Walker, executive vice-president of CIGNA, to senior vice-presidents Ida Schmertz and Rennie Roberts and to American Express vice-president Kimberly Rupert for evaluating my theses against their own experience. Thanks to John Humphrey, chief executive officer of the Forum Corporation, for information he gave me long ago about meetings.

To business consultant Dr. Herbert Selesnick, whose Massachusetts Institute of Technology Sloan School training and critically analytical mind sifted every word I wrote and unrelentingly slashed away at the fuzzy passages and the Hamlin tendency to overwrite — thank you for your dedication and tenacity as well as your perception and knowledge. I look back on the various projects we've shared with pleasure.

Many thanks to Stephen Glasser, president of Prentice-Hall Law and Business, publisher of *What Makes Juries Listen*, for permission to quote from my material in that book.

To Larry Ashmead, executive editor of the Trade Department at Harper & Row, thank you for wanting the book and for your tremendous support and faith in it, and in me. Thanks to John Michel, editor and trouble-shooter, who dealt with the problems and the phone calls and husbanded the manuscript through the Scylla and Charybdis of publishing it. To Dan Harvey and his public relations team, Lisa Berkowitz and Scott Manning, thanks for all your enthusiasm and dedication to the book and your sensitivity to me. Thanks to Connie Clauson, my agent, for launching the book and and to Rita Marcus for getting the whole project started.

Finally, thanks to all the thousands of people I've taught. You've taught me more, and kept me humble and continually questioning in the process . . . .

1
What's the problem?
Why we don't communicate well in the workplace

Hello. I'm Sonya Hamlin.

How can a book about communicating begin from anywhere else, other than acknowledging the typical order by which we all make contact with each other? And then using it, step by step, with you?

How can I ask you to listen to me any further unless I first let you do the usual checking we all do before we start to trust and gather interest in a potential 'teller'?

If a stranger walked into your office and said, 'Change the way you report your fourth quarter results. I know a better way,' would you just do it? Surely not.

Well, you don't know me. Because we can't see each other — a sense that could give you the first fast layer of information — I'll have to unfold our relationship and go through the common order of developing trust through words alone.

Skipping the next order of natural business — the usual handshake, smile, and 'Pleased to meet you' rituals when strangers warily draw closer — I'll move directly to step three: What I have to tell and whether or not you'll 'listen'.

Listening doesn't happen automatically. It's based on how quickly I get to something you can use. You'll stay if I promise some new insights and alternative processes that could improve your life; some ideas that are important and practical enough for you to accept and want to try. Now — have we drawn closer? What have you learned so far?

- This is a rather unusual way to begin a book.
- She writes in a very personal, informal style (says 'you' and 'me' and 'I'll', not 'one' or 'they' or 'people').

- She asks me to think through an almost automatic process — getting acquainted — to find out *what else* is going on and *why* we do things a certain way.

- She organizes her material into visual as well as verbal explanations (the list of ● 'bullets' that visually tell you they'll explain further details of what was just said above).

Okay. Now you're beginning to get an idea about the style in which I'll talk to you and something of the focus I'll take.

What next?

To hold you and draw you in, I need to tell you what you can expect to find in these pages that will be useful to you. And I have to show you that I know enough about *you* — and what you need — for you to stay tuned.

WHAT THIS BOOK IS ABOUT

This book is about getting what you want at work. I want to help you understand what happens in a variety of work situations when you try to express yourself, and to help you develop the new techniques you need for being clear and getting the responses you want.

We'll approach communicating as a complete process involving not only all of what you're about but what other people need from you to listen.

In each aspect of your work-communication we will:

- Focus on another dimension: the unfamiliar one of finding out what else you really want and need *before* you plan your strategy.

- Understand the hidden and predictable agendas on the other side of the desk: what does the other person — the one you're communicating with — want and need?

- Gain information about issues common to all of us: what usually gets in the way as we interact at work: why effective communicating is often so hard to do.

- Absorb some basic principles of communicating and why they work, in order for you to be most effective.

- Show you it's safe to explain yourself — your *true* self.

- Help you learn to listen and hear, and to see so much more.

- Demonstrate how to observe yourself and others through forethought; gaining some new points of view and much more productive goals.

- Learn how to prepare and design what you'll communicate.

- Discover alternative communication processes through practical examples, showing you precisely how to put yourself and your ideas across to the best advantage.

- Practise these new techniques before you actually use them, allowing you to feel comfortable as you rework your communications skills.

Sound ambitious? Too much to promise? We'll see.
But first — there's one more piece of information you need.

How do I know?

Just like the stranger who walked into your office and told you to change how you always did something, I need to answer your next logical questions: 'Who are you? What do you know? Why should I believe and accept your advice?'

I've worked as a communicator all my life, continually trying to solve the puzzle of how to get people — an audience of one or many — to become interested, stay tuned, and then absorb my message. Starting in childhood, as a dancer and musician, creating as well as performing, the challenge was to recognize that my audience didn't know — or yet care — about the message I was burning to give them. I needed to find a way, non-verbally, to get them to understand me.

As an adult, the challenge was first teaching the arts and then working with the most difficult audience to capture — the television audience. Producing, reporting on the arts, making films, hosting my own talk show for ten years — the letters (and the ratings!) gave me instant feedback about what works and what goes astray, even with the best of intentions.

So I turned to look at the real world at what happens to us in our daily lives, at where and how we miss each other, and how I could add some clarity and new techniques to this seemingly simple, instinctive, spontaneous but often unsuccessful process — communicating.

I started working with trial lawyers to show them how their audience — the jury — sees them, what they expect, and what they need in order to be persuaded. I worked with doctors on the doctor-patient relationship and how to eatsblish dialogues, not monologues, in the office. With politicians, the challenge was to get past the initial cynical audience response; to find ways to be credible as well as forceful, interesting, and clear.

The business world presents its own unique challenges, and that's what this book is about. Whether it's my work with chief executive officers, with executives, managers, or staff, the hardest things to do are to find out what you actually want to communicate, and then, in your natural style, to get others to listen and understand.

So — that's why I know.

Now, let's begin by setting the scene: Our basic communications problems; how we communicate in the workplace; and how the three basic work types, Achiever, Affiliator, and Influencer, operate.

WHY WE HAVE SUCH A HARD TIME COMMUNICATING

As I walked into the office of one of my clients, a senior vice-president of one of America's major corporations, he said:

'You know, Sonya, it's incredible. I just walked out of a meeting with two other executives and I still don't know if one of them really *wants* to do this project or whether the other one even *understands* it yet!'

'What seemed to be missing?' I asked.

'Well, I guess it's . . . the *truth!* Ralph just fudges whenever I ask for a direct answer. I can't tell if he'd simply unable to make up his mind or doesn't want to tell me how he really feels. And Jim, he's so competitive I don't think he'd ever *admit* that he doesn't understand!'

Why do we keep missing each other as we try to communicate? How come we end up mainly bad at it, instead of being clear and direct? What has happened along the way, in our development, so that by the time we get to the workplace we can no longer communicate? So much so that I'm called in to work with people on the basic skills of communicating: showing and tellng them how to explain clearly, not confusingly: how not to give false messages; how not to alienate when they mean to be constructive; and so on.

Where it begins

When you were little, how often did you hear grownups say: 'I don't want to hear that from you,' or, 'Now, *don't cry*,' or, 'Control that temper!'? These familiar parental phrases set up an internal conflict that can have a lasting effect on how we communicate.

We live an interesting script as we learn to grow up. We're each born with a sturdy little spirit inside, the essence of our survival, the one that says, 'Me, me. *I* want. I need'. That little self-spirit sees the world through one pair of eyes — its own. It pushes us to take what isn't ours; to hit when were mad; to scream when were frustrated; to cry when were hurt or sad. At that early point our feelings have a direct pipeline to what we say and do. That's how we start.

Our parents' job is to move us into a world where *everyone's* spirit is telling them, 'Me, me. *I* want'. In order to protect us from instant demolition, they have to teach us to curb and hold back, even to deny our self-spirit's outburst of feelings since everyone *else's* self-spirit is doing the very same thing at the very same time! This is the necessary process of socializing, of adapting to sharing the planet with other people — who also want what *they* want, first and instantly.

Socialization

A necessary process but harmful in the way we do it.

In their zeal to get us on the right survival track, parents often teach us to *deny* rather than to modify our first and truest responses to life experiences so we develop a filter, an internal censor that says:

'Before you do anything, run that action past me. There's *danger* in expressing yourself openly. Let's just see how that's gonna play in the big world. Will you get clobbered?'

Now the socialization process works because most of us *do* grow up able to survive on the planet with lots of others. But we pay a big price for it.

That direct line from feelings to action is interrupted, rerouted and detoured so often that most of us run the risk of getting out of touch with the source: How we *really* felt and what we *really* wanted. To become accomplished at *surviving*, we become good at self-deception, denial, and public accommodation.

What we get *bad* at is letting others or even ourselves know how we really feel and what we really mean. And *that's* where the problem in communicating begins. If *we* can't be in touch with how we really feel or what we really want, how in the world are we going to transmit it to others — at work or at home?

How it develops

This process of detaching ourselves from our feelings starts with curbing our behaviour, but it really gets fine-tuned when we learn to talk.

Example: You're a child and you tell your mother, 'I don't like Aunt Agnes.' What happened? You were told:

'That's terrible. She's your aunt! Don't let me hear you say that again!'

What lesson did that teach us? It didn't make us love Aunt Agnes. It made us guilty and taught us the first lesson in subterfuge; 'I do hate her but that's bad so I'll act nice and I certainly won't tell Mum about *that* again'.

If we were given an alternative that would allow us not to like Aunt Agnes *and* learn how to handle it, then we'd accept and deal with how we felt while we learned acceptable ways to express it. We'd learn to choose what to say based on relevance, on how it affects others, and what our major purpose is. But we would have learned what to *do* with the truth — hold onto it — instead of just denying it.

Now, this learned process of denial works well in helping to make us sound civilized and acceptable to others, but it can also have the counterproductive effect of totally *baffling* the people we're talking to. Words provide so many choices, so many nuances, that they enable us to tiptoe our way through a host of delicate shadings that safely mask our true feelings and intentions.

The result? What we *really* means becomes open to others' *interpretations* of what we mean. How could we expect a relative stranger to stumble onto the exact inner meaning of our well-couched phrases? How can we, in the busy, task-oriented world of work, expect others to grope their way through our verbal smokescreens until they grasp the real meaning of what we're saying?

Relationships

Friends and lovers don't fare much better. We groove our relationships into well-worn paths. We talk shorthand and expect those closest to us to understand us with much *less* communication than we put out for those we don't know. But half the time we don't even know how to tell *friends* or *lovers* what we mean!

The process of filtering our true thoughts and feelings long predates most adult relationships. By the time we start choosing friends and lovers, we're so adept at our verbal smokescreens that only a new level of self-awareness plus a very conscious effort at trying to learn another type of behaviour could make us change our hard-won methods of survival.

What we want

What do we want so badly that we would interrupt and subvert natural expressive processes, at such great cost, to get it?

Affirmation. Affection. Approval. Acceptance. Recognition. All versions of love — the most basic 'food'. Not many of us ever experience love *unconditionally*, with no strings attached — or ever get quite enough of it. For most of us, those strings, those 'You'll get it *if* you . . .' last for our lifetime and deeply affect how we communicate.

So — *conditional* affirmation or acceptance is one of our greatest filters: 'If I say (or do) X, then Y will accept/reject me . . . so I'd better say (or do) Z and hope . . .'

Affirmation/acceptance/affection/recognition can come from many sources, in many guises. At work it can be a pay rise, a promotion with more responsibility, a visibly successful project, a clap on the back from a senior. It depends on what matters most to you and whose recognition or what kind of accomplishment has meaning for you. But the gratification of this primary need is at the very heart of the unconscious choices we make as we communicate.

It's little wonder, then, that in those places where we have the *biggest* personal investment, with the biggest need for return, we would be the *most* careful and, therefore, the most withheld. Just compare how much freer you feel complaining about exactly what's wrong to a stranger, like a waiter, than you do to those you work or live with. For many people, the more we have to lose, the worse we get at being direct and explicit.

Therefore, as adults, it's much more rare to see people able to deal with conflict or any other form of self-expression by being direct. The risk seems too great.

So — to communicate in the workplace we need:

- To know what *we* really mean — inside — before it ever gets to the outside world.

- To be able to make informed choices about what we say and how we say it.

- To use some of that instinctive knowledge of other people we picked up in our fight for survival to predict how other people would respond to what we're going to say.

- To discover the best and most productive way to put our requests and to give our bad news.

That's the background to the problem. Now, let's focus on work itself. Let's take a good hard look at how we work and why. What we expect from it beyond the wage packet; where our personal investment — the one that can make communicating difficult — lies.

WHAT MOTIVATES WORK?

We spend three-fifths of our waking hours working. During that time we do not just work; we deal continuously with some of the most critical and stressful problems of our lives — the unresolved personal hungers we try to feed in everything we say and do. We find it hard to acknowledge these hungers in a work environment where the medium of exchange is not feelings but tasks and accomplishments.

Still, those deep and ongoing personal needs continue to create a noisy turmoil beneath the smooth and unreadable facade we try to present in the workplace. They scare us when they surface into our consciousness. We try to banish or conquer them for fear we will sound immature or emotionally impoverished. We work hard at being sure others don't know about them, trying to find acceptable ways of getting what we really want. Let's look at what's going on just below the surface, what hidden emotional agendas we carry that affect, even undermine, our ability to communicate well and freely at work.

Status

We each seek to establish our identity in the outside world through relative status, based on what our society says it admires. Of course, many people come up with different subsets of what's most important — the watch, the car, the fur coat, the title, the corner office — but there are some basic common denominators which almost everyone agrees give us status.

Most of the time, we look to *others* to give us our status, our identity, measuring ourselves through the eyes of our beholders. Therefore, our need for status imbues *other people* with power — power they don't even know they have since we have *secretly* given it to them. This creates a dependency on others, like the people we work with, and makes us see them as having the power to grant or withhold esteem.

You also become the guardian of a secret — the secret of worrying about how *much* respect and appreciation they're giving you, how they see you, what they think of you. Consider the stress *that* creates in your relationship with the company, your boss, your co-workers, or those who work under you.

The need to perform in order to get and keep your sense of identity places major importance — and therefore stress — around how you present yourself and how you communicate who you are and what you want, to those 'powerful' others.

Usefulness

Feeling that we are an integral part of an ongoing process is vital to all of us. It says something we all need to know — 'I matter'. Knowing that your contribution is real and valuable, even unique and crucial, is a major issue in your daily work.

That sense of personal worth and contribution makes us all continue to work hard and stay committed. Without it, jobs become anonymous, automatic, and tedious. Because usefulness is so important to you, you will keep looking for such affirmation. But it's very hard to come by since everyone else is interested in themselves and what affirmation of their usefulness *they're* getting.

Affection/acceptance

The age-old need to be liked, affirmed and accepted by the group is surely vital in the workplace. We each define the 'group' differently, but the need remains. It stays buried at the bottom of whatever seemingly serious, objective pursuit we enter into with others.

Though the size of the hunger and how we feed it may vary, it's a basic force in all of us; so basic that babies in institutions — deprived of expressions of warmth and affection — do not develop and can actually die from it.

The problem is to make this hunger sound, and feel, relevant in the workplace. Trying to deny this force creates a gulf between what you feel and what you're willing to acknowledge and express. Therefore, how to get your hunger fed, how to become more acceptable and likeable (something we all have some basic doubts about) confuses the supposedly simple business of communicating: of asking, telling, and explaining. This is especially true in the workplace, where you are among relative strangers in whose hands you need to entrust such a basic need and who have competing hungers of their own.

Money/security

Money is an uncontested motivator in most societies. It is always more fun to get what you want when you want it than merely to make do, to have to deny yourself and delay gratification. But in the workplace, money symbolizes more than the obvious means to an end and the reason everyone works.

- *Making more money* is a tangible, objective, and visible measure of growth and success — a more concrete process than just hoping to gain status in other people's eyes.

- *Money shows your peers* what your superiors think of you. Therefore, the prospect of not making more — of *not* being given the pay rise, the bonus, the obvious proof of a job well done — seems like a concrete rejection and creates fear and anxiety.

- *Making less money or none* is the biggest fear you have. The prospect of losing your job and its attendant, unthinkable consequences is one of the biggest factors affecting how you communicate on the job.

You know, as I write this, I imagine you reading it. I hear some of you thinking: 'Hmm, you know, that's really true'. But I also imagine others thinking: 'Nope, you haven't got me'.

The fact is that these are very basic motivational forces but they're also broad generalizations. They're intrinsically true for all of us, but

one or another need is much more important to each of us, so it may
be hard for you to identify with *all* of them. But there are other reasons
why you may not readily be able to identify with these motivators:

- *Denial.* Perhaps you've spent your whole working life trying to
deny them, burying them deep so they don't interfere with the
outward coolness and businesslike approach of the workplace.
Probably even before working, you had already developed a pretty
good sense of what's seemly and unseemly, of what you show in
public and in private. So to dredge up your innermost drives and
fears and then to confront and relate to them may be a bit
uncomfortable at this stage.

- *Men vs. women.* Historically, our culture has differentiated between
how men and women have been allowed to acknowledge feelings.
Women have always been given an edge here. So, for men
particularly, these considerations have been kept alien indeed,
especially by their role models in the workplace. While some of
us grow up comfortable with confronting our conscious (and
unconscious) feelings, some of us — both men and women — have
a hard time getting in close touch with them. Asking you to do
that now seems alien and uncomfortable, like talking a foreign
language. You don't recognize feelings because you've held them
at bay for so long.

- *Work personalities.* Another factor that makes it difficult to accept
the existence of such motivating forces as Status, Usefulness,
Affection, and the deeper meanings of Money is the fact that we
all develop different work personalities, based on which personal
needs are most important to us.

- *Achieving, affilating and influencing* are the basic motivations that
shape our styles and personalities at work (described in detail later
in this chapter). Depending on which are your dominant motivators
— concrete achievement or personal affiliation or influence and
power — the needs for Affection, Status, Usefulness, Recognition,
Affirmation, or Money will each have more or less meaning.

Since the goal of this book is to put you in touch with yourself *and*
with your colleagues to discover how and why we all communicate
as we do and how to do it better, it's important to gain some general
information about how *all* of us operate. So let's continue with more
of our basic work habits.

What do we all do to keep each other from knowing about our inner needs and motivators? We design a public image to make us look like we're fine, have no problems, are in control and strong and *certainly* not needy. We want to look independent and self-sufficient, in control. Let's see how, and *if*, it works.

OUR PUBLIC IMAGE

What works, what doesn't and why

'Hi, how's it going?'
'Great.'

'Can you get this to me by four?'
'Sure, no problem.'

'Okay. Now you understand what I want, right?'
'Yes. Sure. Of course I understand.'

Sounds familiar? Do any of these answers usually describe what's really going on? Or are they the answers we give because we'd *like* them to be true, they're *supposed* to be true, and, most of all, we think that's what the other person *wants* to hear?

What am I prescribing instead? Describe what insoluble obstacles you've hit the next time someone asks you how the project is going? Tell your colleague that you can't figure out how to — or just won't — get it to him or her by four?

Sounds like you'd be admitting weakness or ineptitude if you did that. Pretty self-destructive, right?

Wrong! Isn't it more destructive to deny yourself and your colleagues the opportunity to deal with reality? Isn't it constructive and much more efficient to explain what the problems really are, what's not working, and then find a realistic solution *together*?

If the job *isn't* getting done well, your fear of being honest and therefore vulnerable to imagined rejection or criticism can make you experience stress and *still* not solve the problem. What are the possible consequences?

● You may do a less than satisfactory job.

● You may not meet a deadline.

● You may take out your frustration on the people who work for you.

All because you couldn't find a way to deal with and communicate the truth constructively.

Wearing a public image that looks like 'I'm totally competent at all times — I know what I'm doing — I'm nice, co-operative, and always in control' traps you in a cage that can actually hinder your work and diminish your competence. You may spend so much energy continually shoring up this artificial image and filling in the cracks that you have less to give to the actual business of *working*.

And you know those others? The strangers? The ones who've got it made, who have convinced you with *their* public image that none of your concerns apply to them? They're going through exactly the same thing! The same inner-outer conflict and the same fears that you'll find *them* out!

What's the bottom line, then? How can we get to a place where we express ourself as an integrated person? How do we become free enough to tune into *our* personal message and skilled and confident enough to get that message across to *others*, clearly and persuasively?

What we already know

One key to better communication is awareness and discovery. *Awareness* of what's already there and *discovery* of what you've never noticed before, in yourself and in others. It's looking for what connects us.

In some respects, you're really an *expert* on your opposite numbers, your colleagues. Since we all start with the common denominator of being vulnerable, needy human beings, we're all eminently able to know and understand these elements in each other. At work we add the commonality of sharing specific and unique experiences, known only to those who work together.

This means that the knowledge to start solving the problem of how to say what you mean so others listen, understand, and get convinced is *already there*. You own it. The blinkers that get in the way are forgetting how potentially connected we all are, despite our uniqueness.

There are also, of course, differences between us. Mankind is a theme with endless variations. But the ability to understand, recognize, and diagnose these differences is the other key to better communication. Recognizing and understanding human differences helps you change and adapt your communication style. Adjusting your communication behaviour to account for the needs of others gives you the kind of personal power that makes you more effective at work, and in life generally.

With this in mind, let's take a look at the basic work personalities to further define and understand who we are at work and how we operate.

BASIC WORK PERSONALITIES

Achievers   Affiliators   Influencers

We each have a dominant set of motivations that shapes how we work — based on what matters most to us and what seems the best way to achieve the gratification of our inner desires.

Our motivational priorities are established in succeeding waves of learning what is admired and rewarded:

● First by our families,

● Then by our peers,

● Finally by society at large.

Our techniques for striving and achieving are developed from role models, innate talents, and life experiences. We give relative and changing importance to these influences as they occur and as we mature. The end result is:

● Some of us fall for the whole external influence package and strive toward what *others* indicate is valuable and successful.

● Others become anti-players, purposely defying that which is set out for them.

● Still others turn inward to hear and follow their own set of voices.

We respond to our dominant set of motivations by behaving in ways that feed them. This behaviour becomes most apparent in the way we work and exercise our ability to direct others and relate to them. Research has shown that in the workplace there are three distinctly different personality types with distinctly different work and management styles.*

*The following discussion of motivation and personality is based on the published work of Harvard Professor David McClelland.

Achievers

Theme song: 'Climb Every Mountain'.

These are internally motivated people with high, self-set standards and goals. Uppermost for them is accomplishment. Although we all feel we have an achievement motive, research indicates that about 10 per cent of the population is *strongly* motivated by achievement. We find many Achievers in positions of business management.

- Achievers like situations in which they take personal responsibility for finding solutions to problems. They tend not to seek advice or help except from experts who can provide needed skills.

- They tend to set moderate achievement goals, attainable with hard work and ability.

- They take *calculated risks*, preferring to *work* on the outcome rather than leave it to chance.

- They want concrete feedback on how well they're doing.

- They're quite accustomed to having the task itself be enough motivation for them; concepts about persuasiveness and motivating others don't naturally occur to them.

- Communication is often little more than a one-way street for Achievers, related to explaining what needs to get done. They're so strongly goal-orientated that when they look across the desk, the people they see may simply appear as implementors of the tasks assigned, not as multi-dimensional, fallible, needy individuals.

- Entrepreneurs tend to be classic Achievers.

To the outside world, Achievers can look insensitive and unfeeling. Not true. They just work from a different set of motivations than many of us; the software of human consideration and understanding doesn't always seem to be part of their concept of work. Achievers are hard taskmasters for themselves and therefore bring the same demanding standards to others with whom they work.

Consideration such as 'Do you like me?' are usually beside the point for Achievers, though this varies. They give *themselves* love when they accomplish. An extension of that is to have others know of and acknowledge their accomplishments. Achievement is where they find their identity and feel their usefulness. Money may be regarded as a further affirmation of their ability to achieve.

Affiliators

Theme song: 'People Who Need People'

Affiliators care about belonging, relating, how others treat them. This is such a high-priority item that it influences all the choices they make about how they do their jobs.

● They need to gain confirmation of their own beliefs from others.

● They would rather be part of a group than be, or work, alone.

● They want and need to be liked and expend great effort to make sure that happens.

● They prefer conciliation, dislike conflict, and try to find ways to smooth things out.

● They like to co-operate and help others, wanting to be liked in return.

● Willy Loman, the salesman in Arthur Miller's play *Death of a Salesman*, was, among other things, an Affiliator.

Studies have shown that people with strong affiliative needs are often well suited for jobs that involve people: outreach, co-ordinating projects, integrating diverse points of view, mediating conflicts, motivating teams. They are good at sales jobs that require the cultivation and maintenance of long-term relationships.

The high need for affiliation does create problems in decision making, however, since the need to be liked makes them shy away from unpopular choices. They can therefore run a less efficient department than those with more moderate people-needs.

Influencers

Theme song (adapted): 'They Did It My Way'

This category has a semantics problem. We get very judgemental around the words 'power' and 'influence'. They sound underhanded and manipulative — less than pure — and we generally feel uneasy or negative about them. In order to understand this motivational category, we need to look at the influence concept from two points of view: personal power or influence and socialized or institutional power or influence.

- Personalized power is linked to controlling or influencing others for the sake of one's own impact on them as individuals.

- Socialized power deals with leadership of groups such as institutions, business organizations, or even social movements. It deals with inspiring colleagues symbolically and collaboratively to reach for higher goals in support of an organization. It means using power as a leader to strengthen subordinates' beliefs in themselves and in their competence to contribute to an organization's success.

Given these two different manifestations of the influence or power motive, we can now examine a basic set of behaviour traits to describe the Influencer.

- Influencers want to obtain and exercise power and authority.

- They look for positions where they are the ultimate authority or can make a highly visible impact.

- They are not as interested as Achievers are in figuring out *how* to make something work. They care more for making an impact and influencing *others* to make something work.

- Unlike Affiliators, who are dependent on other people for approval, Influencers don't worry quite so much about their critics. They know better who they are and what they want. They are solid in their moves, with few apologies.

- Influencers are self-confident. They have very clear goals, and have worked out their rationale, which includes the organizational or institutional accomplishments they often could foster with their power.

- Loyalty evoked by personalized Influencers is generally of the kind we associate with a charismatic leader.

- Loyalty evoked by socialized Influencers tends to be more attached to the team, the task, or institution.

Studies comparing personalized-power managers with socialized-power managers found the latter to be more effective.

It might help to compare behaviour patterns between all three work types. For example, the kinds of self-help books they would read:

● *Achievers* would read books with sixteen choices about how to do something and what makes any of them work, so *they* could gather the information and make their own individualistic decision about which way is best to accomplish their task.

● *Affiliators* wouldn't like that many choices. They want more *consensus* in their thinking. Therefore they would like the most popular how-to books to make them more successful from a currently accepted point of view.

● *Influencers* would have less interest in either of these types of books, since neither speaks to their desire for *impact* on a situation and its constituents. They would read historical biographies of strong, successful charismatic leaders and what made them effective.

What about sports?

● *Achievers* would prefer individual sports like golf, so they could compare their scores with par or what they did last time. It would give them both feedback and a specific goal to shoot for. They would surely go for the club championship.

● *Affiliators* would prefer team sports or tennis, but might have a hard time fighting for a position or beating a friend. They would have plenty of team spirit and probably be president of the country club.

● *Influencers* would like any team sport if they could be the coach, captain, or manager.

Now, before we get too rigid, none of us is only one type. As strong as the primary motivation may be, other factors also shape our behaviour. We can all find traces, or even large doses, of all three basic motivations in our make-up and behaviour.

Therefore, use each motivation category for quick and easy identification, but always with an eye on where there are spillovers from the others. They can help you predict behaviour and understand your fellow workers. I will use them as a kind of behavioural shorthand throughout the book.

Using the work types

As you read about these three types, I'm sure you not only looked for and characterized yourself but did an instant search for the people you work with — those above you, your peers, and your subordinates. And didn't it help to explain or give some consistency to the sometimes inexplicable behaviour you've seen?

Understanding these personalities — what they want and how they act it out at work — will give you ideas on how to formulate a strategy for dealing with them.

Notice and recognize

Watching and connecting clusters of behaviour with this new categorized set of insights starts you on the road to developing a menu for dealing with your colleagues at work. As you define each type, you'll know whether to choose from Column A, B, or C of your newly gained communication skills and strategies to be most effective with that specifically motivated person.

The next step is harder.

Suspend judgement

A given type may be vastly different from you but, if you can get past 'I hate that' and 'What a cold (cruel, bullying, weak, stubborn) way to be', you will be able to move into action that suits *your* needs and solves *your* problems.

The steps after these two are what the rest of the book is about. But before we go on, there is one more issue to discuss:

Most managers in our business world are Achievers.

A predominance of achievers

Achieving is the predominant behavioural mode taught at almost all business schools; and most top management in many corporations reflects this approach. Since business management teaching had its origins in the engineering schools, it's not surprising that the approach to people is basically task-centred and technical, focusing on the *mechanics* of how to get the job done efficiently and dispassionately, more than on the *people* who do it.

Although the typical executive is an Achiever and this is the accepted mode in a corporate culture, there are Affiliators and Influencers in executive roles, too, as well as in the middle and lower echelons.

A giant step toward developing better communication in the workplace occurs when Achievers (the majority) recognize and accept the skills and behavioural orientations of Affiliators and Influencers (minorities) as being *other* valid ways of doing business and useful *adjuncts* to existing styles, with their own unique strengths.

You must know *all* the keys to play to be the best in your field and at your job. Recognizing, accepting, and learning to deal with all *three* types and their unique drives makes for the most effective communication at work.

This means developing skills and mastering behaviours that may (at first) work *against* your basic instincts and personal style but *with* someone else's. Sounds manipulative? If 'manipulative' means choosing the best techniques to persuade and convince so you can achieve your goals, what aspect of human relations is not? And besides, what do you think the other guy is doing?

To learn more about how we do this — what the basic communications processes are, how they work, and why — let's move on.

2
The basics of communicating
Why and how people listen

Imagine for a moment that you're preparing to make a presentation about an important project in which you have a large stake. How do you start planning for it?

Don't you start from 'I'? 'I'll begin by . . .' 'Then I'll tell them . . .' 'Them' doesn't really enter into it except as the recipients of what you're planning to do. And that's one of the major problems in getting others to listen.

Most of us think of 'communicating' as a one-way process. We get all involved in what we're saying, how we're saying it, what choices we should make to communicate it better. But, in our zeal to achieve our goal and get our message across to others, we forget that at the other end of our message is an 'other' — someone with his own goals, his own zeal, and his own concerns. These often do not coincide with ours, especially at the outset of something we alone have dreamed up to say.

SPEAKING AND LISTENING

The one-sided nature of speaking

Perhaps the greatest single stumbling block to real communication is the one-sided nature of speaking. The first person — very singular — talking from one point of view.

Truly effective communication can't be a monologue in which only the sender is at work. To persuade, inform, or change the listener, both parties — the speaker and the receiver (be it one or many) — must be actively involved. So, true communication must be a dialogue, an *exchange* between you and your receiver. Two (or more) people actively engaged in the *same* pursuit.

Now I can hear you saying, 'Wait a minute — no dialogue! I want them to keep quiet and *listen* to me! I don't want equal participation, especially when I present my idea.' Right. That's what *you* want. You talk and they listen. Seems simple: You have something to say, so you say it. The hard part is '. . . and they listen.' Think about it. Why should they? What would make them want to join in your plan?

The real challenge is to get them to listen by making them actively *want* to.

Listening is work

Listening is an active pursuit. It's demanding, hard work. Most of all, when someone is truly listening, it takes time away from the listener's most important focus — himself.

Normally our commitment and attention space is taken up by our own concerns. We have absolutely no reason, at the outset, to give *you* any of our valuable attention — like stopping to listen. But unless you can get both of you (sender and receivers) equally involved — one giving, the other getting — you may as well deliver your idea or request to the bathroom mirror, where you practised it.

So what's the answer?

Motivation

Making the listener want to hear you is primary.

Right. But now that you think about it, why would someone else spontaneously get interested in your vested stuff? You'd need a propellant — something that could make a difference, something that could *actively* turn your audience towards your pursuit and away from theirs. What?

When what you have to say clearly intersects with what the other person wants or needs or cares about, you have given a primary, compelling reason for listening. You're not actually demanding that he/she give up self-involvement. You're just piggy-backing on some part of the listener's own momentum; his/her self-involvement. You're defining your message as another facet of his or her ongoing life concerns.

Simply put, understanding your listener's needs is the bottom line.

WHAT MAKES PEOPLE LISTEN?

Three basic factors shape the answer to every potential listener's challenging unspoken question: 'Why should I listen?'

● Self-interest

● Who's speaking

● How they say it

Self-interest

Let's not get too theoretical. Since you belong to the same species as your potential listeners, to work out what basically motivates *them*, think about *yourself* for a moment. What, really deep down, is the prime motivator that pushes you to do *whatever* you do — not just listen?

It's that little self-spirit you were born with, the one I mentioned in Chapter 1, the one that went underground but never really went away as your parents helped you get socialized.

Think about yourself. Isn't self-interest at the centre of what makes you, all of us, tick? It motivates you to want, to pursue, to be attracted to anything that looks like it's practical, fulfilling, enriching, or helpful for you. And it never works if someone else simply *tells* you it's good for you. You have to see its applicability for yourself.

Sometimes you even get attracted to what you've learned you *shouldn't* do, because other self-interest components (pleasure; revolt against the rules; 'just this once'; to heck with the other guy) outweigh what the head and the conscience try to restrict.

Gratifying one's self-interest is an instinct that motivates us without even needing to come to the conscious surface too often.

Test yourself. What makes *you* listen or pay attention?

Examples:

● The newspaper. What do you read first and why? What gets you past the headlines? What gets you to turn to the follow-up page? Isn't it that you think: 'I want to know that. I need to know that. I've never heard of that'. It all has to do with fulfilling various needs of 'I'.

● The weekend. What do you find yourself doing? Obviously, with choices, you go for the juiciest version of what you like best. But what about the seemingly negative decisions like going somewhere you'd rather not? If others want to go, and it means keeping peace with friend or family, you weigh your personal first choice against what the other issues are and decide on which self-interest is best served. True? Then you either acquiesce and go, for peace, or decide the wrath is worth enduring and stay. But both are filtered first through what's good for *you*.

● At work. Who do you call back and how quickly? Which projects do you finish first? What stimulates you to learn something new?
   It all revolves around the same motivation: Self-interest.
   People mostly do what they *want* to do.

Therefore, to create an attentive, willing audience, to involve people in that dialogue I mentioned, you first need to direct *your* self-interest beam to shine on the dark recesses of *another's* self-interest. You need to learn enough about your audience to discover *their* self-interest, their needs, their motivations, in order to make them willing to listen to you.

Too often we send our messages without an address. Unless you can point your communiqué toward your unique audience — specific addressees who will become involved in hearing, absorbing, and accepting that message — it's a space shot with no destination.

And it's not that difficult to do. At work, much of the learning about your audience has come from your already sharing so many common experiences. Not just the basic human factors like eating lunch, wanting a pay rise, fear of being sacked and/or a wish for status and attention, but the ongoing reality that you work together.

● You both share a common workplace culture.

● You both know the mechanics of how to get things done there (if not all the same nuances).

● You both interact with the same cast of characters.

● You're exposed to each other more hours in the day than to any member of your family or friends, by a lot.

Therefore, you already have an inside track on your colleague's self-interest. So the conclusion is that the best way to get people to listen is to discover and show them *what's in it for them*. It's to let them know that you understand their self-interest by focusing on their point of view at the start, *before* you tell them about yours. That will motivate them to tune in.

Who's speaking

The next factor that determines whether people listen is their perception of the speaker. Needing to know who's speaking is built into the nature of listening itself.

When you listen, you give power to another. Although the power may be temporary and you keep an active internal debate going inside as you listen, basically you're in a passive state. Something is being done *to* you. You're not in control — yet.

So listening is a big gift, given to the speaker by the receiver. Therefore, who's 'doing it to you', who's getting your gift, matters mightily.

Trust is, and always has been, a hard-won commodity, not freely given. Societies have always devised tests for 'friend or foe'. For example, do you know the origin of a salute? Why the right hand at the brow? It comes from mediaeval times when men in armour lifted their visors with an empty right hand to show who they were and that they had no weapon. And we *still* do it, we shake right hands and make eye contact as we greet each other.

So, whether it was showing the face or knowing the password, before a person was welcomed into our midst the first encounter had to establish his credentials, showing us who he was and how he meant to relate to us. (That's why I introduced myself to you on page one of Chapter 1. It was my verbal handshake, asking you to trust me enough to become your 'speaker'.

Instinctively, we have always been wary of others, needing to know what their intentions are and what to expect before we let them in. We're still wary of others today. When someone says, 'Give me the power to tell you, to sell you, to hold sway while you listen,' our instincts are still alert. We're still asking:

'Friend or foe?'
'Are you *for* me?'
'Useful to me?'
'Trustworthy?'
'What happens if I let you in?'

To answer, we test. We pick up signals, based first of all on our instincts, life experiences, and preferences. This always comes before we decide who we trust or admire, and who's worthy of our attention.

We test in two ways:

● First we notice and respond instinctively to personal style: how the speaker strikes us, person to person.

● Then we reinforce that by intellectually considering some hard-nosed questions about who this person is and how he/she relates to our lives.

(Notice how this also follows the order in which I introduced myself, the contents of the book, and my credentials to you at the beginning.)

Personal style

Who do you like to listen to and who do you resist — whether in a formal presentation, at a meeting, or one-on-one? Could you list some basic characteristics that always attract you? What adjectives come to mind? Look at this list of readily identifiable personal qualities, to see if you find your preferences among them:

warm	honest
friendly	exciting
interesting	knowledgeable
organized	creative
confident	inspiring
open	authentic

Now think about the quick turn-off qualities you've encountered in speakers. Perhaps:

pompous	vague
lethargic	complex
patronizing	unsure
formal	irrelevant
stuffy	monotonous
hyper-intense	nervous
closed	false

Depending on whether you're basically an Achiever, an Affiliator, or an Influencer, your preferences will vary somewhat. But even within those variations the first list has appeal and the second list does not. Why?

Certain basic personal qualities immediately capture us and make us want to spend time with you or listen to your message. This response is rooted in how you make us, your listeners, feel, as well as in what climate your personal qualities create between us.

Positive qualities

Consider the qualities on the first list:

● *Warm, friendly, honest,* and *open* put us at ease. They actively invite us to get closer, creating an environment in which we can relax our guard and relate more directly and openly. These qualities are usually a surprise, a welcome alternative to the guarded way most of us behave. We basically envy and are drawn to the speaker because most of us haven't learned to *express* warmth, friendliness, honesty, or openness very directly or easily, although we *respond* to them with pleasure. We also sense how comfortable one must be within oneself to behave in such an uncluttered way.

● *Exciting, creative,* and *interesting* promise pleasure and make us lose ourselves in a feeling of anticipation and a curiosity about what comes next.

● *Knowledgeable* and/or *confident* are very reassuring. Since the speaker has obviously done his/her homework, we listen with trust and the assumption that listening will be both beneficial and definitive.

● *Organized* satisfies the brain's need for order and logic delivered in the format of how we learn best. As we listen, awash in a sea of words and ideas, we need to see, hear, and imagine the structure that underlies the message in order to get it and remember it.

● *Authentic* gives us confidence that what we see is indeed what we get, that we're down to bedrock: this is a truthful person speaking, without subterfuge.

● *Inspiring* appeals to our deeply rooted willingness to follow a leader or rise above our own thoughts to absorb another's enthusiasm and innovation.

Whatever combination of these qualities we perceive, any one of them can cause us to begin giving centre stage away to become a willing and interested listener.

Negative qualities

The negative qualities in the second list have one thing in common: They make us *uncomfortable*.

By evoking certain responses in us, they create an environment in which we want to find a way out of listening further to such a person.

- *Formal* and *stuffy* styles show us someone operating from a rigid set of rules unrelated to the situation at hand. The speaker's greatest effort seems to be spent not on genuine outreach to us but on hiding behind prescribed and learned behaviour, dictated by anonymous others before we ever got there.

- *Closed* and *false* are worrying. Who *is* this person? How can I predict *anything* about what he/she really means, feels, believes in?

- *Pompous* behaviour tries to set the speaker apart and a step or two above the listener. This creates two problems. First: the listener questions who put him/her up there and on what evidence. Second: you do not automatically want to look up to someone before you *yourself* have designated him/her worthy.

- *Monotonous* speakers turn our already passive state into one of lethargy. Remember the nature of listening: it takes work to keep our attention, since we're not doing anything active. Being trapped by dull usurpers of our time makes us look for the nearest escape hatch — tuning out.

- *Lethargic* makes us mad. If you move into my life but don't feel I'm worth much effort, you've betrayed my allowing you to enter. How can you ask for any of *my* time and attention and not give me the most of *yourself* — a fully-fledged commitment to making me listen and understand?

- *Vague* or *complex* explainers create anxiety in the listener. We hate to know we don't understand. A speaker who confuses or doesn't help us 'get it' betrays the first moments of trust we gave him free, while we were doing our absorbing and deciding.

- *Irrelevant* messages betray the first rule of getting people to listen — self-interest. Who needs to hear something that matters only to someone else, or maybe not even to them?

- *Patronizing* is insulting. If you, the teller, know what we don't know, and ask to tell us, you should be in the position of *sharing* riches, not scolding us for not having them yet.

● *Unsure* or *nervous* behaviour makes us *really* uncomfortable! Since we've all been there and hated it, we recognize it and feel it keenly when we see it in others' and can't bear to watch it. Also — if *you're* not sure of your material or position, how can you ask *me* to get involved? I'm flying blind!

● *Hyper-intense* starts us out at too high a level. Such a person is already at a gallop while we — the blank-slate audience — can only begin with a walk. It presumes the same level of passion and information on the part of the listener that the speaker has, without working on the gradual development that might get us there.

Obviously these are only primary-colour descriptions, thumbnail sketches of the much more complex personal styles each of us develops and gives off when we communicate, whether to one or many. But they serve to help us analyse the process by which people respond when they are asked to listen, to become aware of what listeners perceive, how it affects them, and why they willingly listen to some and not to others.

Since we operate on a primal, instinctive level first, these basic personal-quality perceptions are in the first line of resistance, the first things we notice and respond to. We do it viscerally, instinctively, without thinking, before we go on.

But we do go on. That highly developed brain doesn't like to take a back seat for too long. So we come to the second part of what we do when we ask ourselves 'Who's speaking?' We move up from the gut instinct and engage the brain in considering the request for a willing listener, for an audience.

Are you enough?

Based on the individual situation, and whether one is basically an Achiever, Affiliator, or Influencer, a series of subconscious questions determine whether the proposed speaker has enough credentials to command our attention:

● Do you know what I want (need) to know?

● Do I like or admire you already?

- Can I trust you?

- Am I usually comfortable with you?

- How can or do you affect my life?

- What's my past experience with you?

- Are you reasonable (approachable, rigid, stubborn)?

- What (or whom) do you represent?

Each of us asks, Is this *my* version of what a leader (expert, staff member, colleague) should be and how one should behave?

Look at the list again. What else would you add? What are *your* hidden questions about 'Who's speaking'? Those you don't really need to bring to the conscious surface but that colour and filter how you receive information and enter into a dialogue? Think about them for a moment, consciously.

Can you see how your resistant, wary 'tests' and the opinions you form — often in advance — could shape the outcome of any communication directed at you? That they would shape the *way* you would listen as well as *whether* you would listen.

Instinct + Thought = Decision

The process of deciding 'who's speaking'? has two parts: visceral and cerebral. But they're not distinct and separate. Although you bring your head into it, all the cerebral answers depend on and are filtered through your feelings.

Most of us don't consciously think first. We *feel* first. We like, trust, believe, follow because our sensory antennae tell our heads we should.

Instincts were there before our earliest learned material. Dealing with basic survival, this subconscious system puts up the first row of defence and danger signals as we deal with the world. First comes, stop, look, listen. Then comes, think about it.

Now, listening is hardly life-threatening, but the visceral evaluation system for people's behaviour is in place and we use it everywhere. Therefore, our sensitive instincts 'process' who's trying to tell us something and how we feel about them and about their message. Then our business head starts operating, adding and weighing hard information. It's the combination of the two that gets us to listen and satisfies our wish to qualify the bearer of the message.

Remember that *before* you get to your message — and after you establish their self-interest in listening — you must 'lift your visor'. You must let your audience of *one* or *many* see (or *feel*) who you are, or at least some pertinent aspect of who you are, and what you intend. And if you don't do it consciously, they'll do it for you. They're looking for labels and categories, for recognizable signals seen through your personal approach to them and your task, that help them know 'Who's speaking'?

How they tell it

The third reason people listen is *technique*. Style and technique have become the principal determinants of whether or not we sell or tell anything successfully today. Rather than bemoan that fact and say, 'The validity or purity of the message itself should be the central core', let's deal with what *is* and understand it better: What techniques work to get a message across these days?

How communication has changed

I say 'these days' because the way we communicate — how we give and get information — has been permanently changed in this half of the twentieth century. Our new ingredient?

Television. Mass imparting of information *visually*, with words an adjunct.

Now visually transmitting information is not new. From the prehistoric cave painters to the sculptors of old who told the masses about religion before they could read, we have always found the visual image the most arresting and the most instantly eloquent. In all other times, visual images were evocative, designed to trigger the imagination and emotions of the viewer. But viewing them required work. Commitment. Response. Rapt attention and personal participation to make the pictures or statues be eloquent and to receive their message.

Words, too, used to require effort. To listen and understand, to wait until the end, demanded something from the listener: the willingness to follow someone else's unique style and pace, and then to sort out the ideas and what the words really meant, on one's own.

That's how it *was*. But not now.

Not since television.

The two major differences between how we used to use visual information and words and how that's changed involve *passivity* and *pace*.

To see what makes this true and to discover the effect television has had on us both psychologically and in how we communicate, and then to assess the implications this has for you in your workplace, let's look back at the last hundred years.

How it used to be

We used to *want* to listen — and to read. We delighted in words. They were our major means of exchange. Written language and skilful orators were sources of pleasure. Family entertainment meant reading aloud in the evening. Elocution teachers were the rage. People recited (even wrote) poetry to express their deepest emotions. And we loved to read; to go inside ourselves quietly, let someone spin a web and take us with them. Slowly. To let our imaginations take off from the springboard of another's words and do the rest ourselves.

This reflected the rhythm and phrasing of our lives then. Listening and words took time. And time ticked at a clippety-clop pace, in tune with how we lived. The words went by slowly, seen on foot or courtesy of a horse, touching all our senses.

Every household chore took time.

Going for the doctor took time.

Crafting things by hand took time.

Getting information from afar took lots of time.

So we were accustomed to waiting until we got what we wanted. We could wait to hear the whole story. We actually *enjoyed* the detours and nuances that someone 'speaking' could provide — the little asides, the descriptive phrases that triggered our imagination to hum along and make us an active part of the story ourselves.

Our very lives were lived with more commitment and effort. We were used to — and willing to — go more than halfway to get what we wanted. We didn't depend as much on external help to make our lives better. We developed self-reliant skills and actively pursued what we wanted, knowing it would never just come to us. And that was reflected in how we communicated, too.

But time passed and the world and its timing changed.

We saw our landscape speeding by from the windows of our cars, tightly rolled up.

Aeroplanes distorted our natural world into a geometric collage, where time measured the reward of getting there fast, and earthly wonders, the old realities, increasingly became abstractions.

Technological marvels gave us control over accepted reality. Objects and images — visually magnified, distorted, shown inside out — presented new insights, changing forever how we saw and thought about the tangible real world.

Machines took over our household chores — leaving us extra, discretionary time.

We could *phone* the doctor — more efficient.

Machine-made, mass-produced goods gave us what we needed or wanted — fast. Goods that were anonymous — and just like everyone else's.

The world got smaller for us, courtesy of unseen hands delivering more services. Mechanically.

We became a 'massed society'.

The new watchword was quantity, not quality.

Product, not process or substance.

The 'what' — not the 'how'.

Little wonder that television would evolve. It filled so many of our newfound needs.

- Instant gratification.

- Pleasure without personal effort.

- Understanding just enough without wasting time.

- Group consensus about lifestyles and values.

- Gerting what we need to know to keep pace.

That's the key word — *pace*.

The rhythm of life has changed forever. With that change have gone our old abilities to live life in longer phrases, seeing longer segments. The mailroom boy who worked at the same shop for thirty years, investing in the single, slow rise to the presidency, is now a charming antique fable. We who once were willing to trek across the country, or the ocean, with the hope of a brighter day-after-tomorrow, want it *now*. No waiting.

We used to let time be an active partner and pacesetter. Knowing how to invest and spend it, our activities and our pleasures reflected that. But since we've harnessed most of the means to give us a brighter day right now, the skills that required waiting have begun to dry up, seeming redundant and unnecessary. And of all of these, speaking, listening, and reading top the list.

You see, it takes too long to tell and listen — to wait till you get to the end of a paragraph for me to get the idea.

And reading? A picture rather than a thousand words — that's what we need!

And that's what we have.

THE NEW TECHNIQUES OF TELLING

Here are some 'telling' facts:

- Three-quarters of people get nearly all of their news from television.
- Half get *all* their news from television.
- Many major corporations have their own TV studios.
- Videotapes and videodiscs are commonplace in homes and offices.

Since television is now the major method of giving and getting hard information and factual data today (now that reading and lectures have lost favour), let's look at what new techniques are used for TV communication. And, TV watchers are the general public — including staff and colleagues, buyers, clients, audiences of any size — we surely need to explore further how television has affected us in the way we talk and listen. This is especially true if we wish to build new techniques for effective *business* communication, whose main topic is hard information and factual data — numbers, ideas, issues, marketing strategies.

Basic techniques of television communication

To analyse these techniques and understand their effect on your audience, and also how to use the best of them, let's examine the most common experience of information giving on TV — the nightly news broadcast.

News stories are short

Basically headlines, one and a half minutes long, they're designed for short explanations, not in-depth analysis with background material.

They deal with what's *new*, not what *is* or *was*. This does wonders for the attention span and the desire ever to find out 'how', or 'why', or even if it's all true!

Television compresses time

The common practice of going from the studio (CUT) to a live scene on location (CUT) to a suspended head talking (CUT) to graphics appearing on the screen (CUT) without ever seeing how any of it got there has made us believe in — and expect — magic.

This technological mastery compresses *natural* time. We want information *now* and grow impatient with normal, human methods.

TV reinforces information

Using graphics and descriptive written words to identify and clarify television news teaches us that, 'If you don't catch on, well help you.' 'Don't bother listening hard, we'll tell you again.' Even when pictures are shown, a voice off-camera explains them.

Visuals are the message

Words and *people* are no longer the primary message givers. Now *pictures* tell. Human speakers corroborate and embellish as introducers and voice-overs but are no longer the major source of information. Television has taught the viewer to expect *visual* proof, not to take anyone's *word* for it.

What looks true is not true

Since pictures are edited by the reporter, and their content and point of view chosen by reporter, cameraman, director, and/or producer, what we see is not pure truth. It's technologically altered. Time and reality are distorted with quick, unconnected shots of a scene and close-ups impossible to do with the naked eye. Now, tellers of tales used to edit truth for impact, too, leaving it to our imagination to fill in the picture. But today TV shows what *look* like authentic pictures, thus convincing us they're true and that *that's* the whole story.

The 'talking head' taboo

A 'talking head' (close-up of a person just talking) is considered so boring that it's generally given thirty seconds or less on the air. Television producers, knowing that people are basically garrulous and verbally disorganized, edit most 'talking head' statements into a 'bite' from a speech — taking part of this sentence, the middle of that, and a startling or memorable line to finish. Thus we hear a cogent (albeit manufactured) pithy statement, made *on* but also *by* TV, and not necessarily intended by the original author. Result: we are now accustomed to hearing, ultimately wanting, only the essence — the bottom line — from people. No strolling through the language. Just the facts, Ma'am. And be quick about it.

Seamless flow of words

Consider the TV presenter. Flawless. Delivering his or her message without mistakes. News readers don't look for words or look at notes. They just look at you — keenly, directly, sincerely — and talk. Of course they're reading from a teleprompter, rolling over the lens so their eyes don't move and give it all away. That teaches the audience that people don't stumble or falter or think as they work at communicating with you. No rephrasing or trying again. The only professional, mature, correct way is seamlessly and effortlessly.

Now this is all very interesting, but what can you do with such information in the work world?

In order to know what *else* you have to do to get people to listen to you these days, let's see how the new techniques of TV information giving have conditioned your potential audience. What problems must you know about and take care of as you prepare to speak to anyone?

Communication consequences of TV

Passivity

We no longer have to do very much to gain information. It's all done for us — and for *free*. Delivered in the most painless, least challenging way to ensure the broadest possible audience. TV delivery of information has eliminated the participation which the old forms of delivery required.

And with it the desire to work very hard at trying to find out and understand anything or to like being challenged.

Inattention

Television has taught us to listen with half an ear. In the past, to listen or learn you went to a totally focused environment where that was the only activity: school, college, lecture hall, theatre, auditorium, forum, library.

Now consider the environment in which television gives information and its effect on concentration. Kitchen, den, living room or bedroom. Phones ring; kids play; mums and dads cook, talk, or read. The business of life — eating, arguing, laughing, disciplining, attending to daily detail — all vies for equal time with the tube. Television often becomes an obbligato, a hum or drone in the background. Only occasionally does it rise up to demand total attention from the disparate group pursuing their activities in the vicinity. This from the most powerful communications medium ever created, shared by more people than ever before!

What effect does this have?

We start with the problems we as a species have in *ever* paying attention, under any circumstances. Due to the fact that it takes only 15 per cent of the brain to process and understand language, we have 85 per cent of free 'attention span' left over whenever someone speaks to us. *Any* speaker has to fight for that other 85 per cent in order to keep his or her audience — fight the wool-gathering, daydreaming, problem-solving, random thinking we all do with that free brainpower.

Now television comes along, challenging even *more* of that tenuous attention base. It teaches us that its okay — actually the norm — to listen just a little, from time to time, instead of helping us focus and concentrate. Not good for you, the business communicator who needs rapt attention from beginning to end . . . .

Lack of continuity

We get comfortable about coming in on the middle of a subject. Others fill us in with an even more edited version than the television show itself presents, and that's enough for us to climb aboard and tune in. Otherwise we bumble along till the show or subject comes clear and hooks us, or we resort to our other great power play — changing channels without even getting up!

Vetoing the subject

The ability to snap off communication in mid-sentence, based strictly on whether it has already grabbed us, bodes ill for anyone wanting to impart new, unfamiliar, necessary though difficult information. Click goes the listener, looking for (and being able to find) something that tickles the palate more. The gimmick rather than the message is what we are trained to look for. How appealing are your subjects? Your messages?

Commercials create the rhythm

We are becoming conditioned to expecting breaks in most communication every ten to fifteen minutes. Information — hard or soft — is delivered in bite-sized pieces, and we've learned to expect to get off the hook in predictable segments. Who's going to sit through *your* half-hour presentation without wanting a trip to the refrigerator?

Information is automatically considered boring

We now automatically know what our society deems 'prime'. We are told what information appeals only to a very small, select audience by what is programmed during the best — the 'prime-time' — viewing hours and what is served up when most people are sleeping or out. 'Fact shows' (documentaries, public affairs, serious interview shows) are relegated to no-man's land.

And what's 'prime'? Generally anything that says entertainment and escape. This conditions us to expect to be bored by heavy and serious subjects — the usual fare of business meetings — and to look for the automatic kick and pace that television has trained us to expect. Important information — and a major challenge for anyone who has to present or discuss facts and numbers . . . .

Individual imagination is buried

Visualizing music on pop videos gives another message about how we have learned to process data now. Rather than letting sound into each head and allowing unique, personal visions to develop (remember radio?), we now show that consensus, not individual vision, is the goal. The subconscious message given is that our imaginations can't, or won't, come up with visions on their own and that we need spoon-feeding.

This conditioning can discourage unique opinions and the desire to discover and explore. It can dampen our natural ability to imagine. Not good news for those who need to teach, explain, or present another point of view. Further, it increases our anxiety level about doing anything different from the norm or being out of step with our neighbours. How does that affect management's goals of motivating individuals to step out and perform new tasks, to find original solutions, and to be inspired to move ahead of the crowd?

We expect intensity and shock

The camera zooms in where you and I would fear to tread. Television, in communicating everything, indiscriminately, in full colour and tight close-up, has broken the accepted norms of what we communicate about, simply because we can do it technically. Violence, conflict, and tragedy become abstractions and commonplace. We're used to the close-up of the body bag and the private weeping made public.

Effect? Commonplace, cool, didactic, functional business messages can't hold a candle to what we're exposed to on TV. Hard to generate much interest in just facts without some stimulating visual additives and general razzle-dazzle.

So, that's the current scene: Telling, listening, learning, information giving/getting are permanently changed. Pace matters. People expect an edited, telescoped version of anything new and unfamiliar, amply laced with visual reinforcement. We're a passive audience, needing active engagement to stay tuned in. The attention span is now shorter, the need to think and understand is now dampened, and people are no longer the central truth tellers.

A qualifier

Having just made a great case for the doom-and-gloom sayers about what the failure of our society will be, I need to add another thought, especially since I spent most of my life working in television as a communicator, using those self-same techniques I've just been decrying . . .

Let's not just get mad at television. We can't disinvent it. Like the car it's here. A mixed blessing, and we have to live with the pollution.

There's much to learn about our natural tendencies and how television has built on them. And I still believe in TV's fabulous potential.

At its best, television is the most *effective* method yet devised for giving mass information. It brings every brand of reality into every household, exposing new ideas, social problems, endless types of people, and issues from every walk of life to us all, across the board, without being asked. It can take us where we could never go. It can introduce us to spiritual experiences and cultural joys.

But — TV communication techniques have been damaging to the learning systems of our societies, supplanting more substantive, personally involving ones with the quick fix. To communicate these days, you need to know what's happened and what effect it's had.

Implications for business communication

We need to adapt and adopt.

In these pages we'll learn to offset TV information influences with inventive communication techniques of our own.

● We'll use what people now need to become much more effective speakers.

● We'll remain aware of continuing basic human needs, fulfilling the natural as well as the conditioned demands of any audience.

● We'll adapt the current technologies and other new information about visual learning to make business communication clear, convincing, involving, and persuasive.

Now let's leave the new world of TV and technology, and return to the original one of our *natural* functioning to explore another set of basic principles by which we exchange information and reach each other — those of verbal and non-verbal communication.

VERBAL VERSUS NON-VERBAL COMMUNICATION

How we comunicate

Picture this scene.

You're walking down the corridor at work and you see your friend Jack coming towards you:

> **YOU** (*walking up to him, smiling*): 'Hi, Jack — haven't see you in a while. How's everything going?'
> **JACK** (*backs away hastily, avoiding eye contact*): 'Fine, fine.'
> **YOU** 'What's up? Are you okay?'
> **JACK** (*dropping his papers, scrambling for them, getting up, and quickly looking past you as he shifts from one foot to the other*): 'Yeah, sure, I'm fine. Everything's just fine.'
> **YOU** 'You seem a little distracted.'
> **JACK** (*stepping back, finally looking at you*): 'No, no — believe me, I'm okay (*heaving a sigh*). Everything's — just — uh — great . . . (*looking off*). Yeah, great . . .'

Do you believe Jack? Would you accept what he says about everything being fine? What do you think is really going on: Just been sacked? Messed up the job? How do you know? What clues do you use to give you the answers?

   Go back and read the scene again, but without the directions in parentheses. The words alone don't tell you what you need to know, do they? Actually, the information about how Jack really feels emerges only from what he *does*, in contrast to what he *says*. And if you turned the sound off and just watched this scene, you'd get a much clearer message, wouldn't you?

Multi-messages

We all share a primary human need not just to accept what is communicated to us, but to evaluate it. We automatically filter incoming messages through such questions as: 'What does this really mean?' 'Can I trust him?' 'Why is she saying or doing this?'
   This need to understand fully and to put things in context requires

us to look for as much information as we can.

Go back to that scene with Jack. Look at all the information you would automatically notice and gather from his non-verbal language and consider how quickly you would understand its meaning.

- *Body language*: Jack shifts his feet (can't hold his ground). He twitches, gestures, nervously drops his papers, scrambles hastily for them (can't stop moving, seems unco-ordinated in a simple task).

- *Eye contact*: Jack can't look at you; he looks off, thinking. (Why does he avoid me? What is he hiding?)

- *Space relationship*: You get closer; he backs away. (Doesn't want contact; avoids my personal outreach.)

- *Speech rhythm*: Jack speaks hastily (trying to get done with it); long pauses between his words (reflective, thinking of something else?); sighs as he speaks (expression of inner feeling — disappointment? sadness?).
  And the words?
  He *says*, 'Fine' . . . 'great'. 'No, no — believe me.'

Words and movement

Words may be the basic currency, but non-verbal communication (body language) is the other dictionary we use. Each is powerful and eloquent in different ways, but non-verbals have a much more direct effect on how we process information and our feelings about the speaker.

- *Words are cerebral.* They're symbols, requiring us to translate those symbols mentally into meaning.

- *Non-verbal body language is visceral.* We absorb its meaning instinctively, through the gut, not the head. We *feel* — we don't *think* about what it means.

- *Words are self-edited.* They're controlled. Through training we choose what we say. We filter our choices through the constraints of our self-protective superego. We verbalize only what seems fitting, non-damaging, or not too revealing. Your listeners know that because we all do it.

- *Body language is not edited.* Posture, gesture, movement are unconscious. Involuntary. Spontaneous. And we all know that, too. That's why we use body language as our best measure — our barometer and truth teller — about what's really happening and what any communicated message really means. Remember the scene with Jack?

- *Words are specific.* Although they can suggest, as symbols they mean specific things and call forth the same images for all of us. 'Nose' is nose. 'Window' is window. Words explain concrete ideas and facts.

- *Body language needs interpretation.* Movement, posture, gesture, and space relationships are unique and highly individual, demanding interpretation. They deal with nuance, with feeling, with degree. They can't say exactly . . . but they can say how you *feel* about the fact of . . . Think of — and actually try to do — the gestures that say:

  'Oh, I'm late!' or, 'What, already?' or, 'Finally!'

  The gestures come to you at once, don't they? And they're a little different for each of us, based on our background and who we watched growing up, but they would be universally understood.

- *Words are extravagant.* They can eventually describe and tell, but you need to use many to get depths of feeling across.

- *Body language is succinct.* It shows feelings much more economically, more directly and eloquently. It evokes feeling responses in us very quickly.

- *Words separate.* Not only the difference between foreign languages and our own, but vocabulary and pronunciation define class, level of accomplishment, education, and social station.

- *Body language can unify.* Because life is essentially a series of universal common experiences — birth, death, marriage, children, happy, sad, hungry, fearful — we can understand each other instantly through physical expression. Need a drink in a foreign country? No problem. You'll show them. And in showing them, you also show our commonality. The recognition of that unifying concept by others draws us instantly closer — whether it is tears in Tibet or a welcoming smile at a business meeting in Boston.

Words and movement together comprise a dual dialogue. If they *match* and are consistent with each other, they strengthen and underscore meaning. If they are inconsistent, incongruously saying two *different* things, the viewer disregards the words — the verbal — and believes the body language — the non-verbal.

If you stand there *saying*, 'The figures for this quarter show great strength,' at the same time that you avoid eye contact, clear your throat, and shuffle your papers, you've convinced us only of what you're trying to hide!

COMMON OBSTACLES TO COMMUNICATION

How people feel about learning

New information or information that challenges existing beliefs or systems presents problems to any communicator. As a species, people are grounded in the familiar and in what is proven to work. Exploring is only for the few, not the many. There's only *one* Columbus, *one* Edison, *one* Hilary. Even *questioning* existing beliefs feels dangerous to most people.

Therefore, the first reaction to learning is often resistance. In order to understand what you need to overcome in order to present new information at work, to bring others to accept it or wish to change anything, let's look at some basic obstacles to listening and learning.

Threatened

The ongoing daily business of keeping up — let alone getting ahead — at work requires tremendous effort.

Status, usefulness, acceptance, money, and the other factors I talked about in Chapter 1 push us to try to maintain some sense of security or stability at work while we gather our forces and plan our assault on the next rung or pinnacle. We climb only when we feel ready and strong enough. For someone else to move into our path and say, 'It's time for a challenge now,' can be threatening. Of course, there are individual variations based on levels of skill and personal confidence, but most people think:

'I've just about worked this level out. Why do I want to change now? I can picture the present scene, but not the new one being presented. Better play it safe till I can figure it out. 'The devil I know is better than the devil I don't.'

So our tendency is to push against new ideas or systems, not to welcome them.

Intimidated

Our universal need to save face, to appear confident and competent, to seem grounded in our lives and unflappable, is intensified at work. That's the dangerous, get-ahead place where everyone's watching, waiting to pounce and move in or up — over you. Look at the concern that can be created when someone else (especially someone in charge) comes up with a new idea or initiative. We think:

'*You* dreamed it up, so *you* understand it and know how to do it and why. But *I* am not at all sure that *I* can understand it or be able to do it, especially do it well.'

We hark back to our early experiences in the learning game. Most people's school experience was not without pitfalls. We still remember the smarting embarrassment of being found wrong or wanting in the early vulnerable days. The anxiety about our own competence doesn't ever really leave us. Whenever you, the speaker, present a challenge to move into 'Learn-this, -because-there-will-be-a-test' mode, you call up performance anxiety. Thus the normal human instinct of self-preservation causes us, the recipients, to put our hands up in front of our faces and say, 'Whoa!'

Competitive

Your idea, not mine. That fact can create resistance again. Not only because I didn't think of it, but because of the implication that you were smart enough, creative enough, even brave enough, to think of it. For many competitive people there's also the feeling that if I accept your idea, you're ahead of me and I'm in a weakened position.

Need the familiar

New ideas are usually presented just that way — as *new*. Different. Unlike what's gone before. Bad news! This doesn't give the listener/learner any grounding or context or reason to believe they can tune in. We all need to feel some ownership of turf before we venture forth to the unknown. 'Turf' in this case means knowing that past information and experience, one's background, is valuable and useful in a new situation. New data creates major resistance since one doesn't know how to listen to it, to relate to or even imagine it.

The safest way to discuss new information is to begin with what is known. To start with the familiar and then to add the new as variations or take-offs from the old. To establish and remind one of *what is*, then show how it leads to *what could be*.

Language

Words mean instant understanding if they are used well and if they are within the listener's vocabulary. Since words are exact, stating facts and concepts precisely, we expect them to be accurate and clear to us, making an immediate image which is shared by everyone. We depend on processing words easily, knowing that they are the vehicle that will move us along in our comprehension. We don't expect to get stuck. We are challenged and concerned when we do. Therefore, how we use language has a great effect on how people can take in and understand us.

Effects of not understanding words

● *We stop listening.*
The instant halt to comprehension when we hear a word we don't understand causes us to lose our concentration and the momentum built up by the speaker. We ruminate, scanning our storehouse of language, looking for possible connotations: 'Sounds like . . .' 'In that context, it *probably* means . . .'

But while we do that, we have to stop listening and processing your data. Then, when we tune back in again, we're out of synch and need to catch up. Meanwhile, of course, we've missed something, perhaps the essence of what the speaker is saying. But that's only the beginning of the end.

● *We discover our ignorance.*
The second, and deeper, consequence of using a word not in the audience's (one or many) vocabulary is the discovery of what we *don't* know and what you *do* know.

'And if *you* know and I don't, maybe I won't be able to understand your message. Maybe there's *too* much more I don't know, that you *do* know, to allow me to get the rest of your message.'

Widening the gap between the speaker and the receiver is a major pitfall whenever you use words to inform or persuade.

- *We learn how you feel about us.*

  Even further down in the subconscious is the idea that if *you* understand and know these words and I don't, and if you persist in using them, then you don't know much about me — your audience. You don't automatically know (if we know each other) or didn't bother to find out (if you're talking to strangers) what I understand of your subject; that I don't know the shorthand and acronyms you're using. And if you're not sensitive about that, you don't much care whether I get your message or not. If you did, you'd make a greater effort to make yourself instantly clear. You'd choose words that *would* be readily grasped. You would do *nothing* to get in the way of my continued attention and comprehension. If you cared about my getting your message, *not* just my finding out how smart *you* are . . .

- *The bottom line.*

  There are many built-in obstacles to people automatically accepting and absorbing information. This is true in general, but especially in the specific kind of information you'd like to impart in the work world. You often deal with new ideas, with changing how things are done, with trying to persuade others about your point of view. Knowing how people react to learning is vital to planning your communications strategy.

  And further: recognizing and accepting the ways in which our media have affected us and conditioned our systems of communication helps us to critique and hone our communication techniques.

  Finally, absorbing and understanding the basic principles of how we communicate and why we listen — what works, what doesn't, and why — starts you on the road to a realistic appraisal of what you want to say and how you plan to say it.

The next three chapters will tell you how to prepare for and design what you want to say: How to analyse and develop strategies; how to plan and schedule business encounters; how and when to use visual reinforcement; and what other techniques to consider in order to impart your message.

3
Getting ready to communicate
Forethought for strategies

Whether you're going to have a one-to-one meeting with boss, client, or staff member, give a presentation, or run a meeting, you obviously take the time to plan it.

For most of us, the planning usually starts with a case of nerves: What to say? How to begin? What's the best way to do this? This is usually followed by a series of notes scribbled, crumpled, and flung into the wastebasket or crossed out and rewritten. All the while we're hoping for an inspiration or the definitive word from above.

I propose a much more direct and organized route — a predictable series of steps to give you a solid base from which to plan any communications strategy. It's a systematic analysis using three basic questions that always need to be answered in order to set you on the right path for successful communication.

To demonstrate my system, let's start by looking at a typical business encounter. Let's look at how these usually go and what's basically wrong with the improvised, 'seat-of-the-pants' method of communicating, the one most of us usually engage in.

DEVELOPING STRATEGIES

What goes wrong and why

SCENE:
An executive's office. Staff member is about to be told off.
CAST:
THE EXEC: *a competent, ambitious, hard-working boss who wants*

his staff and their product to work like clockwork.
MIKE: *a staff member who has been getting his reports in late.*

ACTION:
EXEC: 'Look, Mike, I've told you twice now that your reports
          are late. I won't have it happen again!'
MIKE: 'But it's not my fault. It's . . '
EXEC: 'Look. No more excuses. Just shape up. Can you do the
          job or can't you? I want those reports on time. That's all!'
MIKE: 'Okay. Sorry. You'll have them.'

A common encounter. But — read it again. Do you think the Exec
has solved the problem? Do they know any more now than before?
Did they help to solve the problem? And do you think Mike, who's
still solely responsible for getting the reports done on time, will, or can,
truly change what's been happening — permanently?

In order to discover how to effect these outcomes by designing some
different methods of communicating, we need to look a little deeper
at what's going on:

Exec: Needs something and isn't getting it. Typically, they have gone
about getting it by the shortest route possible — complaining, demanding
(or telling), and expecting compliance.

Mike: Hears displeasure or criticism. Typically, he defends himself
or avoids confrontation by agreeing, though he still hasn't figured out
a better way to get his reports in on time.

Whats predictable here?

- The Exec will be angry.

- Mike will not refuse his boss's request.

- Mike's anxiety level will be raised.

- Mike's reports will probably be late again.

In the scenario just described, the Exec must depend on what Mike
says he'll do, *not* on the Exec personally, not on what they can find
out and add to solve or change things. This is not a strong position,
but one probably headed for more heat and frustration without
resolution.

Let's peel back another layer or two. What *else* may be going on
underneath the action? What issues are *not* being addressed?

- *Factual issues:*

  Exec:
  - Late reports make his/her job more difficult.
  - His/her superiors can tell the *Exec* off.
  - Late reports set a bad example for the rest of the staff.

  Mike:
  - He wants to keep his job.
  - He knows he's supposed to deliver the report.
  - To go forward he, like his colleagues, needs the boss's approval.
  - He can't seem to get the reports in on time.

- *Emotional issues:*

  Exec:
  - His authority is being challenged. He delegated those reports and told Mike when to deliver them, and it didn't happen. That's threatening and infuriating.
  - There is concern about having to prove his/her authority again.
  - There is also the hidden fear that he/she may not get total compliance. What then?

  Mike:
  - He feels bad (ashamed, ineffective, guilty) about his reports being late.
  - He worries about the threat of punishment, even losing his job.
  - He worries about the loss of affection and esteem.
  - Since he's failed so far, he fears he may not be able to comply.

Now what can we do with these deeper levels of information?

First: We can see how much of the behaviour in that scene, as played, is predictable, and why.

Second: We can use this foreknowledge to plan a much more active and effective problem-solving strategy.

Effective communication begins by deliberately analysing a situation *before* the encounter. *Then* planning.

Let's see how it works.

What makes a difference

The Exec, if he/she thought about it, would know that a straight frontal attack will surely produce predictable results: Mike would either be defensive and give excuses, or agree to anything just to make it end. Therefore, to be truly effective, the Exec should start the meeting on a totally different tack — information gathering.

By turning away from the predictable fury-and-threat reflex, he/she could start the meeting with a defused, benign (though very active) tone. The meeting then becomes a quest for clues and problem solving; a diagnosis rather than an eye-to-eye confrontation.

The new tack could go something like this:

EXEC: 'Mike, I know you've been having problems getting your reports in on time. I'm sure you don't like that any more than I do. Let's sit down and figure out what's going wrong and how to fix it.'

Now look at what he/she just did. No threat. No anger. (Two modes guaranteed to turn off Mike's thinking part.) The Exec shows recognition of a problem *and* recognition that Mike is probably upset by it and seemingly powerless to fix it alone. The Exec shows his/her ability and willingness to help solve it *and* to help Mike, not just to chastise him.

Mike's response? Disarmed and relieved, he's suddenly able to be very open in confronting the late-report problem. The Exec has established an atmosphere surprisingly different from the one Mike expected after being called to the boss's office — one that encourages honesty on both sides.

Creating a safe environment in which to consider the issue and *only* the issue, of why the reports are late, the Exec is on the way to fixing that. And Mike's basic character, general abilities, or good intentions are still intact, rather than threatened or called into question as in the first script. *Result:* Teamwork and constructive solutions. Mike can get some real help and new information about how to deliver reports on time, and the Exec's reports have a realistic chance to come in on time.

Case closed.

That's it? That simple?

Well — not quite.

Where we get stuck

The problem we have is with that old self-spirit: That powerful internal motivator sets up a stand-off between 'Me *first!*' and 'Who else gets included?'

Our self-spirit's hunger is so great that we can't wait: it's too scary to most of us to *first* pass the plate and say, 'After you!' before we get ours. We have no faith that our turn will *ever* come.

So — we move too fast. Too often, we push to the front of the line, blurt out our needs without thinking, and lose the chance to engage an ally; to piggy-back on the energy of *another's* self-spirit and use that drive as well as our own to make things come out well for both of us. In any *successful* encounter it can't be 'I get mine; you lose', but rather, 'I get (some of) mine; you get (some of) yours'.

This chapter is dedicated to showing you how, in any one-to-one encounter (or larger presentation or group meeting) you can more quickly achieve your goals with a little forethought about your opposite number's needs and concerns. Only then can you formulate a strategy designed for solutions and success, solidly based on motivation — yours *and* theirs.

FORETHOUGHT

You've just seen that spur-of-the-moment improvisation based on nothing but sheer gut-level reaction doesn't work effectively as a system for successful encounters and outcomes.

Once you're in an encounter, you need to be flexible, to seize the moment and go one way or another way. But you need to *start* with insight and build a strategy from that insight. You need *forethought*: to analyse a situation before you say or do *anything*. And to analyse it from more than a simply factual, practical point of view. *Much* more goes into what we do and how we hear and learn than surface behaviour.

Having discovered the huge motivational force that self-interest propagates, we need to learn about the self-interest of your audience.

Who is your audience?

Your audience is the recipient of your message. It could be your opposite number at a meeting you or they call. It could be the group assembled for a speech. It could be friend or foe, client or colleague.

Audiences all have one thing in common. They are on the other end of whatever you're sending. Your message and its possible effects are for them.

What makes a difference

What motivates your audience *before* your encounter begins? How will what you say or do either tap into their motivation or somehow change or affect them?

This is what you need to know to plan strategy, and this information and understanding can be gained only through Forethought. Developed in specific steps, Forethought gives you the insight to see what your audience's basic self-interest and motivations are; where yours and theirs clash or connect; what are the potential stumbling blocks to achieving your goals.

Forethought means going beyond the more obvious outward goals and delving into the inner realm as well; learning about deeper motivations, analysing needs and feelings on both sides.

What you know, what you need

A familiar audience

- *What's easy to know*
  What come to you at once are the specific characteristics of your familiar audience of one or several. You could quickly describe their special foibles: 'Joe? Yeah, he's great but don't mess him about. He's got a short temper!'

  'Listen, you know how long Susan always takes to get back to you. Makes me furious.'

  'Sheila takes her coffee black. Tom, you like tea, don't you? And Bruce, you're still on that decaffeinated stuff, right?'

  Surface behaviour insights born of frequent exposure to others are enormously useful. But they're not *all* you need to know. You also need some deeper insights. *They* can give you what you'll need in order to plan an effective and lasting communications strategy — one that motivates audiences to listen and act.

- *What's hard to know*
  If it's someone — or a group — you know and work with often, it's often harder to be able to answer deeper, consequential questions.

  Familiarity breeds complacency, not continued curiosity or the attention given to strangers. So, it's difficult to force yourself to sit down and look at this person or persons with a clear, analytical eye and answer hard, objective questions.

Example: Suppose you called a conference with two other colleagues about an issue at work. The content could be critical of one of them and could create new problems for the other. To help you prepare and predict what else you'd have to solve, could you answer: What are their goals, not only for this meeting but in relation to their work and their lives in general? What are their fears, their outlooks, their triumphs and disappointments on the job?

Could you predict their feelings, like: how do they feel about the coming encounter? What do they need from you? What do they expect will happen?

These deeper, more thoughtful questions require distancing and objectivity; a special effort. Hard to do when you're thinking: 'After all. I *know* these guys already . . .'

● *The dangers of a familiar audience*
When you address an audience of people you know, not only do you have difficulty knowing the deeper answers; you are also more likely to fall into sloppy communication habits.

Sometimes you don't try too hard because you know them and they know you. The old 'We all know why we're here, let's get on with it' syndrome. You don't feel you have to 'sell' to your friends. This makes it less likely that you'll plan deliberately, with adequate forethought.

Result? If it's a presentation, you may not notice that others are bored, unconvinced, or restless with the length, the preachiness, the predictability, or the sheer 'talkiness' of your message. Just as with your family, you feel you can get away with a lot. After all, you're a *member*! And as they say, 'Membership has its privileges . . .'

If it's a one-to-one meeting or even an informal phone conversation, familiarity can cause you to cut out all the usual niceties (the ones that really *count* in communicating) and to get right down to the task at hand.

So you may find that forethought and planning are often not your priority with a familiar audience. Too bad, you may be losing them more often than you think.

An unfamiliar audience

Here the opposite obtains: they're strangers; no automatic love and welcome. You have to be on your best behaviour and try *very* hard. You know immediately why you need to question who your audience is and what they like and need.

- *What's easy to know*
  The unfamiliarity of your audience makes it easier for you to answer the deeper questions about them. Because you start already removed from them, be it one or many listeners, it's easier for you to be able to see the whole picture, to generalize objectively about some basic truths. You can more readily imagine what they probably care most about, what their goals and needs are, how they would probably take your message as you deliver it or as they sit across a table from you.

- *What's hard to know*
  What you don't know, and often *can't* know, are their individual traits and unique characteristics. But you don't need to know those yet in order to plan.

What you need to know

- *Larger audiences*
  For purposes of planning a presentation to a group, you're looking for the broadest possible common denominators in order to include them all. Therefore, knowing the general facts about them *as a group* is exactly what's called for.

- *Smaller audiences*
  One or several people need more personal, individual information as well as the basic outlook. Your perceptual instincts (which we'll work to enlarge through these pages) can quickly fill in what personal characteristics your opposite number(s) seems to display once your meeting gets going, if you look and listen hard. Then you can adapt and correct your previous plans, if you need to.
  But in either case, you need first to find out about the self-interest or motivations of that audience in order to plan your communications strategy effectively.

We established earlier, with Mike and the Exec, that forethought is able to save you time and unproductive effort. We also discovered how predictable many needs and responses can be. Since your audience's motivations are the key to persuasion, how do you figure out what kinds of questions to ask yourself in order to prepare? How should you organize the answers into a usable strategy?

To codify how to do this efficiently every time, here are some basic principles and techniques — a system.

THE FORETHOUGHT CHART
The basic idea

The best system for forethought is to make a chart describing the motivations already in place and being brought to the encounter.

It's not only your *audience* you need to know more about as you sit down to plan your message or meeting; it's your *own* motivational profile, too. There's some deliberate self-discovery you need to go through to be sure all your bases are covered and that your goals will be achieved.

The chart's focus:

- What does the other person (or persons) want, need, and expect — both specifically and generally? What's important to them?
- What do *you* want, need, and expect? What's important to you?
- Where is the energy and the motivation for action for *you* as well as for them?
- What sources on both sides can you tap into to fulfil your intention for this encounter?
- How do they complement, interact, or clash.

No matter what communications challenge you face, the following chart will give you a basic framework within which to collect your thoughts in a disciplined, orderly fashion. It will organize the insights you need to design how and what you should communicate.

And the chart works whether you are the perpetuator of an encounter or the responder to an invitation or summons.

Why a chart?

A chart forces you to sit and purposefully think about motivation issues; it graphically shows you and makes you consider both sides.

Writing helps to clarify:

- It takes your thoughts to a much more clear-headed level, away from the instinctive, emotional one of operating by reflex alone.
- It forces you to reduce ideas and feelings to simple, succinct statements of fact.
- It makes ideas concrete. They stand still so you can reread and ponder what you're actually thinking.

The process

Let's go back and use our example of Mike and his Exec. How should the Exec go about working out the predictables? How could he/she know how to make the exchange different from and more effective than the initial unproductive encounter I described? By 'coaching' the Exec through the steps of creating a forethought chart and then showing the changes he/she would therefore make in a communication strategy, I can demonstrate, concretely, the uses and values of the forethought chart.

The format

Three categories — objective goals, emotional needs, and probable expectations — will cover the basic kinds of insights you'll need to prepare effective communications strategies. It will look like this:

You (Exec)	They (Mike)
Goals	Goals
Needs	Needs
Expectations	Expectations

I'll fill in a chart, using Mike and the Exec, to demonstrate and explain.

Do it yourself

To make this information most relevant to you and most easily absorbed into your routine, make your *own* chart as you read along, using an example from your own work life. Focus on a recent event, perhaps one that didn't go as well as you thought it should. See if you can gather some new insights about it as you design your own chart based on that encounter. You can also plan for a coming encounter and shed some new light, as we go through the steps of making a chart.

Normally, to get at the truth about what you really think and feel without yet being influenced by what you'll discover on the other side, you should complete the chart vertically on *your* side first — goals, needs, and expectations. Then, when you fill in your opposite number or opposite group's side, you can see the contrasts and differing motivations most keenly.

However, for purposes of explaining and showing you how to develop alternative strategies as we go along, we'll take each category and, completing both sides horizontally, discuss it before we move on to the next.

Objective goals

Yours

Step one is to determine the bottom-line goals of the encounter. Let's begin with the easier part — listing yours (the Exec's). Try filling this part out for *your* encounter and then check below to see what the usual problems are in this section of the chart.

I'll use the problem of Mike's late reports. The Exec has just called a meeting. What results does he/she want?

You (Exec)	They (Mike)
Goals	
1. Get the reports on time.	
2. Be sure Mike gets the message.	
3. Don't want to deal with it again.	

Reading this half of the chart can make you readily understand why the original scenario at the beginning of the chapter went as it did. Read the Exec's goals above, and then go back and read that opening scene again on page 65. See? It's all about 'I want' and 'I need'. None of it even acknowledges that there is another half to the chart, a Mike with *his* goals. This is the most common mistake we make.

Now here's the basic problem: as you just filled out your own chart with your own goals, can you see how one-sided your goals are? And looking at the blank space on the other half of the chart, can you now see, visually, that there *is* another side?

Let's spend a minute stating Mike's objective goals, the things *he* wants to accomplish in this meeting.

'Great!' you say. 'How about a lesson in clairvoyance?'

Not necessary. You don't even need lessons. You already know how to do it! It's based on two single concepts:

Empathy and observation. Major gifts of human nature.

To get the basic picture, the general idea of what *any* 'Mike' would want, empathize and identify with him or her. Just imagine yourself in any 'Mike's' shoes. What would *you* want to happen in a meeting called by the boss, knowing that your reports are late?

Then, to get the specific goals of not just any Mike but *your* Mike, use your perception, your observation skills. What do you know about Mike, specifically, from having worked with him? What makes him tick? How needy is he? How good at his job? Ambitious? Openly expressive or more withdrawn? Think about the opposite number or group in *your own* sample chart. Can you picture what his/her/their goals would be and list them?

Theirs

Let's create Mike's side of the chart. What are *his* objective goals, the things he would want to accomplish in this meeting? What would any 'Mike' want in this situation, based on our knowledge of human nature?

Fill in your own opposite number's side of your chart now. Then let's look at Mike's.

You (Exec)	They (Mike)
	Goals
	1. Keep my job. Get promoted. 2. Avoid the boss's wrath. 3. Try to get reports in on time.

Now what could our Exec learn from filling in Mike's side of the chart? And studying it as he makes his plans?

The first thing you (the Exec) would see is that wrath, recrimination, and desk-pounding would feed right into Mike's biggest anxieties. You'd realize that such an approach could shut down his thinking system and turn up the volume on his survival/defence mode. No ability to make changes then. No chance for honesty or problem solving. Just Mike protecting himself at all costs.

What else? You'd have the time to realize that Mike, along with being scared, would *like* to get the reports in on time and feels embarrassed about it before his peers. Everyone would rather do a job well than mess it up. Everyone would rather have praise than disapproval. This reflection on human nature could lead our Exec to plug into the energy of Mike's goals, his powerful motivating self-interest, to help them *both* solve the problem.

Look back at the goals on the Exec's side of the chart. The Exec wants to 'make sure Mike gets the message' and that it 'doesn't happen again'. How? One way certainly is to open a dialogue: to talk, not just to tell. The fact that the problem recurs tells you that Mike, on his own, hasn't been able to confront or solve it. He needs your (the Exec's) help.

Compare

Now let's put both sides of the chart together to compare both sets of goals as Mike and the Exec go into the meeting and see what they tell us. Then compare your own.

You (Exec)	*They* (Mike)
Goals	Goals
1. Get the reports on time.	1. Keep my job. Get promoted.
2. Be sure Mike gets the message.	2. Avoid the boss's wrath.
3. Don't want to deal with it again.	3. Try to get reports in on time.

Compare them horizontally, point by point. They hardly intersect at all! Not till you get down to number 3 on Mike's goals do you find any mention of the report. And the Exec's major goals have nothing to do with fear or feeling — or Mike, for that matter.

It's important to know that some of our goals can have nothing to do with the other person's, especially in a one-to-one situation. They can even be in opposition. Knowing another's goals is therefore vital. It makes us see many more dimensions to an issue. It tells us about the potential stumbling blocks and shows the path to effective communication.

So step one in designing a successful communications strategy is to define not only *your* goals but also those of your opposite number — the one you wish to influence.

- It makes you get clear about the results *you* want and can reasonably expect to achieve.
- It forces you to focus on the *other* person's self-interest and goals, making it possible to predict their behaviour.
- It helps you see *how* to tap into the energy of their self-interest and accomplish yours or at least part of yours as well.

All of these insights can determine what you select as the communications style and content you'll use; what will be most likely to influence others' behaviour and bring about a constructive outcome.

Emotional needs

Step two is to define inner needs — feelings. This part of the chart is much harder to do.

We're such a product-orientated society, bent on *outward* manifestations of success and external reassurance, that we don't often *consciously* visit inside to find out how we really feel about things and what our hungers are.

Yours

Getting in touch with and admitting what *else* we want, what our hidden fears and desires are, our hidden goals and feelings, requires great honesty. To surface and write them down, you need to give yourself permission to *have* those feelings of doubt, anger, greed, jealousy, ineptitude, or whatever.

Yet, unless you reflect and examine how you really feel and what's at stake for you *emotionally*, you will be ignoring a powerful set of propellants, with an energy and will of their own, ready to rear up and take over at any time. These hidden emotional needs are real and must be acknowledged and included in your communications strategy, since they will keep looking for a way to be satisfied — even at the expense of your logical, well-thought-out plans.

Lets get into our Exec's emotional needs first, with three scenarios, based on our three personalities from Chapter 1 — the Achiever, the Affiliator, and the Influencer. These needs can differ sharply, unlike the more practical and objective goals in the first category which would be universal in nature, based on their work type.

First, the hard-driving, perfectionist Achiever Exec.

Achiever (Exec)	Mike
Needs	
1. Mike should meet the standards I've set for myself.	
2. Must know reasons why not. This affects *my* performance.	
3. I'm frustrated by being stuck. Should have done it myself.	

Because Achievers are task-oriented and accomplishment-driven, this Exec would have a hard time looking at Mike's emotional needs or even understanding *why* Mike didn't get the report done. He/she, in order to improve communications skills, needs to understand that his/her task-driven viewpoint and highly focused motivation leave out a great number of other people who are needy in different ways. Seeing Mike's half of the chart would be *very* helpful in formulating a more effective approach than one based on simply getting tasks done. We'll look at Mike's emotional needs in a minute to see how they would intersect and might actually clash with the Achiever's typically spartan approach.

Now for the Affiliator Exec, who's much more people-orientated and people-needy:

Affiliator Exec	Mike
Needs	
1. Don't want to hurt Mike's feelings.	
2. If I yell at him he'll become hostile and his and my relationship will suffer.	
3. Maybe I'll do the report with him.	

Here the forethought chart serves another purpose. It can put people in touch with those of their *own* feelings that can sometimes work against the original goals.

Affiliators are very sensitive to feelings, so much so that tasks and strong administration are sometimes compromised. This Affiliator, in an effort not to make Mike mad or hurt his feelings, may not insist very effectively that the job get done. With the basic tendency to help out by joining in and doing, Affiliators can keep people from growing and taking responsibility seriously. Take a hard look at the goals section and then at the way this Affiliator Exec's needs may compromise those goals. An Affiliator Exec can satisfy both his emotional needs and objective goals, possibly in this way:

> **AFFILIATOR EXEC:** 'You know, Mike, I don't want to carry on and make a big scene [*taking care of the Affiliator's concern about hurting feelings*]. And I *do* want to treat you like the responsible, capable person I know you are. Let's find out what's wrong right now and solve it so *you* can get the report done by Monday. That's the final deadline. Fair?'

Now for the Influencer Exec, who manages with high personal impact:

Influencer Exec	Mike
Needs	
1. Need my power to be acknowledged and affirmed.	
2. I hate to lose in a confrontation.	
3. If I don't prevail, how will that affect my authority with others?	

How can the Influencer Exec include his needs in building his strategy? Number 1 on the list says the Exec needs to be reassured that he has his power acknowledged and affirmed. What better way than to continue to assert his power not by simply flaunting it but by truly demonstrating it:

> **INFLUENCER EXEC:** 'Mike, you know I used to have to do those reports, so I know what it takes. And since I oversee all the

processes in this department, lets see where stuff is breaking down so we can trouble-shoot our way out of this.'

First of all, the Exec says he knows all about it — the difficulties and the process itself. By asking for information so he can solve the problem, he shows how much leadership and knowledge (power) he really has. The knowledge to understand what needs fixing; the power to make it happen. This cuts the self-importance, the threatening postures, and truly states who's in charge.

This approach also solves need number 2, yet avoids the win-lose confrontation. By changing the encounter to a problem-solving quest, the possible heat and duelling is off. Now this may be at odds with how much some people need to pound tables or vent anger. I understand that, but we're designing *winning* communication strategies, and the temporary silence table-pounding imposes doesn't result in a *lasting* win.

Number 3 — the need to prevail yet concern about what will happen if he doesn't prevail — is also solved since the Exec will help direct the report his way *and* get it . . . his way! Yet notice that he's also saving Mike's pride and encouraging his participation at the same time that he's taking care of his power image in the eyes of others.

Theirs

Now let's get to what the other person needs — his inner feelings and hungers. Let's look at our example — Mike — again. But before we do, to get a more spontaneous response, fill out your half of the *Needs* chart *and* your opposite number's. Don't read Mike's till you do.

You (Exec)	They (Mike)
	Needs
	1. Need to know I can do it.
	2. Need reassurance that the Exec hasn't lost faith in me.
	3. Need to still feel a valued part of team.
	4. Need to be sure peers don't find out.

You can see how readily that new approach shown earlier — the constructive problem-solving approach — would fulfill Mike's needs.

Creating this side of the chart, the Achiever Exec can tune into Mike's emotional undercurrents. Comparing both sets of Goals and becoming more aware of his/her Emotional Needs as well as Mike's, that Exec can now see the challenge: His/her instinctive approach, in this case based on the task-oriented no-nonsense Achiever personality, needs to add some sensitivity to Mike's very different Needs in order to be successful in accomplishing his/her Goals. He/she could try to add the following to a typical Achiever directive:

ACHIEVER EXEC: 'Listen, Mike. Let me tell you *why* I need those reports on time. Actually the whole team does. Your reports are an integral part of how we get the work out of our department. When they're late . . .'

By telling Mike *why* he needs the reports on time, what *effect* their lateness has, how *important* Mike's contribution is to the whole team effort, he not only bolsters Mike's self-esteem and team membership but — more importantly — since he's working from knowing Mike's needs as well as his own, he can provide a major motivation for Mike to shape up. Helping Mike understand the responsibility for others and his effect on the team can make him pull his lateness out of the context of a merely personal foible.

Explaining your needs and the reasons why someone should do something, rather than a simple 'Do it', *always* engages the other person as a partner.

Further, true for *any* Exec, focusing on how Mike probably feels makes him/her think about not eroding Mike's self-confidence and about what reassurances Mike needs from him.

ANY EXEC: 'Look, you're hitting a snag. I know you can fix it, and if you see yourself getting behind, come and tell me before the reports start being late again so we can solve it. That's what I'm here for. By the way, this is a private matter between us . . .'

Bingo! This Exec did three things at once:

- Reassured Mike that he can do it and the boss still believes in him.
- Made a fail-safe device for Mike *and* himself ('hitting a snag', 'come and tell me') so that he doesn't get caught with late reports again.
- Made a safe environment for Mike ('so we can solve it', 'private

matter') to be sure that Mike *will* come to see him.

A special word about Number 4 — the need for face-saving, especially in any group work situation. This is actually a built-in fixture on *any* list of *anybody's* needs on both sides of the chart and must be factored into *every* communications endeavour. It's always there, for all of us. Insensitivity to anyone's pride and instinctive self-protection can sink any communication.

Compare

Now, let's look at the total chart so far, using the Influencer Exec. The Goals would be the same for all three executive types, but let's use the Power-Wielder/Influencer Exec's *Needs* chart:

You (Exec)	They (Mike)
Goals	Goals
1. Get the reports on time.	1. Keep my job. Get promoted.
2. Be sure Mike gets the message.	2. Avoid the boss's wrath.
3. Don't want to deal with it again.	3. Try to get the reports in on time.
Needs	Needs
1. Need my power to be unchallenged or fear I'll lose it.	1. I Need to know I can do it.
2. I hate to lose in a confrontation.	2. Reassurance that the Exec still has faith in me.
3. If I don't prevail, how will that affect my authority with others?	3. Need to still feel a valued part of team.
	4. Be sure peers don't know.

Notice first how much more emotional and personal the *Needs* category is than the more cerebral, impersonal *Goals*. And how much less *Needs* has to do with getting ahead than with getting 'fed' and feeling better. *Goals* is outwardly directed; *Needs* is directed inward.

I'm sure you also sense how powerful the *Needs* are, and how nagging and insistent, how pervasive would be the feelings they arouse. The combination of both categories obviously provides the major motivations for each party to do anything in this encounter. It also provides the motives for blocking and resisting anything that wouldn't fulfill those outer goals and inner needs.

Now you can see the road signs to failure or success in planning your communications strategy.

Understanding and taking care of your opposite number's goals and needs, and truly, consciously understanding and accepting your own goals and needs, puts your planning on a solid plane of awareness and informed choice. *The amount of sensitivity and thought you put out to probe your own goals and feelings and to imagine and understand Mike's is in direct proportion to how quickly you'll get back what you want and need.*

Do it yourself

Compare the two categories you've filled in on *your* chart so far. Pretty enlightening, isn't it, to see the directions in which each side could take you, and pretty challenging to find strategies that would include both?

Before we go on, let's recognize that I've focused more on the personal aspects of the communications problem — how you get someone to 'hear' you — and less on simply solving the task itself. Why? Because my premise is that the best way to get the practical task done is to go *behind* the obvious to start up the *real* engine that makes us work.

Now let's turn to the third category on your chart — Expectations.

Probable expectations

This category deals with the fact that we are all conditioned by past experience to imagine what will or could or probably would happen at a coming communications encounter.

Given previous knowledge of the players — their roles relative to each other, what's going on currently at work, and what reasons there could be for the meeting — anyone could predict a probable scenario, complete with content, style, emotional level, even outcome. It's not only what we've lived that teaches us how to do this; it's all the books, plays, films, and TV we've experienced that show us how people usually are and what they usually do in any given set of circumstances.

So we all walk around with expectations — stereotypic images of people's interactions in a close or a large encounter that we can call on when faced with a coming event. And we all use these to imagine the event because just walking into the unknown creates anxiety. Trying to predict it is preferable to just plain worrying over an impending experience. But curiously enough, we don't do it productively. Just vague, random musings, flashes of images, a general sense of the meeting. Not specific. Not analytical. We don't get added value from this kind of predicting and imagining.

That's too bad. *Deliberately* discovering what you expect will happen helps uncover your mental set and how conditioned you already are toward what you'll do. It helps you scrutinize whether that's the best choice of action, or whether to detour and start on another tack. So much of our communication is based on sheer habit, not designed from current information and deliberation. Anticipating by finding out what you're assuming, and often being surprised at how pointless or self-destructive or negative it is, can be an enlightening and valuable experience.

Even more valuable is trying to predict what your *audience* expects will happen.

Yours

Step three in creating your forethought chart is consciously to imagine what *you* expect will happen and what your opposite number expects; to discover what's predictable. Let's see what our Exec might expect to happen at the meeting, especially if he/she fills out his/her whole half of the chart first, which, as I told you, is the best way to do this.

You (Exec)	They (Mike)
Expectations	
1. I'll be firm and irritated.	
2. Mike will apologize and make excuses.	
3. He'll promise to fix it.	
4. I'll give him another chance.	

Number 1 on the Exec's list tells us that he will probably move into an emotional mode that we've now discovered won't work. Seeing that in the light of both sides of the chart when he fills it all in can make our Exec reconsider and decide against it. Especially after the insights he'd gain from the other two categories.

Numbers 2 and 3 tell us that, no matter what the Exec says, Mike's response is a foregone conclusion. This can alert the Exec to try something quite different, if he really wants to shake Mike up a little and make him think and change. The previous two categories — *Goals* and *Needs* — on Mike's side of the ledger will tell the Exec that more 'firm and irritated' speech isn't going to do it.

Therefore he has a chance now to find his way to the approach I recommended — naming the problem, *without blame*, and then asking questions in order to uncover the underlying flaw, the reason why Mike's reports are always late. This can finally lead to the Exec's helping in the solution.

The 'no-blame' issue deserves an extra moment of thought. The most destructive thing we do when something goes wrong is to spend time blaming and being judgemental. The dynamics are so wasteful and the outcome so predictable. Here's why:

● It's done. Berating for past mistakes cannot fix the past. It can only polarize two people.
● Everyone, just about, gets defensive when they have made a mistake. If a mistake takes place, harping on it can only make someone extra-defensive and therefore resentful and even counter-aggressive. It never 'teaches a lesson'! It only evokes anger.
● Emphasizing what went wrong and how wrong it was in a judgemental way derails *constructive* outcomes such as fixing the problem and ensuring that it doesn't happen again.

Therefore my recommendation is to follow a no-fault policy. The guilty party *is* guilty and generally feels pretty bad about it. Be clear about what went wrong, but let him/her off the defensive hot-seat by analysing the issue objectively and solving the mistakes impersonally. This saves the apologizing and/or excuses time and eliminates the need to counter-attack.

Number 4 on the list, 'I'll give him another chance', tells the Exec that he really *wants* Mike to succeed. That he's *not* ready to make this a last-ditch stand. That his underlying motive is to give Mike another chance.

If that's true, give him the best chance you can. Give Mike new information and tools to climb out of the pit he seems to be stuck in! Help him out! He obviously can't fix it alone or he would have done so.

Theirs

Imagining yourself as Mike, in such a situation, can make you stop your plan simply to be 'firm and irritated'. Becoming aware, and predicting, as you explore your expectations, that he'll probably be defensive or promise you anything just to be done with the meeting, makes you start thinking of a more productive strategy with a more lasting outcome.

An even more important reason to move to the other side of the chart and find out what Mike expects is the element of *surprise*.

The quickest way to get anyone's attention is to do the unexpected — whether it's a pie in the face (not often recommended in the office) or simply behaving very differently from the way someone anticipated.

Knowing what Mike *thinks* will happen, what he *expects* you're going to do and say, gives you the opportunity to come in from another direction entirely. This has the double benefit of not only making Mike give total attention to the new set of circumstances, with no previously conditioned response at the ready, but also making him come up with a much more genuine and unguarded reaction to what you say and do, to really *hear* you. It puts new life and energy into the meeting, into both the discussion process and the outcome.

Given the history and the issues, here's what Mike could expect the Exec would do at the meeting:

You (Exec)	They (Mike)
	Expectations
	1. He'll probably be mad.
	2. He'll demand that reports be in on time.
	3. He won't want any lame excuses.
	4. He wants me to promise to get it right.

Seeing this array, it's little wonder that Mike would walk in feeling defensive and insulated from being able to hear and face the truth, and thus from developing new behaviour.

It's funny. Whenever you assess another's expectations, the other person suddenly becomes much more human in your eyes. You can really *see* them, sitting around picturing you and what you're like and what you'll do.

You can also quickly sense vulnerabilities, anxieties, and aspects you'd never think about if you were only thinking about outcomes and conquering opposition. Imagining that other person and his/her expectations makes you deal with the specifics of that person so much more individually and creatively.

Look at your *own* chart again. Did you find yourself falling into stereotypical behaviour patterns? Surprised to find out what you were probably going to do? How has knowing this added to the rest of your chart, changed your strategy?

Now, let's look at Mike's side and see what would work:

Surprise

First, I suggest you use that element of surprise I spoke of. It takes some self-control but it's worth it. Surprise him by *not* acting mad, although you may be! That's the first splash of cold (actually warm) water you can give him to alert him to the fact that this isn't 'business as usual'.

Instead, start by telling him, in factual and benign terms, that you see a problem:

EXEC: (*calmly, pleasantly, factually*): 'Mike, I think we've hit a snag.'

Then surprise him even further by stating what he (Mike) probably thought would happen:

EXEC: 'Now I suppose you think I'm just going to pound on the table and say, "Dammit, get those reports in on time!" But that's not very constructive, as I see it. Although it would make me feel much better 'cause what you're doing is giving me a lot of grief and creating a problem for the whole group.'

Let's see what this does. You can quickly see that the Exec has defused the situation without losing sight of what he wants to accomplish. He has injected some information about his sensitivity to how Mike probably feels *and*, very important, how *he*, the Exec, feels. A human touch, sorely lacking in most such exchanges . . .

The most important thing he's done, however, is to use that most elusive, difficult element guaranteed to startle — the truth! Saying out loud what both of you are thinking. Being authentic doesn't happen often enough in our daily lives.

The truth is generated to startle whenever we hear it. And to make us feel relieved. It put us both on solid ground and actually draws us closer. For the boss to tell Mike the truth of how he feels makes it safe for Mike to tell the truth and admit to his feelings, too.

The only other ingredient missing in the Exec's opening is a little lightness of touch to get the ball rolling. That's easily inserted. Watch:

EXEC: (*smiling*): 'Now I suppose you think I'm just going to pound on the table and say (*pounding table in an exaggerated way*), "Dammit, get those reports in on time!" But that's not very constructive, as I see it. (*Pauses, laughing*) Although it would make me feel much better, I'll tell you 'cause what you're doing is giving me a lot of grief and creating a problem for the whole group!' (*Then get serious*).

Adding some animation (see parentheses) and humour to any delivery energizes both of you and gives some balance to the exchange.

Humour

It's surprising how rarely we allow that extra dimension — lightness and humour — into our business dealings. Work is serious to almost everyone. Very serious. But too many people lose their sense of humour and proportion as they concentrate on accomplishing a goal.

They particularly don't recognize the *power* of humour, how lightening the atmosphere can actually strengthen your hand. In any meeting or event, being able to use humour shows you in such *control*, and so much at *ease*, that you can afford to lighten up a sober or important situation, and by doing so, lighten the atmosphere for everyone. What control! Powerful! And so welcomed by everyone you're dealing with.

Humour has the additional benefit of *disarming* everyone and cutting tension. To break that toe-to-toe stance allows everyone to put the fists or the defensive armour down for a minute and start afresh.

And isn't that what the Exec wants to do? Doesn't he want to make Mike *listen* and *think*, without the need to put on a show for the boss? To effect some real changes in Mike's seemingly conditioned pattern?

The Exec can afford to lighten up, too, because it's his/her meeting. Since he's running it, he can choose to lighten up whenever he/she needs to.

Compare

Let's see if this approach, the planned surprise based on knowing what Mike expects, would make all that happen.

How would Mike react?

- Surprised at the calm, open environment created by the boss, Mike drops some of his defensiveness and thinks: 'Hey, this may not be as bad as I thought!'
- 'You thought I'd pound on the table . . .' says the boss. Mike thinks: 'That's right! That's just what I was afraid of. He really does understand my side, too. I never knew that.'
- 'But that's not very constructive . . .' says the boss. Mike gets the word that this will be a constructive meeting, not a recriminatory one.
- Exec: 'Make me feel much better . . . giving me a *lot* of grief . . . creating a problem . . .' Mike: 'I never thought of it that way before — "grief", "a problem", for *him*!'
- Exec: '. . . creating a problem for the *whole group*'. Mike: 'What does he mean, the *whole group*? How? It's not about them — it's about *me* and my reports, isn't it?'

See what's happening? Remember the Exec's original goals?

Exec	Mike
Goals	
1. To get the reports on time.	
2. To fix it permanently.	
3. For Mike to get the message.	

Can you see that the Exec really is on his/her way? And it's not just cosmetics. Mike is in a position now to hear and learn. To be motivated to change because he's beginning to learn the full impact of his lateness with the reports and where it, and he, really fit in the scheme of things. What effect he has on others is an incontrovertible truth, unlike the illusions Mike feeds himself whenever he's late and gives himself sole permission to do.

So, we've solved the boss's assignment for forethought. To plan and think through the situation *before* you set out, half-cocked, on a course destined for defeat, not success.

What about *your* chart? What new plans did you develop based on it? At this point there's one more piece to add to this chart process.

A chart for the summoned

Can the summoned person use forethought as well as the summoner? Is any of this process useful to Mike? Could *he* make a chart as he prepares for this meeting with his boss? Would it help *him* be more effective? Certainly.

Mike, or anyone summoned to a meeting not of their own making, urgently needs to anchor himself with some insights. By thinking through his own goals, needs, and expectations — his own motivation — he gets clear on how he feels about the meeting and what he anticipates. He gets even truer clarity when he does the boss's half of the equation as well.

It isn't easy for a person in a lesser, more dependent position to imagine the realities of the boss's position. It may even look to you that all your problems would be solved if only *you* were the boss — in charge, on the *giving* rather than the *receiving* end.

Mike, therefore, will perhaps have some trouble imagining the boss's anxieties, his problems. It's easier for the Exec to look back on *his* earlier days when he wasn't in charge in order to understand Mike, than for Mike to imagine the boss's position.

All the more reason for Mike to try. It will make his response to the boss so much more knowledgeable and effective, so much more responsive to the issues at hand rather than only to his own needs. Mike can then become oriented to my basic premise — give the other person what *they* need, first, and you'll get yours, too. Or at least *some* of yours.

Discovering, as he focuses on the boss's goals, that the boss has other goals entirely; that they are practical and necessary ('How do I get Mike to give me those reports on time?') not just muscle-flexing, makes Mike think again about *his* attitude and what would be a more appropriate approach to the meeting.

As he charts the boss's inner needs ('I need my people to do what I ask them to do'), Mike begins to develop sympathy for the boss's position, not just for his own.

As for expectations, he could recognize that the boss would *expect* him to promise to do better. What else would the boss think Mike would do? Say, 'Forget it. I'm doing the best I can'? So, if the boss obviously expects a promise but will probably not believe it, Mike had better do something else to shore up his credibility.

Recognizing all this, Mike could well begin to rethink his whole position about being late. Why *is* he? What *can* he do to change that? How can he get some good, hard advice about another way to do the reports? This thinking could open the way to Mike himself starting the conversation:

> **MIKE:** 'Before you begin, let me say that I know my reports have been late. I just haven't been able to short-cut enough stuff to get them in on time. Maybe if I talk it through with you, we can find a solution.'

Bingo again! Mike gains points in three different areas:

- He surprises the boss! By *not* giving an excuse or a promise he gets the boss's attention and sets the boss off on another track.
- By taking the initiative, he shows the boss his good intentions and *true* desire to fix the problem. And that he has courage.
- Putting himself in the active 'mea culpa' role lessens the need for the boss to make critical comments and shows another side of himself: Mike as positive problem solver, eager and able to change.

To sum up: forethought is crucial to effective communications strategies. Here's a summary and checklist from which to work your forethought chart:

FORETHOUGHT CHECKLIST

1. *Make a chart.*
   Deliberately writing succinct facts instead of just vaguely thinking about something makes you become aware of all the forces in a coming encounter, whether you're the caller of the meeting or the person summoned.
2. *Take the time to discover and state your own goals.*
   If you dig, you'll find out *all* you really want to happen at the meeting, and you can use that as an agenda to be sure it happens.
3. *Analyse your audience's goals.*
   What outcomes would that person or group logically want from the meeting? See their position clearly. What do they want from

you? Remember that they can't give you the fulfillment of your goals unless they get some of theirs, too.

4. *Be honest about your emotional needs.*
    Without judging whether they are worthy and should be there or not, acknowledge and allow yourself to have emotional needs. Have the courage to find, recognize, and state them in writing.

5. *Uncover the other's emotional needs.*
    Through imagination and perception, become aware of what your opposite number's or audience's feelings probably are in relation to the coming meeting. Reverse roles to find out what you, or anyone, would need in that situation.

    Then, given those needs we would all share, go from the general to the specific. If it's someone you know, use your perception and knowledge of this particular person or group to add to your insights about what they would need emotionally in this situation.

6. *Find out what you expect to have happen.*
    Quell that gut reaction. Make yourself recognize and rethink your conditioned style and response to the coming situation. Analyse whether that's the best way, given what else you now know.

7. *Imagine the other's expectations of the meeting.*
    What do they probably expect? Build on that stereotype of what is expected, going for the element of surprise. Open new avenues to a closer meeting of the minds by using another tack than the one most expected.

8. *Disarm.*
    Use that greatest element of surprise and persuasion — the truth! And don't do the expected: Try a new approach to get attention. And, most of all, don't forget the power of humour.

Forethought for larger audiences

All the processes the Exec went through to understand and better prepare for his one-to-one meeting with Mike work equally well when planning to speak to small group meetings or larger audiences. Here you'd look at the broad picture of what the most common sets of Goals, Needs, and Expectations would be, given the topic and circumstances of your presentation.

You'll find more specifics about how to use the forethought chart to plan meetings and design speeches in the chapters specifically devoted to those topics. Right now, let's turn to the next series of steps in developing successful communications at work: How to organize and structure any business encounter.

4
Structuring and organizing business encounters

Have you ever thought about the following factors as you go about the nuts and bolts of planning and scheduling your business encounters?

- How we all operate physiologically at work: Energy levels, low/high times of day, the hunger factor, and what effect all these have on how we communicate.
- How space and environment affect our creativity and responses.
- What is the best time and location to schedule based on the content of your meeting.
- How communication affects getting your meeting when you want it.

Let's examine some rarely thought of, but basic, truths about people that affect communication in business encounters, and see how to include these when you plan and schedule such encounters.

PREPARATION

To think through what you mean to accomplish *before* you even schedule your encounter, and to organize your preparation, you need to take the following steps. This is true whether you are in power and *calling* the meeting or *asking* for a meeting with the boss.

Choose and edit your goals

What do you want to accomplish?

First, consider what you want the meeting to produce. Make an objective list. Write it *all* down, putting *everything* you'd like to have happen on paper straight off. There'll be time to select and destroy after you've thought about *all* these things you would like to accomplish.

Once you've written it all down, the editing and selecting should be based on three factors: practicality, scope, and timing.

Practicality

Be realistic. This probably is not the last, or only, meeting you're going to have.

Edit your list based on what is actually achievable in this meeting, given the length of time to prepare and the boss's, or employee's, predisposition toward or previous knowledge about your subject.

Decide whether your goals can be achieved in one meeting or need to be accomplished in a series of meetings.

Scope

Consider who else needs to be involved in your plan. Are they already on track? Do you need separate meetings with them before the big one? Should they be included?

Timing

Think about whether this is the *right time* to present this idea or make this request. Consider:

- What's going on in your workplace right now? If your agenda involves a request for money or other resources, is business good? Does it need more sales or new ideas? Can it afford yours right now?
- Your boss's situation: How receptive would he/she be to your subject matter at this moment? Is he perhaps in the throes of some crisis, personal or business? What does she particularly need and can your material dovetail with that, or is it irrelevant right now?
- If your material is out of synch but needs to be handled, how can

you make it more timely? Can you find a connection for fitting it in with existing projects and problems?

- If you're the boss and your meeting involves an employee or staff member, how can you time what you need to say for maximum receptivity? Have you taken account of personal crises as well as the problems at work? How will they affect the employee's or staff member's capacity to learn, absorb, and act on what you want to make happen?

- Approaching holidays also make a difference. If it's a tough or long-term problem or issue, remember that people get into a disengaged, euphoric mood as holidays approach. It might be difficult to make them look hard at ongoing work issues until after they come back.

Length of meeting

Next think about how long the meeting should be. With any meeting ask:

- What do you want it to cover?
- What forms of support do you need?
- Can visual materials be used to shorten presentation times?
- Will research or reports be presented?
- How long are they? How much time is needed?
- Is this complex or sticky? How long will the discussion phase last?
- What's the usual time length for meetings in your shop?

If it's a new subject or a long one with many complex side-issues, you might want to see the initial meeting as one of a series.

You might start by planning a 'pre-meeting', just setting up or introducing the topic with some background on why it's a good idea. Material could then be left behind to back up ideas or plans, thus warming up and enlightening the receiver(s) at their own convenience. This should not be a long meeting.

Plan to give intro material time to germinate. Hold the next meeting for presentations of the major thrust, the nitty-gritty of your agenda. This meeting will, of course, be longer since you'll plan a discussion period so that everyone understands what it's all about.

If it's a shorter, one-shot meeting, think of the length in terms of:

- Whether or not the participants already have enough information.
- Whether presentation(s) can be made succinctly enough to get it all in.

● Whether the multiple things you want the meeting to accomplish are naturally related to each other or belong at separate meetings.

SCHEDULING THE MEETING

After you've selected the basic agenda issues, get your meeting scheduled. But wait. There is more thinking involved before you just take that walk down the hall or pick up the phone.

Optimally, when you call a meeting with boss, peers, clients, or staff, you're looking for people to give their best: undivided attention, high-energy focus, a receptive and open frame of mind. Many factors govern our ability to give all this. They can all be affected by scheduling.

Although the reality of the workplace may not always allow you total discretion about when and where you'll schedule a meeting, I'll now give you the best-of-all-possible-worlds suggestions.

When to meet

Time of day

Choosing the best time of day and day of the week is the first step toward successful business encounters. To customize one-to-one meetings for optimal conditions, your choice should take into account the unique work habits of your opposite number and the demands of his/her work and personal life. For larger groups, some basic truths about all of us and how we respond at different times of the working day and days of the week should be considered. Here are several key factors:

Biorhythms

Everyone operates with a different metabolic clock. Some people are 'chirpers', rising with the dawn, able to move mountains before ten o'clock. Others are 'night owls', whose biorhythmic curve rises as the days goes on. They really hit their stride late in the day and love to work far into the night, while the 'chirpers', losing their speed by mid-afternoon, are happy to put the brain to bed early.

Although we may not all be *totally* one or the other, the general categories of 'chirper' and 'night owl' cover most of our biorhythmic curves.

Therefore, for top attention and energy, become aware of your own *and* your opposite number(s)' energy patterns.Try to take these into account as you schedule your meeting.

If it's a large organization, try to find out enough about the other person(s) from secretary or colleagues to know what time of day to call the meeting based on usual work habits, etc. And know yourself well enough to give yourself a break by selecting *your* best time, too. But if these two times are at loggerheads, put your opposite(s)' preference first. Your adrenal glands will pump you up well enough to overcome *your* lack of energy!

Hunger

Maximum receptivity also has to do with feeding. In our task-orientated work world, hunger sounds like something you should be able to control. But when we get near feeding time, two involuntary things happen:

- Our blood sugar gets low. We feel a real drop in energy as well as a heightened drive to get fed. It's hard to concentrate on anything except wanting food! We become grouchy and see any obstacle to getting filled up as a decided irritant, to be gotten rid of as soon as possible. Not a good frame of mind in which to concentrate.
- Feeling hungry makes us feel depleted and deprived. We become very needy and self-involved, looking for deposits, not withdrawals. This hardly puts us in a frame of mind to give away anything whether it's hard cash, acquiescence to a new idea, or even the benefit of the doubt.

    Therefore, the hunger factor must always be considered. And not only in relation to lunch.
- Mid-morning is often pick-me-up time, when you need another energy charge to feel sated, especially if lunch in your workplace is usually at one o'clock.
- Late in the day also needs a charge to keep us going at work, from a mid-afternoon snack if lunch was early to a four o'clock pick-up if the work day doesn't end till six or beyond.

If you're absolutely stuck with the wrong meeting hour, bring a nibble into the meeting or even just some coffee to take the edge off. No, this isn't overdoing it. Feeding people at a low ebb in their energy not only perks them up; it has the added advantage of putting you psychologically in the position of gift giver *before* you ask for something.

One last thought on this: Don't plan meetings too soon after lunch. Making your opposite number have to cut lunch short to get back to you and your meeting is hardly the mental set you want to begin with. Get some hard information about when he/she usually returns, when he/she will be going out to lunch on the day of your meeting, etc. Give an extra half-hour to allow for lateness and the inevitable messages that are always waiting to be handled as soon as he/she gets back from lunch.

'Rush hours'

Traffic going and coming from work causes many people to make elaborate arrangements, if they possibly can, to beat the rush.

Find out when your other participant(s) likes to leave or arrive at work and how successfully they carry that out. The last thing you want is to face a fuming, irate survivor of the daily transportation struggle.

- Some people love to arrive at 7.00 a.m. to get a head start on their work. They might be very receptive to a breakfast meeting or at least a very early one. (More about the pros and cons of eating-meetings in the next section.)
- People who come in by train have very rigid schedules and begin to get uptight as the witching hour approaches. Asking the boss for a late afternoon meeting can be deadly unless you know that he/she is very loose about which train he catches.
- Bosses should be aware that car-sharing has its own set of disciplines and you may not be dealing with a totally self-determining employee when you call a meeting at the end of the day or first thing in the morning. This creates great tension for an underling who has to ask to terminate a meeting called by a superior, or who comes late through no fault of his own. Very late or very early meeting planners — beware!

Distractions

The last aspect of the best meeting time to consider is: When can you get undivided attention?

- If you're going to someone else's office for the meeting, ask or observe and discover the other person's work schedule.

- If the meeting is in your office, think about when you are least likely to have to take calls or make decisions as well as when your opposite number is least likely to get called away.
- Knowing how things usually go in your shop (when meetings are called, what time of day is big rush or deadline time, etc.) is a start to determining the least distracting time of day.

Work habits

When does the boss like to clear the desk, return calls, read reports, or think, and when is he/she busiest or most pressured? This requires some inside information. If your workforce is small and the boss highly visible, you can probably answer for yourself. If not, ask his/her secretary when you make your appointment. (More on how to do this later.)

Which day

The content

The determination about choosing which day should be made based on subject matter and the follow-up you want.

- Monday finds people needing to get into gear, remember what they left undone from last week, and generally push themselves up to work speed after a weekend of winding down. On the other hand, it has the advantage of still-clear heads, before the week's demands overtake the empty spaces. It also means that you have a whole week to work on something and meet about it, providing some continuity.
- Friday is indeed the day of surfeit, with people generally hanging on till the weekend respite comes. It feels more like ending something than a time to consider beginning something or suddenly having an added factor to think about. Friday afternoons are the worst time to challenge people to just think. It's also difficult for them not to ruminate about when the meeting will be over!
- A meeting about a big subject should happen on a Monday, later in the morning, with a plan to meet again during the week. (Don't neglect the coffee here.)
- One-off meetings of benign information, giving or getting, can happen any day, but keep basic time-of-day principals in mind.

● Bad news or criticism meetings should not happen on Fridays. Friday has an air of finality to it. It gives the recipient a weekend of ruminating and blowing things out of all proportion, coming to work on Monday with a heavy heart rather than with renewed determination to do better.

If you hold critical meetings during the week just before lunch of before going home at the end of the day, you give the person a break and a chance to cool off before needing to go back to work and face you. You also give him/her a chance to recoup within the work-week setting and to get feelings back to normal before the weekend. Additionally, this choice also gives him/her a chance to recoup within the work-week setting and to get feelings back to normal before the weekend. Additionally, this choice also gives him/her a chance to implement some of what you suggest, even to discuss it again.

To wrap up: Timing (time of day and which day) and individual bio-rhythms and work habits are often ignored, but they're a vital tool. They can affect you adversely if you are unaware of their effect or don't offset them. They can guarantee a longer attention span, a more willing listener, a more alert participant, or leave you vaguely wondering why the meeting didn't go too well.

The next thing to consider in planning meetings is where. Although this is not always at the planner's discretion, let's discover the best environment for a meeting or encounter.

Where to meet

Work spaces are meant to be practical and are analysed first for their functional aspects, but we also respond *emotionally* to our work environments.

Our need for personal space

Think about yourself on a long plane ride. Did you ever notice how quickly you stake out your territory at your seat and make it uniquely, cosily, familiarly yours? Where and how you put your hand-luggage for best access; how you arrange your blanket and pillow and how that quickly becomes a personal comfort zone; how you carve out a little work space right there; and how suddenly it loses its meaning when you arrive at your destination and no longer need your own unique 'space'?

We snuggle in and do that same personalizing with our bit of ground at the beach, in a hotel room — whenever we find ourselves in an alien environment. Our basic sense of nesting and shelter and our need to make *our* dent in an impersonal world prompt us to make any space we're in for a while our own.

Therefore we become sensitive to the messages any environment gives us and we all respond to the space we're in. So it's important to look at what messages and responses meeting environments generate.

'Turf' and power

The most important thing to consider about spaces at work is the relative amount of power that differing work environments symbolize. Therefore, depending on what you wish to accomplish, the choice of meeting location must be carefully considered from the power point of view and for the messages it sends.

- Who's calling the meeting and for what reason?
- How do you want your opposite number(s) to feel?
- Do you want them to be aware of how much power you have?
- Do you want to downplay the power so your opposite number(s) feels more secure?
- Are you trying to neutralize the power issue in order to motivate and build a team spirit?
- Do you perhaps wish to add a personal touch? To relax your client, employee, or colleague?
- What effect does eating-and-meeting have?

Let's look at each of the most common meeting environments for the statements they make and the effects they create. We'll focus on the players, the subject matter, and the desired outcome.

Your office

The most important effect of 'my office' is one of turf. Be aware of the obvious ownership and power your office symbolizes. Look at it. It's filled with *your* things: *your* calendar, *your* urgent work spread before you, *your* trophies and awards displayed, *your* pictures and momentos on the wall — in short, *your* turf.

This fact creates the following response: It makes the other person feel like a fish out of water — *his* or *her* water. Your office obviously sends 'someone else's seat of power' messages to whoever enters it. It speaks of someone *else* exercising sole discretion and judgement about how things are done in that space. It's clearly not the space where the visitor does that, too.

Your office is therefore:

* Challenging to a person who also feels power, or needs to.
* Threatening to a person who doesn't feel power.
* Official and serious, even scary, to an employee — almost like going to the headmaster's office when you were at school.
* A plus if your employee wants the reassurance of your power, which may then be used on his/her behalf.

The challenge in your office is to reassure meeting participants that although you *do* have the power, you can be flexible and responsive, too.

Their office

Going to someone else's office implies respect.

* It gives him/her extra turf, especially if you're the senior person.
* It puts that person at ease, because we all respond with comfort to familiar surroundings. Our eyes subliminally send us the message that 'all is well, we're in our own cave, nothing can get us here'.
* If you're a peer, going to someone else's office gives him/her a leg up, but in certain circumstances you might want to do just that: to flatter and thus disarm him/her in order to get a more receptive audience.
* If you're the boss, going to a staff member's office has the element of the unusual and the noteworthy. Employees don't usually get a visit from the boss.
* If you want to do some motivating and team building, the informality and gesture of appreciation that going to his/her office implies is very effective. Again, remember to tell your employee and make a real appointment. You could still keep it casual and

relaxed by saying, 'let me drop by your office tomorrow at about three to talk over a few things.'

- It's very informative to see where someone else works and to discover what symbols *they* use to say 'power' and 'comfort' and 'mine' to themselves and to others.
- It tells you something about someone else's work habits (cluttered desk or cleared and organized, reference books all over the place, other interests suggesting a sense of balance and proportion, etc).

If you wish going to someone else's office to have a benign effect, plan it. Don't just drop in! That's a real shocker and brings up panicked thoughts like 'My office is a mess!' 'Why didn't I put my lunch away?' and so on. (Of course, having the boss see you as such an avid worker that you don't even leave for lunch is not all bad!)

Neutral territory

A conference room or other generic work area that has no unique personal identity is still another meeting environment with built-in messages. This kind of territory says: 'Concentrated, objective *work* done here'.

- It implies focusing on a subject, on problem solving, not on each other.
- It speaks of leaving the daily considerations of the job outside while you both (or all) direct total effort towards a separate topic.
- It speaks of the anonymous and transitory nature of the meeting — that no one makes a real dent or leaves a mark here, and that the waters close over and erase what you did as soon as you leave, making ready for the next users.

The disadvantage of conference rooms is that they are very impersonal. Effort must be made, if the meeting is a lengthy or intense one, to warm up this environment and make it personal.

- The colours and objects in such a room have a great bearing on how much such an environment invites people to give their all for an abstract idea and how stimulating it is creatively. Notice that ambiance and use it as a decision factor, too.
- Conference rooms need to be made more nurturing environments if you want people to put out and give much of themselves. Meetings

in conference rooms should therefore include feeding, both for its break-in-the-proceedings value as well as for two sensual messages it sends to the participants: the feeling of being 'stoked up', which encourages people to put out more energy, and the feeling of being valued and cared about because someone is aware of and giving to them.

Consider going to a neutral territory conference room if one of your goals is to equalize the proceedings and get everyone focused on business, not on oneupmanship.

To lunch or not to lunch

The advantages

The greatest single attribute of a lunch meeting is getting to know each other better and gaining the kinds of information you can tuck away and work with at your leisure to pad out the picture of a person you're dealing with.

- Lunch can be a uniquely disarming experience, giving the lunchers a chance to discover other personal aspects that would never come up at work. The usual discussion of food, complete with likes and dislikes; the choices you each make; how fast or slowly each of you eats; your table manners; what, or if, you drink; how you each handle the waiter — all of these added dimensions give great meaning and value to lunch as a meeting-time choice, especially if you notice and absorb the personal information.
- You break into the middle of the day but solve that hunger problem I mentioned earlier, the one that causes people to be unreceptive and ungiving. Actually getting fed as they listen and talk causes people to feel more generous and less threatened.
- The kind of small talk you can engage in over lunch is unique in terms of typical work encounters. Sitting around a table automatically puts people in a much more relaxed and unwary frame of mind than any office meeting. The informality, the sense of community, of belonging, of jokes and chatting — the pleasure that eating itself brings — all these conditioned responses subliminally colour any lunch experience. They generate a more outgoing and revealing flow of talk about any subject than the product-orientated discussions of focused meetings in offices or conference rooms.

- People have a tendency to tell you more about what they care about and believe in — much of it unconsciously — over lunch. This provides a great source of knowing more about what makes the other person tick. The conversation can flow from what motivates them and what evokes resistance to what their private lives are like all the way to who are/were their heroes and what are the meaningful influences in their lives.
- The sense of sharing and closer ties you both walk away with, if you can relax and thus get to know each other better as people, moves your relationship to a new level at work and is therefore a valuable investment.

The disadvantages

If you mean your meeting to be very productive and efficient in a specific way, lunch creates problems.

- There are interruptions for ordering and eating which may disrupt an important moment.
- The defocused time spent chatting, although beneficial if you know what to do with what you're learning, can also cause you not to get to a tangible result.
- Writing notes or working with documents is very difficult at a table full of pasta and Perrier.

Lunch is much better for generic kinds of fact finding than the pointed office meeting huddled over a desk. It gives you information of a more informal and personal nature which you'd probably never get in your office. It's a good place to generate or test ideas and get responses, but not a good place to try to come away from with an exact written product.

Breakfast meetings

The advantages

The best aspect of breakfast meetings is the uncluttered nature of everyone's mind at that hour of the morning. Able to focus tightly before the daily demands move in and fight for equal time, your meeting mate or mates will be very receptive to focusing on your wavelength.

The disadvantages

Breakfast meetings are a burden and a chore if you're a 'night owl' and not a 'chirper'. 'Night owls' think grim thoughts about the caller of such an ungodly and uncivilized get-together. Know your invitees!

To wrap up; The decision of where to meet depends on what your meeting is about. The working atmosphere you choose or create can help or hinder your results, as does your timing.

I think I can hear some of you saying, 'These ideas are very useful if you have several choices, but I'm in a small business and have no other place to meet than my office.' There are several techniques I will show you in the 'Openers' section of Chapter 6 on Close Encounters about how to neutralize or change your office's power impact when you have your meeting.

The next step, after choosing *when* and *where* and *how long* a meeting you'd like, is to go about making it happen.

GETTING ON THE CALENDAR

How formal you need to be in setting up the meeting depends on your work circumstances and relationship(s) with the person(s) you want to see. The key watchwords are sensitivity and flexibility as you go about scheduling to get on someone's calendar.

Techniques

'How long?'

Be very clear, before you ask for the appointment, about how much time you'll really need.

Don't get unrealistic and back down about this when faced with someone's busy schedule. Stay flexible, but remember to allow enough time to get the material covered and your message across *and* to have a question-and-answer discussion period. Always opt for the longer time when you're offered two time slots. You can always end sooner, but it's hard to stretch a meeting when the next appointment is waiting.

'What's it about?'

● If it's something you both (or all) know about, mention the subject since that builds in an already existing interest and the reassurance that there won't be too much challenge or surprise. Add some new wrinkle to make the meeting more compelling, like, 'There's something else to think about in relation to X.' Don't give away what that something is. Just gear your opposite number(s) up to thinking a little more about subject X.

- If it's a complex or innovative kind of meeting, you may need to be vague. The big goal here is to create a receptive environment, but not give an abbreviated version of the topic itself. Say just enough to interest, but not enough to challenge too soon. 'Some new thoughts on that project that I think will interest you,' or, 'Something to do with making more money for the company' (that'll get them every time). What you're looking for is enough information to create some positive anticipation.

- If you're the senior person and the thrust of your meeting will be a negative one, the less defensiveness you can create, the better. Don't give it away, allowing the other person to build up a head of anxiety. Try something general like 'I haven't talked with you for a while and there are some things I'd like to go over . . .'

'I'll get back to you . . .'

Be sure you are clear about how you will get confirmation of your appointment. Either get it right then, through the person involved, or from the secretary, if she has the authority to do it on her own. Asking her to confirm with the boss brings up a ticklish subject: The 'I'll get back to you' syndrome.

Don't let go of your options at this moment. If you say, 'Okay,' when she/he says that, or volunteer it by saying, 'Please get back to me,' you have no recourse but to wait passively for a call or to call if you don't hear and become an unwelcome nag.

On the other hand, if you establish that *you'll* be the one to call back and confirm, *you* keep the initiative. You then have the *right* to call, to press a little and, generally, to keep actively running the show.

Say, 'I'm going to be out of my office a lot in the next few days,' or, 'I'll be at meetings and hard to reach,' or, 'I need to confirm this rather quickly so I can get materials together. Let me call you this afternoon.' In any case, ask when she/he can make it definite or when she'll see the boss to confirm. Then make an appointment with the *secretary* about the best time to call back to get the exact meeting time.

Person-to-person approach

If the atmosphere at your job is informal, with a small cast of characters, you can simply suggest a time directly to the boss or person(s) you wish to see. (This presupposes that you've gone through all the 'what, where, when, and if' planning considerations.) Select and ask for the best time first, but have two more possibilites at the ready to allow for the other's schedule needs. Be sure your other choices also have *your* timing considerations in mind, so you don't get caught short.

Always try to make this approach in a place where the other person can get to his/her calendar easily. It is useless to get verbal agreement and then lose it to reality. By the way, as you discuss the meeting, notice the response to your request. Use it as an indicator of how he/she anticipates the meeting, and use those clues in mapping your Forethought Chart.

Through a secretary

- *Priorities and goals*
  Think *first* about the secretary's priorities and goals. Her/his job is to keep the boss's schedule workable and to protect him/her from overload or uncomfortable situations. This protects the secretary from an irate boss, so it really matters.

  Therefore, secretaries want some information up front; how much time, what day would you like to *start* talking about (you rarely get your first preference), and probably something of what it's about, since some bosses like their secretaries to screen such requests and/or consult with the boss before giving appointments.

  These priorities and considerations are at the top of the secretary's self-interest column, and you know that her/his self-interest needs to be satisfied before she/he can be receptive to yours.
- *Personal needs*
  A secretary also needs the affirmation that her/his job is important and that you appreciate that fact — and them. Secretaries need you to see and value their individual identities and to treat them as such.

  A major turnoff to any secretary is being treated like a cipher. (Sounds obvious? Ask a secretary how often it happens!) A secretary on your side as you try to schedule can be enormously helpful; a hostile one can find many ways to block your entrance.

Through a familiar secretary

For those who have difficulty making small talk.

Begin by taking a moment to share pleasantries, asking about a holiday, etc. Always learn a secretary's name! Remember what you learned about her/him on your last encounter (vacation in the Bahamas, plays football on the company team, new baby, etc.) and ask for an update. Share something of yourself as well (comment on the season, a news or personal event, etc.) before you state your case. Then:

'I need about thirty minutes with X' *Before* you say when, ask what the schedule looks like for the next week or so. This is also an opportunity to get the timing and work-habits information on your opposite number.

In talking, you might casually ask what time her boss usually likes to have meetings: morning, afternoon? Does he/she usually work late or need to make a train? And so on.

Or you can be more direct, depending on your style: 'You know, I'd like to catch him at a good time, maybe before all the pressures of work get to him. How about early morning meetings? Does he do those?'

Or, 'So we don't rush through, tell me what time does she generally go off to lunch? When does she usually get back?'

If your questions are put on the basis of finding a mutually agreeable time that will best take into consideration the well-being of the secretary's boss, she/he will probably be very amenable to answering.

Ask about major pressures coming up (such as board meetings that require preparation, visiting firemen, etc.) or if the schedule is relatively free. This last can also give you the additional information on your timing and how receptive his/her frame of mind would be right now to your meeting topic.

When the secretary asks what the meeting is about, use the answers about content that I suggested above.

However, if it's urgent business, you must get that across, too. If you have a problem to solve, state just that, without saying what it is ('I'd rather discuss it in person'), unless you need to get specific to increase the sense of urgency.

A secretary you don't know

Your powers of persuasion are brought into full play here. Start with something like, 'You're just the person who can help me.' This establishes both your need and her/his power. Then, 'I need to see your boss for half an hour and I know you're the keeper of the book.' What follows is probably 'Who are you?' 'Does he/she know you?' 'What shall I say it's about?' Titles are vital here, if you're a stranger, but the big seller is to say *why* the boss should see you.

Remember about motivation; *his first!* Not, 'I want to show him . . .' but, 'It's about developing a new market for his product . . .' Be intriguing about what your thrust will be — always keeping that self-interest beacon before you.

If you're in the organization somewhere, your mutual interest in the good of the company is your primary link.

If you're from outside the company, you'd better come up with a good reason for that person also to need this meeting . . .
Okay. Now you're on the calendar. The wheels are in motion. What's next? Designing what you have to say: the content, the order, the pacing. It's also time to work out the best way to present: what to *show*, what to *tell*, and what to *leave behind*.

5
Designing presentations

What captures attention and understanding

There you sit.

You're scheduled to make a presentation. Now you have to decide *what* you're going to say, and *how*.

'How should I begin? What's the most effective/persuasive/informative thing I can do or say? What's the best way to explain this complex (or disconcerting or negative or unexpected or demanding or costly) message? Should everything be explained only verbally? When should I stop for questions? What if they disagree or get hostile?'

You sit there picturing your audience.

'He/she/they could look bored. Perhaps confused. Glancing at their watches . . .'

If you don't imagine at least *some* of the above, please do.

You are embarking on an extremely difficult task.

You want to move your listener(s) from an inert, self-involved state to actively participating in *your* subject. It takes a major effort to capture and energize them so they rise to *your* occasion (which you hope to make *their* occasion).

You also want them to understand what you will explain: something *you* understand and care about but that others don't, or may not even *care* to understand. And you want to persuade them enough to buy your idea, product, or point of view. Even to be willing to spend money or effort on it — two things no one gives away without a struggle.

What you need are some foolproof fundamentals about what best makes people listen and understand, so you can design a presentation that will work for you and help you reach your goal in all kinds of business encounters.

The good news is that there *are* some proven communication

guidelines to help you make *choices* for better presentations. There *are* known ways in which people learn and absorb information, stay interested, and get persuaded. There are also some basic principles that govern what turns people off, what makes them resistant, and what confuses them.

GUIDELINES FOR DESIGNING PRESENTATIONS

What kind of presentation are you faced with?

- A speech to a peer group or to a first-time audience?
- A presentation of a report at a meeting?
- A one-to-one or one-to-several explanation of an idea?
- A sales pitch?
- A request made to the boss?
- A reprimand to an employee?

It's odd, but the same content design process applies to all of these 'presentations'.

There is a general structure and pattern which we use when we think and listen. Your progression from topic to topic and how you build toward your final conclusion requires that you use these already existing, ingrained thinking and listening systems in order for your listeners to follow and understand you.

Let's find out what these learning/listening systems are.

How we think

The human mind depends on order and logic to absorb data and formulate answers. It relies on previously programmed material to make sense of, and process, new information. Your brain cannot accept a message when it:

- Lacks enough or the right kind of information;
- Has no frame of reference;
- Is unable to find a familiar hook or frequency on which to tune in;
- Can't connect the parts of what it's hearing.

Our minds prompt us to ask for help when we don't understand: 'What did you say again?' 'What do you mean?' 'Wait, I don't understand.' In casual conversation that works, as we make the speaker slow down and re-explain or try another tack to help us understand. But there are two problems:

- In a formal presentation, we *can't* ask till it's too late — and by that time it doesn't matter because we've already long since lost interest.
- Most of the time we *won't* ask. It's our nature to prefer staying confused to losing face by admitting that we don't understand what was just said. We often see the work arena as too dangerous a place to admit we don't understand and to ask for help.

So in the workplace, as elsewhere, we are left to depend on others; on the skills of 'tellers' and explainers to be clear and give us what we need so we can understand because we won't, or can't, ask. Unfortunately, those 'skills of others' are often fumbling or sorely lacking, so we sit through endless experiences wondering, 'What is this about?' 'Who cares?' 'How boring — wasting what could have been a time of real information gathering and exchange.

Most people, when called upon to 'tell', are still only amateur talkers, *not* skilled orators, naturally gifted rational and coherent explainers, or trained and inspired storytellers. Our instincts don't automatically bring us to present information systematically, with logic and order.

This state of affairs conditions us to *expect* to be bored or confused whenever we hear the word 'speech', or 'report', or 'presentation'.

It's time to demystify the communication process and set about purposefully learning what works, what doesn't, and why. The final responsibility for your listeners getting your message is yours, the 'teller's'.

To help you develop foolproof techniques for organizing and presenting material so that your audience of one or many will stay tuned in and get your message, here are some principles about how people absorb information best. They'll also help you be aware of pitfalls, of what kinds of presentation techniques *don't* work, and why.

What we need so we understand and stay interested

For maximum efficiency and minimum audience confusion and

resistance, you, as a 'teller', need first to tune into the learning/listening systems already inherent in our brains.

The mind demands order

To plan any presentation of information, you must create a coherent system that is readily apparent and recognizable. Not only the information itself but also how you present it must follow a systematic, orderly plan.

Information giving must follow the laws of logic

Chronology and logic are built into the human brain. They are definite, predictable ways in which we gather, organize, and interpret information.

To introduce new material to an audience, you must allow their brains to hook into old, well-known, comfortable information-processing systems. To absorb new material or make sense of *any* material, your audience needs you to follow a *logical* progression. In real life 'A' does truly come before 'B' and 'C'. So it must in your presenation. Start at the beginning . . .

Television has conditioned us to logical progression

Since television news, talk shows, and documentaries are now the major vehicles by which most people accumulate serious information, it's efficient to use the ways TV has conditioned us to process information. This conditioning has trained your audience to respond to a certain pattern of information delivery that facilitates and speeds understanding. As you read the next paragraphs, picture an issue or idea you want to explain. See how these techniques can apply to *your* information giving.

On TV, new information is edited to be shown in three stages: the long shot, the medium shot, and the close-up. (Now you'll have a *professional* reason to watch television, so you can see how it's done.)

● *The long shot.* This is the orientation shot. It shows us the room, the street, the whole head of lettuce. It establishes context: Where we are; who's there; what they're doing. It familiarizes us with the general size, shape, colour, concept; the parameters within which sits what we're about to learn.

- *The medium shot.* This draws us closer. It peels away some of the outer leaves. By tightening our field of vision, it draws us further into the idea or event, beginning to eliminate the unimportant features. It makes us start concentrating on where the teller is going, on what the heart of the matter might be. By giving us some more detail, the teller intrigues us to want to know still more as we absorb the more focused data we've just been given. Then we move in for:

- *The close-up.* Now we're at it. This is where the teller was going all along. *This* is what he/she wanted us to consider and think about. This is where we will stay, to learn and discover the message the teller already knew.

This sequence of zooming into the details *after* you first establish the general context and the basic idea works best as an information-giving system because it makes instant sense to us. It establishes chronology and order, making sense out of context and detail. Using this logical and familiar system of going from the general to the specific doesn't get in the way of absorbing the data; it helps us.

We cannot understand from just a pile of lettuce leaves what the leaves do and how a whole lettuce looks. We need to either break it down from the whole or build it up from its parts. But in either case we need grounding in a basic context.

Order of presentation affects how we absorb data

- *Starting with the whole*
  Peeling back layers makes us more curious about what it is and how it works. It's easier to get us engrossed in gathering more data as each succeeding layer is revealed when we know what we started with.
  Example: Opening a package. As we remove the wrapping, open the box, unfold the tissue, our interest rises the closer we get and the more we keep discovering and anticipating. This is one way to explain an idea. Like giving a gift.

- *Starting with the parts*
  Building up from the parts to form the mysterious, previously unseen whole is another way. This makes us focus on the final product.

We're much more curious about seeing the finished whole than we are about the properties of the parts themselves.
Example: A jigsaw puzzle. The essentially abstract pieces serve as tools to get us to our goal — constructing the whole. By themselves they have no particular value. They do intrigue us to want to put them together and see how they fit and what they make. Explaining an idea this way is very intriguing but there must be some early indication (like the picture of the completed puzzle on the box) that the whole will be of some value and worth the wait. Its best use is to show the importance of the parts, how they fit, and what their role is.

● *Cutting through to the heart of the matter*
Getting right to the core issue in one shot is also a familiar system and possible for us to understand. The 'pronouncement' approach. This can startle us and intrigue us to draw closer, or it can stand as a complete statement by itself, telling us the bottom line. *Example*: A newspaper headline. We know that we're getting just one statement. We subconsiously recognize that the *gradual* accumulation of information as well as the ability to gain more data and detail has been edited out. Just a shortcut to the end product remains, making *only* the end product of primary importance. Its best use? Making a major definitive statement or a final conclusion right at the beginning to startle us and entice us to learn more.

Opposing natural information-processing systems disturbs us

Because it's easy to follow the familiar systems, we sit up sharply and take notice when something is presented in direct opposition to them, like unrelated objects, random ideas, haphazard connections, illogical reasoning, or unfinished phrases. Use such techniques, like presenting something out of order — i.e., medium shot, close-up, long shot — consciously and deliberately. Be aware of their effect. Use them only *because* they engender special attention. If you are simply negligent or disorderly, you'll lose your point and audience.

Do not frustrate the listener

If you choose to go out of sequence and confuse or at the least intrigue the listener, realize that you also startle, surprise, or unnerve the listener.

Fix it fast. Get your effect, then explain, to keep your audience with you.

Starting in the middle of something, a speaker needs to stop and say something like: 'What's going on?' 'Why am I saying (doing this)?' and tell them why. Audiences get frustrated quickly when they don't get what's going on and feel left out. Needing to stay oriented as we make demands that the teller not let us down, that you keep us on your track at all times.

Unclear language and unfamiliar words lose and anger listeners

When you say something I don't understand and leave it, you are making me notice how stupid I am and how clever (knowledgeable, sophisticated, competent, different from me) you are! Is that ever useful? It creates these effects:

- *You lose me*
  I have to stop listening in order to start thinking about what the word or phrase means. While I do *that*, since I come equipped with only one brain, I have to stop paying attention to *you*. You rattle on, oblivious to the fact that you just lost your audience. This is particularly so if I'm struggling to understand complex, unfamiliar, or technical material, not well explained.

- *You make me angry*
  No one welcomes the messenger who shows us our own incompetence, ignorance, or unpreparedness. Beware of this response universally, but especially when you are presenting to a superior who may need to know *something* of your speciality but not the in-depth knowledge you have. Making him/her ask for clarification about technical, unfamiliar words and concepts instead of your simply providing it is an obnoxious, if not downright threatening, posture to take. Studiously avoid exposing your audience or competing intellectually with the boss. Be clear, self-edited, and helpful.

Oral presentation is difficult to follow

You not only know where you're going and what your subject matter is but have created *notes* and documents to help you. Your hapless first-time and once-only *listener* is more than ever in the dark next to you.

Since your information is new, the only anchor you can offer is *order*; the basic skeleton of how you will present your material.

For your listeners to follow you, the structure and organization of your presentation must be very clear. So clear that your listeners could almost visualize and write your outline as you go along. Knowing what to expect next and where and how the pieces fit into your whole scheme is a vital requirement for anyone trying to understand you. Since they don't know your *material*, at least they feel grounded in the *logical order* in which you give it.

Knowing your order increases attention

If the structure of your oral presentation is clearly explained and easily followed, then the listener can use all his/her time and energy just absorbing and understanding your message. Otherwise, much of the listener's attention will be spent on just figuring out where you are and where you're going and how the different pieces fit together.

People have a very short attention span

Here's some bad news for all 'tellers', you who need to keep your audiences listening:

Language is so exact that the human brain requires only *15 per cent* of its power to understand language, if we're both using the same one. Eighty-five per cent of the brain is actually not needed for your listener to grasp what you mean.

Implication? *Eighty-five per cent* of your listener's brainpower is left, like a loose canon, to do whatever it wishes! That doesn't necessarily include listening to you . . .

Think about what *you* do: When you're not really absorbed by what's happening, your brain goes on holiday. It's free to (and does) daydream, worry about other things, make lists of various duties, wonder about dinner, the weekend, who's winning the cricket — in short, *anything* but the business at hand, being earnestly presented by a . . . a . . . (dare I say it?) a bore!

Therefore, *never* take your audience for granted. It's a continual uphill struggle to keep them with you, to fight for more than the 15 per cent you automatically get when you begin. You must build in new devices to keep *100* per cent of the listener's brain occupied.

Clear introductions and transitions are a must

Unless you let your audience know when you begin a new topic or end it, your whole presentation can sound like one endless paragraph. In order to help your audiences follow, you must make verbal indents, endings, chapter headings, paragraphs, and transitions.

Remembering how vital a clearly self-evident structure is in helping the audience follow and stay tuned in, you must let them know where you both are, when to stop thinking about *this* and start noticing *that*. Transitions help them change gears, to actually 'turn a page' in their minds and start off afresh with you down a new path.

Now that you understand how the brain basically absorbs data and what information techniques work and why, let's put them into practice. We turn first to planning your message: What's the most effective agenda order and layout in which to subdivide it?

STRUCTURING
A PRESENTATION

Outline form

The most universally recognized system — and the simplest one — for organizing and subdividing unfamiliar or complex information is the outline. Luckily, if we learned anything at school, we learned to outline and we remember that system. Therefore we easily recognize it when it is described and referred to verbally.

So the basic presentation format should be an outline. But within that framework there are many other issues to consider as you plan.

Order of presentation

Presenting or explaining, teaching or selling something is like taking people on a journey, with you as the leader and the guide. You're telling people where you've been that they haven't and what you know that they don't. Having just learned how people absorb information best, we need to use those guidelines to create some order in your presentation so that your audience can follow your material and stay with you on the journey. Here is the most effective format:

- Introduction
- Movitation Opening
- Outline of Agenda
- Content — section by section
- Recap each section
- Transition to next section
- Wrap-up
- Conclusion

To help you use this format to design your presentation, let's take apart the various steps to see what's in them and why they're necessary in this order. (The actual techniques of presentation and examples of what to say and how to say it are the heart of Chapter 7.)

Introduction

You're opening to a clean slate, to a fairly open mind (excluding previous prejudices), a mind at least a little curious about what you want to present. Your introduction should set the tone and the theme for your presentation. It should instantly focus one or many on what the presentation is about and what you hope to get across.

To begin planning your presentation (formal or informal), establish what you think is the essence, the theme, and the one or two major points you're going to cover. No details yet, just the overall basic one-line theme. That's the heart of your introduction: 'I'm going to talk about X today, how it affects Y and Z, and why we need to change it.' That's your introduction. Next: motivation.

Motivation

- *Tell them why to listen*
  You know why you asked for the meeting or are making the presentation. Tell them how your topic affects *them*, what good will come of their listening, how important they are in the equation, and how your two interests intersect. That's the Motivation aspect of step 2.
- *'Lift your visor'*
  Another aspect of your opening is to let them know who's speaking: to help the audience get to know you, the speaker, better. To

recognize your style, your persona — to get the first impression.

Give them the outline

Tell them what's to come:

To help them follow, give them the structure of your presentation. 'I'll tell you about X. To do that, I'll start with A. Then B, with an explanation of 1, 2, and 3. Then we'll discuss C, which is also a part of the issue. I'll wrap it up and conclude with some ideas I have about what this means to us and what we should do. Then we'll open to questions and answers. I've brought some exhibits to demonstrate B and C and will leave copies of them with you.'

People need to know what to expect in order to get interested. To follow you, they need to understand and picture the organization of your material. Telling them your outline helps them do that. It grounds them by telling what will be predictable, giving them landmarks to look for. It also builds up some anticipation about what they'll learn, and gives them an incentive to pace themselves to stay with you till the end.

Content: present your basic idea

Now it's time to get right to the heart of the matter: Tell them what your message is about. Here is your 'long shot', creating the context your audience needs in order to listen to your presentation. Explain the whole idea first so whatever further explanation comes next can be hung from the framework you create right at the beginning. This is the time to give only the general picture; no details yet.

Example: Suppose you need or want to introduce a new way of doing something. Knowing your audience of one or many and anticipating their possibly negative response, you could start by capturing the essence of the problem and why you suggest change:

'Today we'll deal with a difficult subject — something that makes people anxious, even angry sometimes. We'll talk about change. Many people see change as a threat. I see it as a challenge; an opportunity to make things better, to grow, to open new possibilities.' Or:

'Our X system isn't keeping up with the times. So we need to take a hard look at it. I plan to show you why it's becoming obsolete and what we can do about it.'

Begin to break it into segments

Next, break the idea into its component parts and generally describe what they are. Now you're moving down into smaller segments of the whole idea. This is your 'medium shot': the capital A, B, C topic headings. This makes for an easier explanation from you and easier digestion for your audience as the logical progression and order of your presentation emerges in bite-sized pieces.

'Let's start with A. Here's the basic problem. There are three reasons why it fails us.'

Present each segment with its details

Now you can tighten the iris for a still closer look. This is the 'close up'. Each segment with its topic sentence and the 'bullets' under it gives us information in a still greater detail: 'Let's start with A. The basic problem is ... There are three reasons ...' The bullets serve as illustrative examples, adding dimension and support and providing a more intense, searching look at the heart of what you're talking about. Details work now and not before because your group now understands the whole idea and is drawn into learning more.

Recap each segment

Build in a recap at the end of *each* segment before you finish and go on, for reinforcement and for additional clarification about how you're building your case.

'Now what have we just discovered? That A has actually been out of synch for quite a while. That it's an outmoded system because of 1, 2, and 3, and that it's keeping us from moving forward.'

This catches up the slower listener as well as the inattentive one and makes sure that everyone is ready to move on to the next portion together with you.

Make transitions

Remembering that your audience cannot see your notes or know your next step until you take it, you need to build in a purposeful transition to each new topic so you let everyone know you're all about to go there. This helps make your outline structure continually clear as you move from A, through your small-number 'bullets' listed below it to the recap, and with a transition sentence or two, on to B. Be sure that as part of your transition you introduce and set up your next subject as you move into it.

Example: 'So there's the problem. Now let's turn to B — why we didn't know and how we found out.'

Wrap-up

At the end of all the components, wrap up by restating the whole idea, hitting the major points, and referring back to only a few of the most memorable and telling details you've explained for fuller illustration.

Example: 'Let's look back at all of what we just discovered. We've been living with an outmoded system. It's caused us to lose business; remember the three cases I told you about? And we weren't asleep! We didn't get the message because of . . . , something we surely shouldn't do again! And now it's time for a change. Time to develop a new system like the one I just described that can . . . , and move us onto a new and much more productive track.'

Now, logic says you should go to your conclusion, and many times you would. But if yours is a subject with built-in controversy or that could draw major objections, you might sometimes want to try this, depending on the circumstances, on your audience, subject, and goals. Also, on what your forethought chart has told you to expect. Some research has shown that sometimes the one-sided approach is more persuasive, but often this approach can be very useful.

Pose and answer possible problems

List and discuss as-yet-unresolved problems. 'Okay. Now that I've got you convinced we should do this, let me take a realistic look at what still stands in the way . . .' Show not only the good but the difficult side, making the listener aware of your responsible, realistic, clear-headed thinking and planning. Give your answers and the possible solutions you're working on. Then go on to the next step.

Raise and answer anticipated resistance

If you say what *you* think the opposite number's reservations or resistance may be *before* you give the other person(s) a chance to, you can turn the ensuing discussion toward ways of resolving whatever the concerns are, since you've alreay stated them. If not, you'll have to wait and hear them, and then possibly find yourself in a much more defensive and less constructive position.

Example: 'One more thing. I've been watching some faces in the group who look decidedly sceptical, even negative! They're probably thinking, 'Sure sounds great, but can we handle the cost?' Others might be thinking, 'What happens to my department if we do this?' Well, let's talk about these two issues . . .'

Now it's time to finish. With a flourish.

Grand wrap-up and conclusion

Finish memorably with a grand finale — bringing together all the elements of your presentation by succinctly reviewing the highlights and restating your major argument, now backed not only by all your data but also by your answers to the negatives.

Pick out your best, most telling points. Illustrate with your most graphic, dramatic, or innovative examples. End by saying why your idea should happen.

Open for questions and discussions

Now it's time to give your opposite numbers the floor, too. Open it up for further clarification, explanation, discussion, and for countering opposition. Focus on getting responses to your idea and finding ways to solve the problems (perhaps together) or to discover what you need to do next.

Checklist

Here's a chronological checklist for you to use as an organizing tool when preparing any kind of presentation or report:

- *Opening*: State theme and general message
- *Motivate and identify with audience*: Tell them why they should listen
- *Give agenda*: Describe content and structure of presentation
- *Content*: Present basic idea
- *Break each into segments*: Logical chronology of A, B, C

- *Break into subsegments*: 1, 2, 3 of details and examples
- *Recap into segment*
- *Make transition to and introduce next segment*
- *Wrap-up*: Recap highlights of whole presentation
- *Pose and answer problems* (optional)
- *Objections*: Raise and answer anticipated objections or resistance (optional)
- *Grand wrap-up*: List persuasive points
- *Conclusion and recommendations*
- *Questions and discussion.*

Creating the order of any presentation or explanation makes you narrow your sights on what you mean to cover, what you'll say, and how you'll say it. Which brings us to the next step. Should you only *say it*? Or should you *show* some of it?

MAKING MESSAGES VISUAL

'Seeing is believing', 'A picture is worth a thousand words'. These concepts are not just old-fashioned homilies. Research has shown that we remember *85 to 90 per cent* of what we *see* and *15 per cent or so* of what we *hear*. A sobering thought for all you talkers . . .

Why use visual reinforcement?

Whenever you present new material to people, you should be aware that it's clear to you but not yet even imagined by them. They cannot yet visualize it as you already do. Therefore, you must do some very effective things to bring them on board.

Visualization is a prime source of information giving, of explanation, and of reinforcement with any subject. Visual demonstrations are very helpful in presenting facts clearly, especially in the new areas of technical mastery, as well as advanced financial concepts, where there is great disparity in what is common knowledge. Visual support can often make the difference between the audience staying with you or shrugging their shoulders and losing interest, bored and disappointed. This is particularly true when explaining complex material or advanced financial concepts to a client or to a lay or less knowledgeable audience. In case of wandering attention, the fastest way to catch your listener up is to *show* them what you're talking about.

Perhaps the most important reason is that we are now a visual society, courtesy of TV. You can't just talk; you must also show. Making ideas or facts visual creates information plus impact.

What to show; what to tell

Now that you're a firm convert to what visuals can do for you, how do you decide what kinds of information to show and tell and what works with telling alone? The difference between using visual aids and just using language alone is subject matter. It's what effect you want your message to have and which aspect of the brain you're appealing to.

Which subjects need visuals

The organizing, data-collecting, cognitive, fact-orientated, list-making side of the brain gets the full message most clearly and convincingly with visual documentation and explanation. It responds best to concrete images and incontrovertible, collectible, hard-nosed data.

Presenting a business plan, asking for more budget, introducing a new system, or needing a hard-nosed decision? Consider adding visuals for greater persuasion.

Here are some categories that can use visual suppport and the impact it creates:

- New data, known only to you.
- Data known to all, but never presented in this context or with this interpretation before.
- A message which needs documentation or support from objective data in order for people to believe it.
- Numbers, facts, quotes, lists, trends; information that people do not or cannot collect and remember only by hearing it.
- Chronological data that needs to be repeated and remembered from one segment to another.
- Comparisons

When you need a factual, analytical approach, backed by data — explicit, logical, clear — visual support is most often the answer.

Which subjects only need verbalizing

In general, the material that lends itself best to just telling is material that is narrative and dramatic in nature. To spin a web, to weave a yarn, to marshal the troops, to inspire, you can often rely on the charisma and energy of the teller alone.

The creative, imaginative, fantasy-making, instinctive, emotion-driven side of the brain responds best to the imaginative, colourful messages of feelings. These messages leave room for individual interpretation, not uniform acceptance of the facts. Each listener's unique personal imagination can get engaged and respond. There is no right or wrong sum here. Just feelings. Unique. Individual. Intimate.

Being able to *talk* visually, to elicit pictures through words and excite the imagination of your listeners means relying only on language and style, on analogy and metaphor. These, if you will think about it, are all actually *visual* too! But delivered personally . . .

When the task is building morale, gaining loyalty, running for office, anything that needs feelings attached to agreement, you need a lot more emotional, less documentary approach. You don't need charts and graphs. You need a quiver in the voice, a higher or lower decibel, personal eye contact, and emotional commitment.

Visual and verbal

Sometimes you need to mix both. You need to be logical *and* factual to set the stage and show the new system you propose.

But then, to get real gut agreement — for example, to get the commitment to try hard or harder — you must change gears to appeal to the more emotional level.

That's the time to set the charts aside. To slowly close the Magic Marker. To walk forward a step or two, or sit on the side of the table. And just talk. Person to person. Intently. Intensely. With genuine feeling.

Before I show you how to go about planning and designing your visual aids, let me suggest one more area to think about as you plan your presentation: what materials to leave behind for further thought and later discussion.

'Leave-behinds'

Unless your request or discussion is a quick and simple one, almost everyone likes time to think things over before they commit themselves to anything.

Therefore, built into your total presentation should be a packet of materials you prepare to leave behind for further study. During your presentation you can focus only on the main issues and what you can show and explain succinctly there, knowing that you'll be giving them back-up material for later perusal and thought.

Don't let them 'read along'

If you give your listeners material to real along with you *while* you talk, you lose your audience!

- They can read much faster than you can talk and will be ahead of you and all over the place while you're dutifully still on page 1.
- Reading while you're talking, they draw their own conclusions from the printed word — which seems like 'harder' information — rather than from your verbal (and self-serving) explanation.
- You lose contact with your audience. having spent some time developing rapport with your audience of one, several, or many, why would you want to release centre stage and abdicate in favour of the anarchy of everyone reading for themselves? You want them to look at your graphics *with* you! While you're making eye contact and continuing to persuade, *you're* the answer giver. Handouts are for *after* you've explained and finished. When they go home and want to remember your data.

But, because they would like to see what you're reading from, or review again the data you've introduced, you can promise them that, *after* you do all the explaining, you will provide each of them with this data for their personal use.

What to leave behind

- *Copies of what they saw.* Very reinforcing and already familiar. Best of all, they have the benefit of remembering *your* explanation when they reread it.
- *Extra documentation.* Documentary evidence that you will not introduce during your presentation. Background material: articles, previous reports, excerpts of speeches given by others (in your company or not), reprints of speeches or memos by the leader, research data, and so on. Items that back up what you said.
- *Your background.* What additional information do they need to know about *you*, if you're speaking to a new group? Here is your

chance to put together your subtle "I'm terrific" packet: résumé, client list, past accomplishments, etc.

Checklist

Your package of leave-behinds may include any or all of the following:

- A summary of your ideas.
- Reproductions of the most important, comprehensive visual aids you used in your presentation.
- Documentation of why what you *say* is so, *is* so.
- Examples (if possible) of what you (or others) have already done.
- A résumé and other personal reference data if they don't know you too well.
- Groupings of related background materials (like research, articles, reports, etc.).

I don't mean to leave them a 5-pound package. Be selective and edit well, but just remember what your stickiest points are and what data you have (and they need) that supports your position best.

Now, to create visual aids for what you tell, you need some guidelines about what makes graphic sense to us and what's most persuasive.

Here are some of the most important techniques for making visual materials extend and clarify your message. This is information you need whether you will design simple visuals and execute them yourself, or want to be more knowledgeable (and critical) if you get the art department or someone to do them for you. They will help your own creativity understand what you can make visual and how to do that best, avoiding pitfalls.

DESIGNING VISUAL MATERIALS

Basic guidelines

Visuals dominate talking

Whenever you introduce a visual demonstration, your audience will stop looking at you and instantly become absorbed in looking at, and trying to understand, the visual.

We are always drawn to action over just listening. (Notice the next time a door opens and someone enters a meeting room.) Since a visual aid engages the audience and gives them independent work to do, they are immediately drawn to the more active role. Knowing this, you need to choose your visual aids with care, to be sure they *support* you and don't just compete with you.

Which medium and why

Form follows function. First decide *What* you want to say. Then think about which form says it best; chart, slide, diagram on the board, list on a flip chart, video piece? Different media forms create their own conditioned responses from earlier association. Decide what effect you want: informal and improvisational, or professional, top-of-the-line, well planned.

Exhibits can be simple

Don't think that bigger and more expensive is better. There are many times when the best visual medium would be an informal, interactive one like a blackboard or flip chart. Direct and personal.

Good design makes a difference

Be aware of colour, shape, size, layout. Look for advice on eloquent design. There are good and bad ways to make charts, graphs, and so on, that can enhance or detract from your message. Quality counts.

Use colour

Colour is loaded with information, creating dramatic, emotional responses. An invaluable source of visual communication, it affects how we see and respond to hard information. It creates warmth, drama, contrast, variety, credibility, and interest in your otherwise cold, factual information. There is a 'corporate conspiracy' about using black slides with white letters. Born out of sheer habit and the mistaken emphasis on 'what shows up best,' this technique has been putting hapless audiences and board rooms to sleep for years! Why not use the extraordinary power and emotional dimension of colour — or many

colours, of contrasts, of variety and of sheer pleasure — in your attempt
to persuade?

Is every slide you show *equally* important, or unimportant? Surely
not! Do they all deal with the same subject? In the same way? Are
numbers, graphs, lists and phrases designed to do the same thing to
get the same response?

Add to these challenges the fact that black and white is also the
driest, dullest, most unaffecting combination there is. No juice! No
feelings! No persuasion or motivation on its own.

It only requires a little nudge and the willingness of executives and
graphics departments to rethink an old habit for the business world
to get on the colour standard and make slide presentations as persuasive
and effective as they really can be!

Research placement and scale

Go to the room you will use to give your presentation. Examine how
far away everyone will be and where they will sit. In order to make
something big enough but not too big and to find the optimum size
for your letters (be they pre-printed or written by you at the moment),
you need to get a clear picture of the requirements that room dictates.
Practise by writing on chart or blackboard in that room and seeing
the size from the audience's viewpoint. Notice the lighting for best
placement.

Control the information

The single biggest mistake I see in my work is the tendency to *overload*
visual aids with too much information at once.

Result? You lose control. While you're explaining the upper left-hand
corner or column one, they've reached all the bottom lines and are
roaming all over the place making judgements, and, incidentally, totally
missing *your* explanation of the upper left-hand corner or column one.
Therefore you must control your visual information.

Only give one piece at a time — just show as much as you can explain,
in small, self-contained pieces. Then add the next point and talk about
it, then the next, and so on. Whenever you add a point, you challenge
your audience to keep thinking, to stay active and involved.

Adding information

In order to control each piece of information you give, add additional pieces visually. And only when you are ready to talk about them. To help your audience stay with and absorb only *your* explanation, when *you* give it, not their guesses as to what you mean, try these:

- If you're using a blackboard or a flip chart, draw or write *while* you explain and stop till you're ready for the next point. Don't reveal great gobs of information and then talk. Introduce, then draw and explain as you do. Your material will then unfold naturally, and only when you're ready to add it.
- With prepared charts use transport overlays, if possible. Separate your data into individual points, time lapses, chronology, or new information, each of which modifies previous data. Add them one at a time or draw on a slick transparency to make each new point.
- When creating slides or overhead transparencies, use the 'build' system. Slide one has only the basics or the outline. Add a piece of data with slide two. Add more with the next. Keep the style and layout consistent so the audience can focus only on the addition of new material, not a new layout each time. Use colours to design newly added material.

Accumulate the data

Accumulating the data gives much greater impact and makes logical progressive sense as you go along. By building on, point to point, and leaving the original data still visible, you keep making your first point stronger. The audience can see how the evidence mounts. The sheer weight of visibly accumulated data gives additional clout to any argument.

Make material consistent

Use the same symbols throughout. When using a black board or flip chart: if you start printing, don't start writing after a while. Don't put 6/22, then July 5th. Lists should also stay in a line under each other for easy comprehension.

Make visuals self-explanatory

Label all unfamiliar items with a line connected to them and a label out to the side so your audience can readily identify them whenever they look.

Create a glossary

If you're going to use technical or unfamiliar terms, create a glossary, adding to it as you go along. Put it on an easel or on the side of the board for ready reference by your audience as you continue explaining. It will cut down on redundancy and will ensure that everyone knows what you're talking about, as they keep checking it while you speak.

Techniques for using visual aids

Let them look

If one reason for using visuals is to engage your audience — let them look! Hold still, be quiet, and let the visual impact itself take over. Visuals *are* eloquent. They do captivate. They are more exciting than just talking. Learn to wait. Work *with* visuals and let them help you.

Build anticipation

To increase their appetite, tell your audience what you're going to show *before* you present it: 'Let me show you a chart that demonstrates this trend.' Then, present it and wait a moment. Let the eyes roam, get adjusted, and absorb. *Then* you can become more specific and focused. You'll get maximum attention when you prepare your listeners in advance and then let them discover on their own a little. This gives audiences a sense of power and independence, therefore the desire to learn more and stay tuned in.

Keep materials organized and neat

Nothing looks worse than messy, disorganized materials. Keep transparencies neatly stacked in boxes, charts in portfolios. You'd be surprised at how carefully your audience notices small details and gives bad marks. It not only looks unprepared but shows less respect for *them*, as though you approached this encounter very casually.

Stay active with your exhibits

Use them as an extension of yourself, to underscore your points. Learn to handle them comfortably, to master whatever medium you will be using. Write and underline often, to show your control of the subject and help your audience get your point.

A *final note*: Lots of people feel uncomfortable about using visual aids. They think that visuals look too pedantic, sterile, stuffy, deliberate, etc.

I suggest that you try a few — in the interests of your audience. Not only do they really work and vastly improve your listener's comprehension; we are now such a visual society that you can buy a much longer attention span by making ideas visual.

Try it . . .

The bottom line on designing presentations: Unfold your material with full awareness of what learning/listening systems we, as your audience, use to understand you. Choose different styles for further impact but always keep the basic progression logical and orderly, letting your audience 'see' your outline and your material.

Now — on to Close Encounters.

6
Close Encounters
One-to-one

The difference between one-to-one encounters and the group interactions we've been talking about is the level of intensity: it's personal visibility without dilution. You can't get away with as much in a one-to-one situation: the margin for error is *very* small.

This makes the give and take a little harder than in a group, where you get some relief because of the numbers participating and the time *that* gives you to think.

Now, close encounters *can* be benign, like mild get-acquainted or informational sessions; they're not all acute, emotional, or confrontive. But the process of two people interacting in a business setting *is* up three or four stress notches from anything else you do at work.

So our work in this chapter will be to analyse each segment of a close encounter; to understand and find good communications solutions to the various aspects; to give you options as initiator or participant. Let's begin with the underlying structure.

A one-to-one encounter has four segments — openers, substance, special issues, closure. The *function* and *quality* of each segment determines what kind of communication is needed and how to deliver it best.

OPENERS

As we've already discovered by the pains I took to 'open' this book well and invitingly for you, those first few opening moments really count in *any* human encounter, but especially in a one-to-one.

First impressions etch deeply because they're written on a clean slate, when nothing else is going on except curiosity and the alert collection of data on both sides. They not only establish you to each other; they create the environment in which your meeting will continue.

Before you begin

What's your goal? To be cool? Secure? Efficient? Open? To create an environment of support, reasonable discussion, or whatever? Decide on your persona and what quality would suit this occasion before you begin. Base it on all that pre-planning we talked about in Chapter 3 and the strategies you developed because of it. Then use it, especially at the beginning.

Change gears

Until your meeting began, your 'other' was all involved in something else. It required an active stepping on the brakes, stopping, then putting the work engine into another gear to make him/her go from *that* focus to the new tack *you* wished to take.

Therefore, making a personal dent and helping the other person change gears to focus on *you* is the first order of business in the 'openers' segment of your one-to-one encounter. In order to do that, you need to take a little time to help the other person slow down, stop, and restart with *you*.

The next group of suggestions will do that, and more. I'll focus on both visitor and meeting-caller, to show you how to create the most productive and appropriate environment, at the beginning of your encounter.

Warm-up

How you greet

- *To shake or not to shake*
  Women, particularly, ask me about this. They're concerned since many men don't offer a hand and it looks like such a male gesture if *they* do it. Since it's such an expected gesture when business people meet each other, my advice is to shake hands and to offer yours if it's not offered first. That initial physical gesture can help establish a businesslike, professional atmosphere. By the way, for anyone,

if your hands are very cold (or damp) because this is a high-stress meeting, rub them together *hard* before you go in. No sense betraying that calm exterior . . .

● *Smile*
Animals do it to signal friendly and non-threatening demeanour! We need it, too. Sometimes in your rapt concentration you forget to smile. A concentrated face can often look forbidding or even angry. Be aware.

● *'Jack' or 'Mr Hill'*
The new informality in the workplace generally dictates first names. However, the content, the relative age and positions, and the intended outcome of the encounter make all the difference in how you make this choice. The culture in your place of business and the particular style of the individual you're meeting with also count. Using someone's first name *is* taking a liberty. Be careful about sounding intrusive and presumptuous. The safest route with someone you don't know well is to start with 'Mr Hill' till *they* say 'Jack — please.'

Small talk

Hardly 'small'! The next few moments that you spend (or *should* spend) chatting are an untapped gold mine — if you know what they're for and how to use them. (They're not only for helping to change gears.)

One important use: Small talk helps you each get accustomed to the other's style, voice, and speech patterns, if you don't know each other.

Another: Small talk covers the slightly awkward moments of settling down and settling in, whether you know each other or not.

Perhaps the *most* valuable by-products of small talk are:

● To connect and get to know each other (or start the ball rolling, if you already do) with a most relaxed, non-product-orientated, personal kind of contact.
● To develop a source of personal information you can use within the meeting.
● To let the other person begin to relate to you.

Here are some small talk suggestions and why to use them.

Visitors

You're now in someone's personal space. See what you can learn. People are *extremely* revealing in what and how they choose to create a personal environment. *First*-notice, *then*-comment.

Everyone loves their precious or meaningful objects to be valued and admired by others (especially if they display them on the walls and shelves of their offices). Look and you can discover *personal passions* (fishing; photography); *other human dimensions* (family, kinds of books, antique furniture); *awards, diplomas* (is *that* where she's from!); *controversial subjects* (he's a member of the National Rifle Association and you're against guns!).

These personal observations can have several beneficial results:

- *Bonding*: 'I see *you're* a skier, too. Where do you usually ski? We go to . . .'

  Contact! You've opened a conversation vein, discovered something in common, and had the opportunity to tell him/her something about yourself, too.

- *Personal* (to someone you know): 'Your family's really growing up! (Almost everyone has family pictures around.) Doesn't that give you a turn, when your boy starts borrowing your ties?'

  Contact again! You can spend a few moments listening to his atittude towards the passage of time (comfortable or not) and something more about his family (everyone has something to say about *that*). It also lets you share something about *yours*, and you . . .

  Or: 'You know, we're expecting a child next month. Think I'll pop in for some advice!' Again, opening a third dimension before you zero in on just business.

  These kinds of personal asides are a much smoother transition into your subject than just an abrupt 'getting down to business'.

- *Informational*. You can also ask questions: 'What's the story behind that picture (fire helmet, autographed football, Kermit puppet, etc.)?' or just appreciate and admire: 'What a view', 'What a great desk', etc. All of these will generate 'small' but *useful* talk.

  Note: Always be sensitive to how small talk is being received and when it's time to move on to the next step. Pick up signals about impatience, time pressures, and so on.

Host

As host, making small talk with a visitor is equally important. Of course it depends on your goals and how you want the meeting to go. Generally speaking, taking the initiative in establishing some mutual conversation puts everyone at ease.

General talk about the latest news or weather all the way to more personal 'Have you been away yet?' or, 'You're looking very fit and trim' (to someone you know), or, 'That's a wonderful colour you're wearing. Makes me feel as if spring is really in the air' (to someone you don't know) are all good beginnings. What you say should help the visitor add to the conversation and help to get the ball rolling. Lots of people need a little help to get started.

If it's someone you don't know very well, the welcome you put out can establish the tone of the meeting, helping the other to settle into the business at hand in a shorter time span, with less need to oversell, over-impress, or stay very intense.

Where to sit

The issue of where to sit is a delicate one. Since there are places in the room where the power gets equalized and places where it tilts very much in one direction, this is an issue to think about.

Visitor

Don't sit right down. 'Case the joint', as they say. What are the options? Is there more than one area in which to sit? Stand and/or walk around (ostensibly admiring the view, etc.) until you decide where you'd like to sit. Now you can't just wander. But you *can* redirect and not accept what is offered immediately. Find an altenative (which I'll explain) and give a good reason for sitting *there*. Here are the usual options:

- *Sitting across the desk*
  A weak position: The office owner has all the marbles on his/her side with memorabilia that says, 'This is mine and you're an intruder or a petitioner'. Avoid this at all costs, if possible.
- *Sitting to the side of the desk*
  Next best: Pull a chair up to the side of the desk. This lets you both share in looking at documents from the same angle. It also

allows you to move to the corner of the desk so that there is no physical barrier between you.

● A *neutral corner*
Optimum: If the office has a couch or two chairs and a coffee-table, *that's* where to go. A round table in another part of the room is also great. In either case, you start out much more visually equal, and that affects how you present and how you're perceived.

● *How to get there*
Have a reason for wanting to go to the neutral corner or moving your chair to the side of the desk, if there is no neutral corner: 'Since I have some figures (materials, product) to show you, perhaps we could sit where we can both look at them together, like here . . .' or, 'Maybe there's more room over here for my portfolio (report, etc.) . . .'

Office owner

Knowing the above, you can select where *you* want the visitor to sit, based on your strategy for the meeting. The more power you have, the greater the need to think about this particular non-verbal aspect of communicating. People are usually at least a little uncomfortable in your (someone else's) office. See how you can put them at ease.

Now let's turn to another role; you as host.

Amenities

Host

The gift giving implicit in the simple gesture of offering a cup of coffee has many more ramifications than just being polite.

● *Sensual* What! At a *business* meeting? Yes, the person you're dealing with has bought *all* his human responses into your office. Feeding *is* sensual. It makes us feel good, warm, cared for. Therefore, offering and sharing this experience is a great welcoming gesture.
● *Physical activity* The coffee ritual affords one something to *do* on both sides. It can get some of that runaway adrenal energy under control (probably better use *de*caffeinated coffee . . .).

- *Feeding before taking* Especially if you're about to give criticism, bad news, or ask for a big commitment, the idea of giving before getting sets the visitor up in a more sated, open frame of mind.
- *Informal talk time* Just attending to the business of 'milk and sugar', etc. can be another level of small talk.

For all these reasons, the 'hosting' posture you can attain by offering something to drink or personally arranging for coats, gear, and so on to be cared for is a valuable adjunct to the ice-breaker aspect of the opening segment.

Visitor

What if your host doesn't offer and you're nervous and need a little more time to get into your subject? It's really quite all right to say something like, 'You know, this is the first moment I've had all day. I'd just love to get myself a cup of coffee before we begin. Okay?' But pick your host, if he/she is formal and snappish, swallow and go on!

Body language

For both sides, this is a *great* clue giver as to the general attitude toward the encounter and what else you might want to do to counteract what you see. These are the areas to look at:

How they sit

- Forward on the edge of the seat = tension, anxiety.
- Lounging back = not necessarily relaxed. Sometimes this is an attempt to *look* relaxed. Need other clues to verify this.
- Changing positions = too much movement means they literally can't find a comfortable place; it's hard to settle down. Sometimes the result of the adrenals overflowing at the beginning of a meeting.

Or — it could mean they're getting impatient . . .

Hands

- Clasped = perhaps tense, but notice *how* tightly they're clasped. Do they open and close their fingers? Another sign of tension and nervousness. For some people, clasped hands are a sign of orderliness and doing things correctly, like in school, remember?

- Open and relaxed = a good indicator that this person *is* feeling in control.
- Fiddling with objects = unsure; needs tangible touching to feel comforted. Also signifies highly charged overflow of physical energy.
- Clutching chair arms = holding onto reality. Needs an anchor. Another sign of tension.

Eye contact

- How and/or *if* we make eye contact is a most eloquent source of information.
- Steady gaze = calm interior; sense of security and strength about oneself.
- Shifting glances = obviously unable to hold his/her ground; to confront you.
- Looking over your head or down = solo monologue, not taking the listener into account.

Look for anger, impatience, hostility

Throughout the encounter, stay tuned into the other's body language. Notice what else is being transmitted non-verbally if you want to know more about how your opposite number is accepting you and your material.

So — Openers are for getting you started, warming up the environment and helping the opposite number to feel comfortable and more in touch with you. But they're also to help make the first quick evaluation we're all so good at, and to use that information in the encounter itself.

Now, to what the meeting's about.

SUBSTANCE

Up front: agenda, goals, time

If *you* called the meeting — introduce your subject by starting at the beginning, as we discussed in Chapter 5.

- *Agenda*
  When you begin the substance section of your encounter, tell your opposite number what you have planned. Describe your agenda in simple, bullet-like terms. Hit only the highlights. This is to explain the *organization* of your information, not to *give* it just yet.
- *Goals*
  Everyone who's busy at work wants some bottom-line orientation. So the next things you share are your goals for this meeting; why you're having it, what you hope to accomplish; perhaps something about how your opposite number relates to this material.
- *Time*
  Unless you negotiated the time when you scheduled your appointment (as I suggested), you must now ask how much time you have and do your editing right there. Even if you have already negotiated it, remind your counterpart how long you expect to take and ask if there are any problems with that time.

Sharing the power

Decide on how much power you need in this encounter. Depending on who called the meeting and what the subject matter is about, one important aspect of a one-to-one is finding ways to balance the power between two people.

My work has taught me that people communicate best when they feel on solid ground. Not only the solid ground of knowing their subject and being committed to an idea but also the solid ground of being able to share in how things will be done and that he/she can make things happen at the meeting, too.

How much can the boss share?

Boss
It requires inner security to know that you *do* have power and that you therefore can share as much as you like because you're not *losing* it; you're only *lending* some . . .

You surely know that subordinates worry about your power. Calling a meeting puts you in a powerful position indeed.

To make maximum listening room in a subordinate's mind or to ensure an honest exchange if you wish to get something clear or find something out, you need to let your subordinate know that he/she has power, too:

'Susan, we'll talk about some issues that may have controversy attached to them. It would be most constructive if we got those out as we talk, so let's agree that you not only *may*, but I *urge* you to interrupt with questions and take an opposing stand, if you feel that way.'

Be sure that you *mean* it. Don't patronize or make statements of form, not substance! This must be genuine, or else the first time Susan speaks up and you get vague or fight back or don't listen, she'll know not to do *that* again!

How much can the subordinate or peer share?

How much power *you* can hope to exercise in this encounter depends not only on the subject matter and circumstances of the meeting but mainly on your opposite number. Some people *need* to feel in total control, for many different reasons, of course. Think: What are your opposite number's major motivations and style of working?

As long as you feed his/her primary need, you, too, can share in the power by questioning within that framework, suggesting but not threatening or becoming too stubborn or resistant. Examples:

- *To an achiever boss* (who responds to tasks): 'I understand *that's* how to do that project. One more addition, maybe, that would get it done even faster — how about X . . .' or, 'The task must *definitely* be done. But I have a problem with Y. Help me try to deal with it so we can get right to completing the project.'

  In either case, you've given him/her the power by agreeing to do the task *and* put your suggestion or objection in his/her terms — how to get the task done best. This then allows you to negotiate from *your* needs and get some power of your own.

- *To an affiliator boss* (who feels powerful through a sense of being needed): 'That project is a really *great* idea! I'm flattered that you asked me. I'll need your help in sorting out the opening steps, but I'm sure we can do it.'

  Again, by playing into the affiliator's greatest need, to feel connected, you can also rearrange the project to suit your needs as well.

- *To an influencer boss* (who needs affirmation of team leadership): 'You know, our team can put that project together with some real substance, because of the expertise we've got. By the way, could you get me involved in the Z part of it? I think I can make a major contribution.'

Knowing that the influencer has a vested interest in organizing and leading a successful group, you could then ask for your preferred assignment acknowledging his power to delegate it.

Motivation

When you present an idea or discuss an issue, identify what aspect of it would best fit into the other person's motivation. What would be his/her prime concern? Saving money? Gaining new influence in the workforce or marketplace? Developing a new product or system? Would it make the other person look good? Use this appeal to core motivation as the opening wedge to get your listener's attention and to persuade him/her.

Telling and explaining

This is such a vast subject that I've handled it in three different chapters! Organizing, structure, and visualization in Chapter 5; presentation techniques in Chapter 7; and explaining and answering questions in Chapter 8.

Therefore, let me focus here only on some specific ideas about how to enhance your explanation or statement in an impromptu fashion, without pre-planned material, as you talk and things come up.

Making ideas instantly visual

Explaining, as we have discovered, is very hard to do purely verbally. Also, people often need to keep seeing the 'before' so they can evaluate the 'after' — what effect it has or how the whole process gets connected.

Example: Suppose you're planning what happens if you route a product through the usual system (as your opposite number is now suggesting) vs. rerouting and including a new loop in the system (which *you* think will work best). You see that the other person isn't getting it. To be convincing, this explanation needs visualizing. But how, on the spur of the moment? You could:

● Draw it as a diagram. The plus side is that it's very simple to do. The minus side is that it is a flat, two-dimensional portrayal, inanimate and uninteresting. It can only give the bare-bones information, and you need to draw several diagrams to show the extra possibilities or do a lot of crossing out and mish-mash. I find the next way better, more succinct and more persuasive (also more fun).

● Use a few tangible objects on the desk or coffee table, or on your person, as symbols of the various parts of your idea. Cups, paperweights, ashtrays, paper clips, pens, etc., work very well. Designate each one as a part of the routing system: 'The cup is a . . . and the two ashtrays are the . . .' Pens and pencils make excellent 'arrows', showing directions and connections.

Then set up the current route (your opposite's preference). You can talk about each step as you build it (what it's for, how it moves to the next place) and actually move the objects around. You can get your opposite number involved, too.

This provides three-dimensional plus tactile visualization (much more interesting). It's more colourful and more active. It can show movement and retrace steps to show variations with the same basic objects. You can set up two systems, side by side, for instant visual comparison. It's a novel and original way to tell, bound to capture interest and attention as well as better comprehension.

Ask before you tell

To get someone involved right at the beginning of presenting an idea, start by asking them an interesting question. A few startling bits of trivia relating to your subject: 'What do you think is the biggest?' This approach engages your opposite number in trying to answer and being properly surprised by the right answer. It also establishes your expertise very quickly *and* it's a different way to start, not openly aggressive or sales-orientated.

Discussion

Create a positive environment

Primary in any discussion is the environment in which it happens. If it's a challenge session in which the goal is to put you on the defensive and make you answer negative comments, it's not a discussion.

Host and visitor should both be aware of the optimal circumstances for discussion and work hard to keep the exchange factual, easy, and friendly. One big advantage of a one-to-one discussion is the fact that there are only two people, so, unlike a group meeting, you can each have *lots* of turns and be heard, and can also focus more directly on each other's ideas and subtext.

Listen

We usually start out *trying* to listen. The problem arises when the sides differ and the discussion deteriorates into a series of interruptions and counterarguments.

How to fix that?

What do you think of: 'Look, Dan, I keep trying to make my point and you cut me off'?

Well, it's truthful. But is it persuasive? Not really. It's very judgemental and critical of Dan. How about:

'Look, Dan, we're both so hot to get our point across that I don't think either of us is listening! Let's each take five minutes each and present our point of view, uninterrupted'?

The advantage of the latter idea is that the speaker said *both* were not listening (which has to be true because the person who is interrupted spends some time seething, *not* listening!). This allows both to save face and begin again.

Consider the idea

Stay open! Give credibility to each idea. We do have a tendency to close down just because it isn't our idea.

Ask

Before you go off half-cocked, ask questions! Be sure you understand the *whole idea* before you answer, defend, or counter-punch.

Be clear

In order to be convincing in a discussion, listen to yourself! Sometimes when you talk of something very familiar to you, you use shorthand and your opposite number may not understand it.

Notice and comment on what's being discussed

'I see you want to know more about X. Is that an important issue?' Become very conscious within a discussion about the underlying trends of the subject matter. Not only should you notice in order to pick up clues on what to answer; you also can find out about the hidden concerns of the person you're talking with. Good to know for further motivation and persuasion.

When you mention what else is taking place, 'I see you want to know . . .', it's generally very disarming and also focuses the discussion. How they deal with the answer is also important to notice.

Know when to get out

You need to develop a sense about when you've been around the track enough times and learn to end it and get out.

'Well, I guess we could keep pulling this apart but perhaps we've explored it enough for now. Let me suggest that I leave (or send you) some materials for you to think about.' Or, 'I hear what you're saying. Let me think about it for a while and then we can talk about it again.'

These approaches work whether you are the originator of the meeting or the one being questioned or perhaps disagreed with.

To sum up: the techniques for presenting an idea or explaining yourself are as important here as in a large speech. You need to capture and hold your audience of one, too! Don't forget about motivation when you want to persuade. Be sure to bring substantive visual materials to bolster your point and to leave materials behind for further consideration.

SPECIAL ISSUES

So far, the steps within each segment have followed a chronological order. But there are also particularly delicate communications issues that often crop up in a close encounter and they need special attention.

Creative criticism

We often forget that the main purpose of criticizing is not to be negative but to be constructive! To *fix* something! one of the most difficult things to do when you need to criticize someone for a job not well done, or for a major mistake, is to reassure and encourage at the same time that you're criticizing. Unless you can give them the reinforcement that they're capable of fixing it, most people won't be able to get past the negative 'you screwed up' message to listen to you and try to do better.

Accentuate the positive

'Harry, that writing job you did was short and to the point, just as I requested. It made good sense and was well written. Thanks. Now — let's look at something that needs fixing . . .'

Before you tell him/her what was *wrong*, spend a little time on what went *right*! It sounds so self-evident but it's a common human failing. We get so focused on exploring the mistake that we don't hear how negative it all sounds, or realize that *something* went correctly.

If you praise before you criticize, people are more likely to listen to the criticism with both ears, knowing that you're not *totally* displeased and they're not *totally* deficient.

Be specific

'Ruth, I didn't like the way you did the report, at all! It was generally dull and not too convincing. Do it over and make it shorter, and more interesting.'

What does Ruth do with this kind of criticism? What's 'interesting'? And 'shorter'? It *all* seems important; what should she leave out? (Also, notice that put-down of an opening line!)

General criticism is destructive. It doesn't lead anyone to know *how* to fix things; it just makes people feel bad. We all have different verbal and visual styles and conceive different ways to say the same thing. But, unless you can explain specifically, you haven't started *fixing* anything.

To help the criticized person know how to fix what *you* object to, define *exactly* what went wrong and why it is unsatisfactory. Most people are generally so sensitive to criticism that they'll say, 'Yes, I understand,' when they actually don't, just to get the criticism to end. Specific examples for improvement as well as specific descriptions of exactly what you mean are a must.

'Ruth, it's too long. To fix it, why not take out the detailed background sections? That will leave you with only the current status, which is fine. Then you could include some examples and those customer letters as well as some visuals, perhaps. *That* should make it more interesting, which it needs, to be more effective.'

Stay with the facts, not the person

'Look, this job wasn't done correctly and only a very sloppy person who doesn't pay attention would have let that go through!'

It's often a temptation to pull in the whole kitchen sink when all you need to criticize is the tap. We sometimes get carried away and attack the *person* — their ability, intentions, etc. — when all that needs to be discussed is what *thing* or *process* went wrong.

'Well, this job went wrong. Somehow it was allowed to go through. It would help to figure out why so we can fix it.'

Getting at the truth

Behaviour is predictable, given certain kinds of circumstances. What do you think people normally do when they're accused of something, criticized, or asked to discuss something incriminating? Wouldn't they naturally be self-protective and careful of what they'd say? Wouldn't *you*?

In one-to-one encounters where the subject is incriminating — like finding out why or how someone made a mistake or uncovering a weak link in the system — you as truth seeker need to counter the usual self-protective responses with some strategic moves to get to what you want.

Describe the expected response

Before you start, clear the air and surprise him/her.

'I was thinking before you came in about how I would feel if someone asked *me* to talk about . . . and asked me about X and Y. I guess I'd be pretty careful with my answers. Is that how you feel?'

This opens the conversation on a healthier note of allowing for people's natural tendencies. It sounds understanding. It helps the other person feel safer and encourages them to tell you how they feel before you go for the hard information. Then you can deal with fears, anxiety, reluctance to chat and so on.

Tell what you want to know and why

Your intention has very much to do with *how*, and *if*, someone will answer you openly. If the reason sounds useful and valuable to the ongoing good of the business or the group, you have begun to provide motivation. The other person can then select from what you want to know about and feel in some control at the same time that they answer you.

Tell what you'll do with it

The next worry people generally have is:

'If I discuss this openly, what will be the result? What will he/she do with it? Why should I be a party to that?'

If your issue deals with fellow workers there is the loyalty issue to contend with, and the feeling that the troops bond together, not necessarily, with the leader. There's also the consequence of lapsed privacy and secrecy. So tell them what you'll do with the information and how, as much as you can.

Help by leading

'There are probably two things you can tell me about that. You worked with the . . . so you could start there.'

Leading people toward some organized direction instead of saying, 'What can you tell me?' is very reassuring. Since the concerns are generally as we have described them, it helps to have *you* edit and eliminate, rather than leaving them to flounder in a sea of choices, most of which look dangerous. Starting them talking helps you to ask follow-up questions to pinpoint more specifically or to move off to another direction.

If you're not getting what you need

Say it. Tell the person being questioned what the problem seems to be and what's missing. I don't suggest too many manipulative cross-examiner tactics, especially if you have no training in this. If someone feels backed into a corner, they will become even more defensive and guarded.

Handling anger — yours and his/hers

The major clue to handling anger successfully is: first, agree it's there! Generally, we try to deny it or pretend it's not happening, on both sides.

In a business setting, the person with more power allows him/herself to express anger much more commonly than the subordinate. Yet there are many levels of seething or hostility, and you need to learn to recognize the many faces before you can deal successfully with anger — yours and his/hers.

Perhaps the best way to tell you how to do this is to tell you a story.

I was the host of my own TV chat show in Boston for many years. Nothing makes you learn about human communication and what doesn't work faster than trying to interview, talk with, or handle people on live TV before almost a million viewers and hitting a wall! Talk of damp hands!

Here's how I learned about handling anger: I was scheduled to interview a famous film star who was making a film on location near Boston. We had promoted it very heavily on air. Yet, although he had initially agreed, he had put us off several times, and we were now at the last possible day for shooting the interview. Armed with a definite appointment, we packed a full TV crew and went trekking off (in mid-December) to a cold bleak forest glade where they were shooting the film.

Our film hero again stalled us, with a rather acid greeting:

'Oh, of *course*. We'll just stop shooting this silly little movie and do *your* little old interview.' Here's where the lesson begins.

My approach was to smile sweetly, turn the other cheek, and placate by saying:

'No. No, please. We'll just wait until you're done.'

A clear case of denying the anger — to myself *and* to him!

Result? We waited all that freezing afternoon (overtime clock ticking for the crew) until our hero was ready for us — at 5.00 p.m. Five p.m. in Boston in December means *dark*!

Again, ignoring the seething messages we were getting, we scrambled around, rigged up lights in a by-now *freezing* setting, and sat down to begin our — er — talking/sharing/listening/experience. Right.

The next experience provided Lesson Two — one I have never forgotten and that I teach as a major strategy all the time.

Still denying the truth of what was really going on, I started what I hoped would be a pleasant interview with a . . . snarling tiger. The more questions I asked, the testier he got. I continued on my Goody Two-Shoes path of pretending all was well, convinced that it was my fault. I kept looking for a great question and he kept being more openly abusive and ridiculing. All of this was, of course, being captured in living colour by our TV cameras, to be edited and shown the next morning, as advertised. Finally, my producer signalled the cameras and me to wrap it up and, undaunted, still smiling sweetly, I said, 'Thank you,' and called it a night.

And ran to the truck and broke into tears. Do you know what? I didn't blame our film star. I blamed *myself* for being so inept! I felt that if my *questions* were better, I could have made him turn around.

I learned then how unrealistic, harmful, and useless it is *not* to deal with anger as soon as it happens and you see it.

But don't let me leave you here. Of *course* there's a happy ending and a moral to my story.

Now, what could I do with this disaster of an interview — to be seen by my audience in a very few hours? I decided that because it was such a great lesson for everyone, we should show it, with an introduction from me telling about my terrible failure and wanting to share it with them so we could all learn something from it.

Learn what? What *should* I have said? I should have said gently, non-judgementally, simply as an observation:

'You know, Mr Film Star, you seem to be very angry,' and let him respond. Putting the ball in his court, we could both have dealt with his anger and been on very solid ground. Then I could have dealt with what really *was* happening instead of what I thought and hoped *should* have been happening.

Telling this all to my audience and showing parts of the interview, I then filled in with many common experiences we all have like that; not dealing with what's really going on and hoping it'll go away, or get better on its own, or blaming ourselves for not being able to fix it 'somehow'.

Not yet a happy ending, you say? Wait.

Time marched on. A whole year of time. I had really learned my lesson. I handled many hot topics and hot-under-the-collar people according to my new technique of simply, benignly, saying what I saw happening, right away, and then being able to defuse and deal with it effectively. And it worked!

And then, my turn came around again — with our self-same movie hero! Back in town to promote the now-completed movie, his people asked to book him on my show.

What happened? It was wonderful. I did everything I taught my audience and myself to do, based on my bitter lesson. He and I talked of the last time we'd seen each other. He vaguely remembered the occasion: 'Something about you weren't prepared and ready for me,' he said. I said, 'No, that wasn't how it was at all,' and proceeded to tell him what actually happened.

Again, he became angry, saying that TV interviewers ask too many intrusive questions, etc. I said, 'Hey, we're doing it again. I see you're getting angry again.' And do you know what he did? He laughed! 'Yep, ya got me.' he said. And *then* we had an absolutely splendid interview . . .

Enough said.

If you're angry, *say so*. 'This really does upset me (make me mad, etc.) because . . .' This allows others to deal with your anger and help move the conversation to a more productive place.

If someone can't say it and you see it, then *you* say:

'I see you're very angry (or upset or whatever). What aspect of this upsets you?' Then leave it, giving him/her a chance to vent it and calm down. Then deal with *that*.

(There's a whole section on handling hostility with many more tactics in Chapter 8: The Art of Being Questioned. Read it for more ideas.)

Now on to Closure, the last segment of a close encounter.

CLOSURE

This seemingly simple segment is very often mishandled or quite forgotten. Here is where the nitty-gritty takes place. Unless you both know *exactly* what happened and *exactly* what you both expect from each other next, your whole encounter was for naught.

Recap and clarify

'Now, let's go over what we talked about, just to be sure we're both on the same wavelength.'

Sounds simple, yet it's funny how often people forget to do that. Each person thinks the other understood what *he* understood, and that's rarely the case.

We all use selective listening. Tuned into *our* major themes, wanting to be sure we got *our* particular goal achieved, we don't notice too much about what else took place. Therefore, recap is important.

If it's your meeting, do it very methodically. Start from the beginning of your agenda and go down the list. Check off each item with notes about what you both decided: send those notes to the other for mutual sign-off.

Take the opportunity to re-discuss any issues that still seem unresolved. This is your last chance.

If you're the other participant, be sure you speak up during this part of the meeting. Don't just agree. Sometimes this is a better place to make, even win, a final point. When other parts have been resolved and there's only one sticky place left, a little distance from the initial discussion can bring cooler heads to bear.

Just a simple 'You know, that *still* makes me uncomfortable', or, 'I'm still not altogether clear about our intention from now on' will open it again. Then resolve it into its final form.

List next steps

Again — methodically. Make a real list. Write dates for upcoming moves; who else will be involved; what else you need, to continue; and so on. Again, it's important that all this be memorialized in a memo that states it in writing for mutual sign-off.

If you're with a client, not a peer or staff member, this is still a necessary step. Writing down what you decided and sending a follow-up letter makes your mutual decision that much more binding. This is the time for clarifying what you really plan to do.

Follow-up

Who, *how*, and *when* often involves checking with others and getting back to your original meeting partner with additional data. Make *that* clear as well. Immediate against long-range plans need to be defined, and the process for checking back and checking up on progress made also needs to be discussed and decided on.

End on a high note

Whichever role you played, the final exit lines and the mood created at the end are very important.

You should leave, if it's not *your* office or *your* meeting, with some vigour and some 'onward and upward' quality. If the meeting was dour and even critical of you, you need to impart a sense of energy about tomorrow and optimism that you/he/we can and will fix it:

'Okay, Sam. I heard it all. I feel there are many things we (or I) can do to change the situation. Let's get started!'

If the meeting is process-orientated, or relating to a new idea, try something like:

'I must say how enthusiastic I am about the new plan and how eager I am to see how it works out. I'll give it my best.'

If you're the meeting convener, and it was a tough one, this is the time to heal and soothe. Walk with your opposite number to the door. If you're comfortable with physical contact, this may be the time for the proverbial (and literal) pat on the back.

'I think we got a lot done. I feel you heard me and I *know* I heard you. Let's make this the basis for our next talk together. I know we can work things out.'

If you've just given a tough assignment, give an inspiring send-off:

'Karen, if anyone can do this job and do it well, it's you. I look forward to our next check-in meeting to see how it's going. Meanwhile, since it's pretty complex, if you need me, I'm here.'

In general, 'high-note' send-offs by a convenor at the end of a meeting should reverberate in the hall as your participant leaves, making him/her feel good, purposeful, re-energized, and capable.

'High notes' from the departing visitor should leave the meeting convenor with some positive thoughts about you as you close the door and disappear. They should provide a moment of reflection about how you handled yourself and the material and about how fired up you seem about going forward.

Don't forget or short-change closure. It's very valuable; saves phone calls and extra meetings, and has a great by-product: The last word . . .

CHECKLIST

Here's the short form, to help you remember and plan:

Openers

- Change gears; make a personal dent
- Warm-up; small talk

- Office as turf; where to sit
- Amenities; the 'gift' of coffee, etc.
- Body language; the key weathervane

Substance

- Up front; the agenda, goals, and time
- Share the power
- Make an open-exchange environment
- Consider motivation
- Tell and explain
- Discussion

Special issues

- Offer creative criticism
- Get at the truth
- Handle anger — yours and his/hers

Closure

- Recap and clarify
- List next steps
- Follow-up; who, how, and when
- End on a high note!

Now, let's turn to presentations, understanding audiences and giving them what they need; positioning your presentation; techniques for writing and delivering them.

7
Presentations
How to make memorable speeches

This is such an easy subject to get into. We've all been in audiences: suffered in them; gone to sleep in them; been inspired and moved in them; been hopelessly confused in them. In short, we know a lot about what we don't like, something about what we do like, and not much about exactly why.

It is also fair to say that we generally don't know exactly how to make audiences work for us and respond to us? Especially on a regular basis?

Well, the quest for answers stops here.

In this chapter we'll uncover the secrets of audiences — small or large. We'll find out how to make speeches and presentations that will make an audience listen, understand, and respond on your side.

UNDERSTANDING AUDIENCES
How audiences feel

We know how we feel when a speech is not working or we become disinterested. But it's not only the fault of the speech.

There are actually a natural set of givens, responses created by simply being in an audience and listening to a speaker, that affect us and make our basic mental set quite predictable. Though they're subliminal, they're basically how we respond to being members of an audience.

Knowing what these givens are will help us to understand what we have to do to prepare the presentation and deliver it effectively. Here are some of the problems that attend us as audience members. We feel:

Passive

Unable to get information unless the speaker gives it and powerless to change the way things are going, audiences feel basically inactive and uninvolved. The by-products are lowered physical energy level and a lessened ability or motivation to stay with you and your topic.

Disenfranchised

Audience membership puts us in a receiving mode when we have been quite accustomed to running our lives and being the teller or activator. This makes us feel that we've lost our turf. It's hard to sit back and just let someone else take over.

Anonymous

You, as the speaker, are instantly visible. You are listed in the programme or, at the least, are introduced. We the audience may also feel distinguished or at least competent but know that to you, the speaker, we're only a sea of faces. Anonymous listeners. One amorphous bunch, rather than the individuals we pride ourselves on being.

Competitive

'Let's see your stuff !' It's typical of us, when we feel even some of the above, that we would also feel competitive with the person that put us in those states. 'Who are *you* to tell *me*? What do you know that I don't know already?' We become not only an audience but a jury.

Put upon

Often, presentations are either gratuitous, useful for the teller, or upon an audience because 'this is good for you'. Audiences are not in charge of either the subject or the length and manner of presentation. This can create resentment, especially if the speaker isn't impressive.

Manipulated

Since most presentations, large or small, cast the speaker as the champion of a cause, the seller of an idea, or someone who wants the audience to do, think, or agree with something, audiences have a natural tendency to see themselves as being manipulated. They see the speaker as 'doing something to them'. Not a wholesome, open-minded state.

Resistant

The common outgrowth of feeling manipulated is to draw the line. 'Don't tell me what to do' is as old a response as the first time we disobeyed a parent. There is not only a natural tendency to resist any salesperson for the sheer feeling of strength or personal integrity it gives us: we are also, due to our ad-happy culture, very sales-shrewd and seller-suspicious these days.

Challenged

Whenever a new idea is presented — or an in-depth, detailed, or alternative version of an old idea — we as an audience are challenged to rise to the occasion and understand it. Especially since you — the speaker — already, and obviously, do. But people learn at different rates and come to such a table with different skills and differing levels of comprehension. Therefore, the very act of being in an audience, trying to understand, can be threatening. Especially since, very often, it's material we *need* and *want* to understand.

Bonded

Because we're all in it together, in that time and place, sharing that special experience and those possible discomforts, audience members do feel connected to each other. Singling any one of us out makes the whole audience feel affiliated with and protective of that person. (Just watch the TV game shows if you doubt this.)

Now let's add the physical realities of sitting in an audience to the emotional responses and consider the effects *they* could have:

● How hard are the chairs?
● How long have they already been there?
● What else has gone before?
● Is it hot? Cold?

- Can they see? Hear?
- Are they hungry?

All of the above affect the receptivity of your audience. Using them as guidelines, let's move on to phase one of making a speech.

PLANNING YOUR PRESENTATION

Profile your audience

What do you especially need to learn about your specific audience to be sure that your message goes right to the heart of what they care about and or need to know?

You need to create a group portrait to be able to predict what their goals, needs, and expectations are; in what style and at what level your presentation should be delivered.

An unfamiliar audience

Demographics sound so market-research-orientated, but in truth isn't that what we want? With a disparate group of strangers, you need to start narrowing your sights about who's coming to hear you in order to be effective with them. You need to learn about:

- *Age and sex*
  The age (under X, X to Y) and sex (all male, mixed, all female) of your audience matter because they will affect the choices you make: choices in language, allusion, metaphor, allegory, reference points, and so on. Not useful to talk of the current heavy-metal range to a group of over-forties. Not effective to bring up the old Hollywod morality plays to a group of thirty-year-olds. Sports analogies, family issues, historical references, old-boy networks, disenfranchisement: all these have more or less interest, aptness, and symbolic meaning for one age or sex than another, based on where people are in their lives. Therefore, knowing about these two general categories begins to help you winnow the range of choices you make in preparing your speech.
  Please understand that this is only a start in *generalizing* about who's in your audience and what they probably care about and

respond to. (No female letters about football fans and male knitters, please. I know they're there!)

- *Professional level*
- Are you sharing new data?
- Introducing them to your methods?
- Altering an existing belief?
- Solving a common problem?

What you're trying to say and how to put it must be based on whether these are hands-on people, management, staff, customers, or laymen. Therefore, find out what they already know about and how deeply they know it. How much experience have they actually had in dealing with your subject? Most of all, from what point of view do you wish to talk to them?

- *Educational level*

The choice of language and metaphor as well as how deep you go is also determined by where your audience stands educationally. Talking over people's heads is the most patronizing and self-destructive thing you can do as a speaker. It's guaranteed to turn people off and make them hostile.

For less well-educated audiences, never make the mistake of becoming *simplistic*. Learning what people don't know should challenge you to *simplify*, to *edit* and make *clear*, but *not* talk down.

Another aspect of knowing about the educational level of your highly trained audiences, accustomed to research and lectures, your horizons are opened for a lengthier form of explanation (although *everyone* has a cut-off point). For less informed listeners a more practical, less theoretical approach should probably be taken with more time spent on why they should listen at all and where this subject fits in their lives.

- *Socioeconomic level*

Granted, we're working from stereotypes when we presume to know an audience merely by knowing their salary levels and probable bank balance. Yet suburban home owner, inner-city solo loft dweller, or apartment renter with room-mate are all conditioned by their social and economic experiences and can respond from very different mental sets.

- *Ethnic differences*

It's also important to be aware of the different kinds of belief systems and morality issues that are shared by ethnic groups in various parts of the country and how *that* might affect how you structure your message.

Coming in with a very avant-garde plan, for example, blissfully unaware of the conservative family and business traditions in a certain section, is a one-way street to being turned down. So learn something about the unique make up of your audience and how their background or belief systems could affect the way they hear you.

A familiar audience

If yours is an audience you already know, you may already have the answers to many of these questions. Going through them, though, and creating a quick profile helps you focus.

There are a few questions uniquely relevant to an audience that knows you which can help you pinpoint their key elements and some predictable responses.

- How do they feel about you? Do they know you well? Is your relationship casual and friendly or more distant and formal? This could help you decide how relaxed and informal you want to be.
- What is their perception of you and your work? Do they know your responsibilities, expertise, power, status? What do they think about that? Are you on the same level as, below, or above your audience in terms of job status and knowledge?
- How does your work or position affect them? Is there a little awe and wonder, if you're a very senior person? Maybe some resentment and stereotyping? Can you be seen as dangerous to them? Threatening? Or inconsequential, perhaps, which would make you sharpen your focus on being extremely relevant, with crisp, enlightening information?

Answering these questions is obviously vital to your preparation — both for style and for content.

Why are they coming?

Find out why your audience is coming. Knowing that will tell you what their mood will be when you begin and what you might want to change or upend right at the start.

Take the time to ask this question of the people who arranged the talk, if it's an unfamiliar audience. If it's a familiar audience within your own workplace, ask a few of your fellow employees or whoever organized the meeting. Spend a moment putting yourself in their place, thinking about why they will be at the meeting and how that affects them.

Coercion

Are they being told to go? Although this won't make you happy, you'd better know it beforehand. Knowing this would affect how quickly and thoroughly you must intrigue them with your topic and how relevant to them you must make it right at the beginning. And how hard you'd better work!

Personal interest

Are they coming to hear *you*? Perhaps it's because of your reputation in the field or because of recent publicity. Maybe your job and resultant experience makes you the person they want to hear from, either from genuine curiosity or because it relates to their work in some way. In this case your presentation should be quite personal and sharing in nature.

Subject-matter interest

Are they coming because they want to know more about the subject and you're the conduit? Then you need to know more about what aspect of your subject they want to hear about and how it relates to what they're already doing. This would mean a more in-depth look, if they're in your field, or a well-presented, comprehensive overview if they're newcomers.

Politics

Maybe they're coming because it's the 'right' thing to do — either within their own firm or because it's an industry get-together and they need to be seen. This challenges you to make them glad they came and to do it early. Give them a new message or a twist on something you all know about that they may never have thought about before, blowing the irrelevance with which they view your speech, and to do it early.

Hostility

Your audience could also be made up of people who disagree with you; representatives of another point of view; people who are being negatively affected by what you do or propose to do, or by whom you represent. Major challenge! Knowing this prior cast to the audience helps you prepare a presentation that could begin by listing all their grievances and dealing with them up front before you even try to turn them around to your way of thinking!

Indifference

You may be the strong proponent for (or opponent of) a particular issue. Your audience may not care much and be on a totally different emotional wavelength to you. They could even be attending because of something else on the programme. Knowing the space between *your* commitment level and theirs can help you start at a much lower speed and tone and build slowly, as you feel the audience come with you. If you come in at a high level of intensity and they're still at the starting gate, you've lost them from the opening gun.

Regular attendance

Your audience can be a weekly staff meeting group. People who know you, who expect a certain number of reports per meeting and perhaps have a jaded view of how exciting the proceedings are going to be. The great challenge here is to up-end the usual snail's pace or perfunctory level of presentations. Make 'em sit up and take notice! Make this the memorable meeting 'when Jack (or Jill) gave that really great report . . . '

Whatever the reason, understanding why your audience *is* your audience is a vital aspect of helping you design your presentation.

Physical realities

What else has been affecting them is a major factor in how well they can listen to you: time of day; when you appear on the programme; what else they heard; how long they've been there. These will obviously affect your audience's receptivity and you need to think of them to adapt your speech's pace, approach, and style to these burdensome factors in order to counteract their effect.

Timing

Remember the section in Chapter 4 about Timing? About hunger and energy level and when to call a meeting? Well, take it seriously when it comes to looking for a receptive audience for your speech as well. Effects?

- *Lunch*
  Before lunch = unpredictable and impatient; right after lunch = slow and sleepy; During lunch = noisy and possible talking at tables. Get prepared for what energy level and special effects you'll need to fight that.
- *Coffee breaks*
  Find out about when there'll be a coffee break and how near to that you'll speak. Remember to give coffee breaks if yours is a lengthy presentation. Everyone needs a stretch and a bathroom visit, no matter how good you are . . .

Setting

Where is your presentation to be held? Hotel room? Large? Long! A raised dais? Air-conditioned or not? Lighting? Acoustics and amplifiers? How hard *are* the chairs? Being prepared for the physical realities of your presentation site and knowing in advance what problems of sight and sound your audience (and therefore you) will have to deal with is also important and helpful.

What has gone before

Find out what kinds of programmes they have already lived through to understand what effect that would have and how your presentation will be greeted. Long programme? Many speeches? Intense subject? This consideration is true whether you're addressing a large, unknown crowd at a convention or just the folks from the office at a weekly meeting. People have only so much attention span and so much tolerance for being talked at. You need to build in a change of pace and new life to keep them.

So — here's your group portrait, your audience profile. Knowing this helps you customize your speech for them. Now, what will you say?

DESIGNING YOUR PRESENTATION

Positioning the speech

What level will you talk at? What approach will you take? It's time for the old forethought chart. (Just for review, check the steps in Chapter 3.) Since you know your audience well enough now to make generalizations about them, begin to strategize, making sure that your half of the chart is filled in, too.

Seeing what the answers are to your Goals, Needs, and Expectations as well as those of your audience is step two in preparing your speech.

Now what next?

Challenge yourself: Why should your audience listen to what you have to say?

Why they need your information

Ask yourself:

- Why, in the pursuit of their daily lives, is your subject relevant?
- Is it within the scope of their work?
- Is it not yet in their orbit but should be?
- Can it make their work better? More rewarding? Easier? More effective?
- Would it affect their life outside their work and be relevant to them on that level?
- Do they need to be inspired to do more with what they already know?

Making yourself answer these questions about a subject you care and know a lot about is a real eye-opener. Nothing is more important in terms of getting you in touch with your audience than recognizing the space that exists between them and you about your topic.

What do they care about

Before you can design your presentation, you need to take a look at where your audience is in relation to your material and why they should listen. This can tell you how to pitch your subject and, most importantly, in what capacity you came before them as speaker.

How much do they already know

To pitch your presentation at the right level find out how sophisticated your audience is about your topic. (Even if you can't find out in advance, ask them as you begin your speech: 'How many of you know much about XYZ!' to get yourself on target.) It saves so much time and boring overkill if you come in on their informational frequency. Knowing in advance will also help you prepare your visual materials more effectively, since you'll know how simplistic and diagrammatic or detailed and complex you need to make these.

What role should you play?

Expert? Teacher! Prophet? Critic? Representative from another sector?

As you continue to develop your presentation, keep posing the question to yourself about what you are for your audience. Here are a few alternative roles:

- *Sharer/guide*
  Suppose this is a situation in which you have to give information or expertise that the group doesn't have. Your role here has to be non-threatening — not a 'Here I am, folks, world expert' posture. You need to be non-judgemental, sharing your knowledge with enthusiasm, obviously dedicated to being sure they can get it, too. It's to be their guide through a rather forbidding jungle that you've traversed often and know well — that you won't let them get lost. You need to assure them that you know the pitfalls and will stop so they can catch up. This protective sharer/guide quality you need to protect softens the distance between what you know and they *don't* know and makes them able to hear you. This encourages them to listen and learn.
- *Inspirer*
  Suppose you have to ask for more commitment and an extra measure of work from staff, colleagues, or even the lay public. Your

audience is either reluctant, resistant, or without motivation. What role should you play?

You can't start telling people what they'should' do for the good of the company, etc. That breeds resentment. Instead, you have to lead, by example: to lay out the need or the issues, and to show the solution. Before *they* see the need or the issues, and to show the solution. Before *they* see the need, they can't move towards action. Then — to answer why they should do anything, you need to move into engaging your audience to see the point of your message or solution.

Here's where you need to show *yourself*, your zeal and dedication. You need to use your energy and commitment and your persuasive powers to make them follow your lead. Your 'troops' need to find someone to follow with enough reasons and passion to overcome their natural inertia or resistance. You need to be inspirational.

● *Hard-nosed (though optimistic) realist*
Suppose your job is to tell your audience negative information. Times are tough or problems have developed or what they expected is not going to happen. Just flat-out 'bad news giver' is not a constructive mode in which to cast yourself.

Here your role must be to tell the bad news and some of what went wrong in objective, impersonal terms — factually and quickly. Having got rid of that, the very next gear for you to move into is a constructive one. Now you need to present clear steps toward fixing the negative turn of events and telling everyone specifically what needs to be done and how. And — most of all — you need to let them know you believe they can do it and that it can be fixed.

These few examples can show you that your audience needs more from you than just your message. The effect of your message *on* them and the result you want *from* them both demand that you fill a unique role for them. Therefore, know — before you take centre stage — what role you need to play for your audience and what relationship they need from you, so they can really *hear* you.

Basic organization of a speech

Structure

The checklist in Chapter 5 sets forth the underlying structure of any speech to make the most logical and easily followed design for any audience. Although unique occasions and subjects may call for abbreviated versions or a very different approach, this is the simplest, most orderly format to follow, with the most flexible sections within which to design your message.

Selecting the content

'But you can't leave *that* out! This is so important! How can they learn this without first hearing about *those?*'

Strength and courage are required. Editing is a fact, unless you want to hand out pillows as you begin your speech. You must find a method of selection that will counter your tendency to tell too much.

Start out knowing that what makes a speech great is the feeling of giving 'just enough' to your audience.

● Just enough *background material* to be orientated to your point of view.

● Just enough *information* to let them understand what you mean and stimulate them to think about it.

● Just enough *examples and explicit visualization* (graphic or oral) so they can make up their own minds.

To help you select your content, I have created a little motto:

> Tell them what *they* need to know,
> *not* all *you* know!

Give them the kinds of basics to bring them into your orbit and, at each step, give them enough to be able to move on to the next.

What to make visual

Chapter 5 describes when you should make your material visual and the best ways to do that.

SHOULD YOU WRITE IT?

Witten vs. oral speeches

Now I enter stormy waters. Most people's tendency is to 'write it all out so I get it straight' (or 'right' or 'well said') because they're afraid to search for the words at the actual moment, in case they get stuck.

But, *reading* a speech is not the optimum technique for *oral* communication or an audience. I know that some speeches *must* be read for legal or policy reasons, but barring that, the method of delivery should be extemporaneous, from notes.

Oral communication at its best should feel like a live dialogue between the teller and the audience.

It's personal. You talk, and they feel that you're talking just for them, to them, about them.

It's immediate. Of the moment. Live. Unique. Unduplicable.

The written word

This is designed for delay. Delay between when the message is created and when it is received. Delay in how the message itself is taken in.

When words are read, the eye has the leisure to go back over the things it didn't understand, to reread and re-assimilate. Reading a written message, we take in information at *our* pace, not the writer's. Words alone create the sound of the author's voice.

You, as speech *writer*, rely on that process, too. You design your words to say it all. Then, you criticize by reading and rereading them, testing to see if the words — as read — give the message.

But that's not how your audience will receive it. So you're analysing a very different version of your speech from the one your audience will get.

The spoken word

Oral communication is instantaneous and doesn't reply on words alone. It depends on and is heightened by your delivery. Pace, rhythm, inflection, phrasing, pitch, facial expression all shape the message and define the author's 'voice'. The words serve only as *part* of what is communicated.

Oral communication cannot exist without the speaker.

Performance

Reading a written speech leaves little room for performance since the speaker must continually return to the printed page. This gives your message the quality of being extremely controlled and withheld.

Extemporaneous speaking from notes leaves the speaker free to move; to use different parts of the stage, to gesture spontaneously — all adding to the image of a live, fully committed performance given as a gift to the audience.

Flexibility

Extemporaneous speech is interactive, not one-way. This means you can see and 'feel' your audience *at the moment* and know just how it's going — 'too slow', 'too big a bite', need to go back again'. Since you're creating at the moment, you're flexible. You can add, subtract, and explain again based on what's happening to that audience, right then. No guessing in advance about how much is enough.

In a written speech, you're stuck. There is no flexibility. You can't stop and fix anything if you feel you're losing your audience. God forbid that you stray away from the text and try to improvise! Finding your way back in as you fumble through the paragraphs is a disaster, and when you do get back in, you'll usually find that you've already just said some of the text, and differently. You're thrown off your pace, have blown your cool, and feel like an idiot.

The use of language is different

The spoken word uses much shorter sentences. Because you see your audience as you speak, the tendency is to be much more informal and conversational, using simpler words more commonly used. You also know, subconsciously, that you can rely on the vocal, physical and performance aspects of communicating to help deliver and explain your message.

Writing is a much more formal means of communicating. What's called to mind when you write a speech is explicit textbook language (a little dry and long-winded) and formal phrases (a little stiff), as well as the professional shorthand language used most often in written memos from above. When you write, rather than thinking of the most direct, simple way to say something, the tendency is to fall into pattern and cliché based on what you think sounds professional and smart.

The effect of written speeches on the audience

Marching up, speech in hand, and plunking it down on the lectern to read brings forth to audiences mainly negative images. The usual effects of reading a speech are that:

- It creates a conditioned reflex born of all the boring, professorial, or sermonizing speeches your audience has ever heard.
- The authorship can be suspect; who actually wrote it? Since most written speeches are devoid of personal touches, nothing feels like your particular hallmark.
- Your natural conversational style is altered into a more formal, removed, and stilted one. This presents *you* as formal, removed, and stilted, too.
- Seamless delivery without faltering or looking for a word, neither backtracking nor trying another explanation, is not how you, or most people, normally talk. So the audience sees and hears someone unfamiliar and very unlike them.
- If it's an audience you know, they will contrast how you usually talk and behave with this very different image.
- You can't make continual eye contact with your audience; you cannot be genuine or personal as you would be without your head buried in the pages. Nor can you judge if they're understanding it or getting bored.

The effects on you, the speaker

Written speeches

- *Energy level*
  It comes from your paper, not from your audience. The best of your energy was really left in your office or your den, spent there as you wrote for an audience you imagined then. Reading and rereading your speech as you imagined how they would respond to each point or turn of phrase was when you were involved in the *real* process of communicating.

To stand before your audience and re-say it for the tenth time (because, of course, you practised your head off !) is but a pale copy. It's an exercise, not a vigorous, creative effort.

● *Security*
'But I like writing it out. I feel more secure that way.' The fact is, reading creates a bigger worry — losing your place. Since your active, creative mind is turned off when you're reading, 'ad-libbing' and trying to flow back into your pre-canned message makes a real problem. Also, you give your audience a chance to glimpse the 'real' you — genuine, animated, a trifle hesitant, and human . . .

Oral speeches from notes

● *Energy level*
By keeping eye contact with your audience, you allow them to become your catalyst, your energizer. They become a continual reminder of what you're doing and why you're doing it.

Working from the audience, rather than from the printed word, gives you a tremendous push forward. You present your material at a much better level and it puts you at a more intense and committed pitch.

● *Security*
When you improvise from an outline that just tells you where you're going, you actually make your job easier. It's much more secure to work from notes because your brain is alive then, thinking of what you're saying and where you're going next. Therefore, backtracking, rerouting, changing your mind, and explaining in a new way are easy.

Most lay people are simply not good enough actors to make a written speech sound fresh and new. Your audience is in a much more passive mode.

Effective speeches, providing good contact with your audience and making your personal presence felt, should be extemporaneous — from an outline and notes. Then your speech is really *you*. It sounds, looks, and feels more *natural* to you and your audience.

For addicted speech writers

I know, I know, I hear you saying, 'Yes, *natural* . . . and *rambling*, and *fumbling*, and not very *articulate!*'

But that's about concentration and ways to organize thinking: things you can learn to do with much greater rewards than the security blanket a written speech offers you.

So, to all of you addicted speech writers: try it. Begin to experiment with freeing yourself by delivering a message from notes in a small presentation. Let the same head that puts all those words on paper, privately, manufacture them right there before your audience's eyes and ears. Those words *are* yours! You *do* know your subject matter! The words *will* be there when you need them, stimulated by the actual performance setting. *If* you have good, usable notes . . .

For extemporizers

To those of you who do speak from notes, hooray! You're on your way. Let me help you with some more effective systems for writing your notes.

So let's find out how to write *usable* notes that will give you a base from which to improvise — notes so eloquent they virtually compel you to move to the next step and show how to deliver your next thought.

MAKING USABLE NOTES AND OUTLINES

For you to stay free, to be able to think *and* talk, your notes must:

- Be immediately understandable.
- Be written in such a way that the order of where you're going is made visually simple and clear to you, instantly.
- Feed your information in short, catalytic bursts that make their translation into speech self-evident.
- Signal their various levels of importance in advance.
- Tell you in what quality, form, and style they should be delivered as you see them.

Now, here's the problem: The notes and outlines we're accustomed to writing were for studying *later*. But when you're speaking, you don't have the time to read and decipher what you meant and decide on their relative importance and values in order to deliver them well, at the moment.

Notes must speak to you so succinctly that you can see and process them *on the spot* and use them as a springboard to launch the next idea towards your audience. Here's how.

The basic process

The biggest mistake people make when writing notes from which to speak is that they write out too much. The secret is to write your notes as catalysts — one or two word 'bullets' or phrases — action words designed just to remind you about the next point and push you into it with momentum. They should give you a clue about where this fits in the whole picture and an indication of what delivery style to use.

Just seeing key words like 'basic plan', 'budget', stumbling blocks' can trigger a response in you. You know what they stand for and why you want to talk about that point. The rest of the words will come through as you begin to speak.

Use whole pages

I do not recommend using little index cards. You can only write a few lines on an index card and everybody watches you shuffling the cards. It doesn't make any sense since you can't hide them in your hand and that surreptitious little peek looks so false, as though you think we don't see that you really have notes. We see you and we know it!

We, as audience, give any speaker permission to bring and use notes. We *want* you to be prepared! But full-length pages are the way to go because they can give you both an instant overview and a sense of continuity. You can write much more on a page and it can tell you not only where you are but what's coming up next.

Short words

The hardest thing to do is to reduce the phrases and ideas to a form short enough to be useful as speech notes. The essential problem with writing actual sentences that use pronouns, prepositions, and adjectives is that the mind is automatically put in a reading mode — moving the eyes to the right *horizontally* to get the whole idea. That stops you and interrupts the desired springboard effect notes would have — the *vertical* process of 'Look down; get the idea; bounce your eyes up; make audience contact; talk.'

Don't lose eye contact

Since the human eye can see three long or four short words at a time without needing to move to the right to read them, use only essential, descriptive words with one, two, or no more than three words on a line. Seeing more than that throws you into a horizontal reading mode, stopping your 'see-think-talk' process.

New symbols

When you use an abbreviated outline form as a springboard for oral presentations, you need a series of symbols or signals to tell you *in advance* what's coming and how to deliver it. You need to know that the *next* thought is important, that the list of words you see will culminate in a major statement, or that in the upcoming section you must shift gears and change the mood from a cool, logical one to a softer, more intimate and personal one. You need to give yourself a hint about what each section is about.

Example: Here's a visual outline of the above paragraph, designed for *talking* notes. See how I've adapted the material into symbols and a kind of shorthand.

A. **Need new symbols**
   1. **Abbrev. outline**
   2. **Springboard**
   3. **Advance signals**
      a. what's coming
      b. how deliver
      c. quality next thought
      d. what list means
      e. statement
      f. mood shift coming

Personalize

Design your own set of visual symbols to alert you to deliver the next words or thoughts in a different way. We all respond to different visual stimuli — layout, spaces, accents, indents, contrasting colours, underlines, capital letters.

Discover what you respond to most, what colours and symbols are most eloquent to you. Then develop your own system of visual shorthand to signal the other dimensions of your outline words — to remind you of your basic themes, of relative importance, intrinsic drama, or building to a climax.

The above two paragraphs could look like the following:

Paragraph one (starts 'Design your own set . . .')

B. Design own symbols
1. Indiv. responses
a. page layout
b. spaces   (*colour underline*)
c. accents

Possible   d. indents
designs   e. contrasting colours
f. underlines
g. capital letters

Paragraph two (starts 'Discover what you respond to . . .')

Before I began it, I would signal myself by writing, in colour, deeply indented, so I would notice it:

Mood shift: More personal

continue with outline:

(*use different colour
for mood change*)

C. Find your symbols
1. Discover own respns.
Conclusion   #### 2. Make personal shorthand
● remind basic themes
● relative importance
● drama/climax

These are the symbols that work best for me. Notice the techniques I used:

- Spaces and layout for idea separation
- The layout and the margin notes explaining each section. You want to be able to shuffle quickly or rearrange the order.
- What's underlined and capitalized and how that helps distinguish whole new ideas.
- How bullets and lower case letters are used to explain that this list is made up of examples of one idea, not separate ideas.
- The mood shift instruction, places where and how it is, in a colour that describes the mood (mauve for personal; possibly red for important or green for positive). It alerts you by its indentation and total separation from the text. It gives you advance warning and tells of the quality coming up as well, so you can change your delivery *before* you say the next sentence.

About underlining

Underlining works, but not as universally as you think. It speaks of only one gear. How 'loud' should the underlined word be? How different is it from the next underlined word? Does it mean *loud* or does it mean *important, heavy, thought-provoking*?

Therefore you may want to make different underline symbols like:

= = = = = = versus _____ versus ☐

Decide how to differentiate your 'underlinings,' and, by all means use colour! This really makes instant response and a major difference between meanings.

Colours

Underlining or writing out certain kinds of thoughts with coloured pens is extremely useful. If you decide that *blue* means basic principles, *red* means key points, *green* means details and examples, *orange* or *purple* mean emotional or personal concepts, you can give yourself a visual cue for presenting many kinds of ideas with the proper weight, mood and style. Choose your colours based on your emotional response to them. They will have an impact on your consciousness and therefore affect how to give your presentation.

Lists

A vertical list is an automatic organizer. As soon as your eye sees one, you know that these are several connected points that explain what has just gone before. Use numbers of filled-in bullet dots ● before your words to make them even more visually organized-looking. Keep the list consistent — all ideas should have only one line apiece, to make them look like they have the same general importance and character. Don't interrupt the rhythm you see unless it serves a purpose.

Spaces and indents

Words are written just as you see these words you're reading now.

What happens to you as
you read these words?

Did you read them more slowly? Did you read them putting more weight on each word? How would you say them aloud?

This device is excellent when you come to your key, big sentence, your smashing put-'em-away thought. It alerts you, slows you down, and tells you right away to deliver it differently.

Another really effective device using space in your layout is to insert more than the usual amount of space between ideas and to indent even further, like this:

A major thought is really noticed
when placed this way on your page.

To identify the key sentence even further, box it in. Use colour to underline or box it. You can also make the letters larger.

Typed vs. handwritten

How do you learn best? By writing something yourself or by reading something typed and memorizing it? Decide which visual form suits you best; what helps you remember, what triggers you. Then decide whether to write your outlines yourself or have them typed. You might like the combination of having your basic outline typed, and then going over it making extra notes in the text or margin, using colours, underlining — in other words, *personalizing.*

To sum up: You need visual catalysts, not just words, to help you add emphasis, feeling, and verbal order to your thoughts as you extemporize from notes. To present your ideas well and persuasively to your audience, you must be able to see and absorb your notes with logic, order, and an inkling of the quality needed *before* you deliver them.

Now let's go to the behavioural stuff: How to make it (and you) believable, persuasive, interesting, and memorable. How do you build in the fireworks? Where are the dynamics? What about style and ways to handle content? Language? Audience involvement?

TECHNIQUES FOR DELIVERING MEMORABLE SPEECHES

Everyone has heard speeches. Everyone is conditioned to assume they're mostly boring. How do you make yours different? How do you make audiences sit up and take notice and follow every word of that dynamic speaker (*you*) who has them in thrall?

Attention-getting openings

'That reminds me of a story . . .' Did you ever stop to think about why every speech seems to start that way? Actually the goal the speaker is trying to achieve is the right one: To warm up the audience, get their attention, and start on a friendly, pleasant, informal note.

What's wrong with the 'story' technique is that not only does the story commonly not apply to the rest of the speech, but ninety-nine times out of a hundred, that's the last bit of laughter, warmth, or informality you'll get for the duration of the speech! Funny-story openings promise something they never deliver. They create a visible space between 'that's the fun part' and 'this is the real speech'.

What openings should do

Your opening must establish your theme and why it is valuable for the audience to listen. But the first thing your audience wants to know is who you are and how they will relate to you, even before they want to know the essence of what you're going to talk about. Remember — we're still basically as suspicious of strangers as we ever were. Therefore,

your opening needs to let your audience in on a quick personal portrait
of who's telling — without ever telling them that's what you're doing.

Sounds difficult? Actually, it's instinctive. Watch what you do when
you just get introduced to someone at a party:

- You smile ('See — I'm a friend').
- Shake hands (a short-cut physical contact to experience each other
  more closely).
- You circle, subject-wise, looking for a common interest, or
- Make a joke to show your personality and charm, or
- Comment on the party, weather, etc.

Why? Just to get the ball, and the get-acquainted process, rolling. In
every instance you're looking for a common meeting ground, a way
of identifying with that other person to show who you are and to get
a little closer. What you're really saying is:

'This is me. Different from you, but not really. Let's draw a little
closer. Look what we have in common. See how much I know about
you, us, work, life, etc., and how I'll use that in the rest of my speech.'
Now you've satisfied the 'Who's telling?' question you can go on.

The best approach is an informal, personal one, bridging the space
that separates you from the audience, not only physically but
symbolically.

Example: 'You know, preparing for this speech, I sat and imagined
all of you. You'd be sitting there thinking. "Now, what's this going to
be about? How long will it take and when's lunch . . .?" '
What does this kind of opening accomplish?

- *It sets you among them, not apart.* By predicting what they're
  thinking, you tell them that you've been there, too. Like them,
  you've also anticipated boredom and wished you were somewhere
  else. 'Hmm, sounds like a pretty ordinary sort,' thinks your audience.
- *It has warmth and humour.* Demonstrating that you not only have
  that but are very willing to show it before a large group is another
  surprise and brings you closer to your audience. The wry touch
  of humour, the relaxed manner says to them: "This speech is going
  to be a little different; not stuffy or formal. It'll deal with the truth
  and it'll be on my wavelength. Probably enjoyable, too."
- *It shows that you care about them enough to even spend time imagining
  them as you prepared your speech.* This bodes well for the substance
  of your speech. It'll probably be about something *I* care about,
  not only what the speaker cares about.'

- *It suggests you're a pretty secure person.* To dare to say at the outset that they probably think you will be boring is to get a laugh and a doff of the cap. People don't often make fun of themselves, especially in public.

Telling a surprising, human kind of truth as an opener is one of the strongest beginnings. But, it's not for everyone! Some of us feel very comfortable being personally revealing like that. Others, because of background and conditioning, may feel very *uncomfortable* talking like that. If your father was very formal and never loosened his tie at the dinner table, it may be hard for you to present an informal image that will also make you feel professional.

Other possible openings

Be true to yourself. Find an opening that feels comfortable, now that you know what it needs to do.

- *Shared experiences*
  You can begin by telling them about an experience you both share: 'Like you, I work in steel. I've been at this plant as long as some of you, maybe longer than most, but not as long as Albert Brown over there.'
      This kind of 'levelling' approach moves you in among them and also gives you the opportunity to toss a personal, friendly greeting to one of their own. Audiences always feel they share in kudos for one of their own and love to participate with applause, a few cheers, etc. A little involvement right at the start is great.
- *Shared background or interest*
  'I come from Sheffield too, originally, and remember when the old steel mill was down on . . .'; or reveal a hobby you share with some of the audience like:
      'On a lovely day like this what are we all doing in here? I know we'd like to be out in the fresh air instead of listening to speeches!'

- *Shared goals*
  Another approach is to use the subject matter as a joint jumping-off place:
      'Well, it looks like the company is in the best of hands. We need commitment and we've got it. Here you are, interrupting your day

to hear about how to make better widgets, and you must surely know how *I* feel about that.'

● *Shared values*
Still another area to work from is to let them in on some aspect of what else you care about besides business, and then let that lead you into your subject.

Yesterday my daughter left school. The first child. A big milestone for us. Maybe some of you have just experienced that. Gives you a bit of a twinge, doesn't it? To see how fast the time passes and how much things change. I don't feel too removed from school myself and here she is talking computer jargon that makes me feel really past it!

'There's a lesson there. We certainly can't sit back and feel satisfied with what we know. It's outdated before you know it! Frightening, don't you think? So, come with me while I take you on a trip to Tomorrow-Land. To see what's new in the marketplace and how we need to gear up to absorb and use it.'

See what these do as openings? You touch a feeling part, not a thinking part, first. Get them where the feelings are! Much stronger than the head alone . . .

You told them something personal about you that they can surely identify with. Children, leaving school, 'where is the little girl I carried?' kind of nostalgia.

You identified a common fear — becoming outdated — and let them know you think it's frightening, and that's okay.

You told them that you're there to help by bringing them the new news and showing them how to use it.

One more approach:

● *Relate to an important current event or local occasion*
Anything that makes them see you as generally aware *and* aware of *them* is a helpful opening message. It helps you lead into your subject more gracefully than simply starting with paragraph one of your speech.

Clearly, there is no one perfect opening, good for all occasions. Just be continually aware, as you plan yours, of the purpose of an opening:

● To find a common meeting ground;
● To identify yourself with your audience;

- To let them know something of whom you are by your style, choice of language, and approach;
- To connect into the body of the speech in a seamless way so the opening obviously belongs to *this* speech and *this* unique audience, right now.

One last thought: Your audience's highest point of concentration and pure attention is within the first one-and-a-half to two minutes of your speech . . . After using your opening, establishing your theme, and showing why your audience should listen, you move into the body of your speech. What techniques can you use to continue to hold onto your audience's attention?

Audience involvement

Why audience involvement?

Look again at the first few pages of this chapter to remember the basic emotional responses people have toward *being* an audience. Now let's add some of the physical problems they can face as part of a captive sitting audience. Many forces are fighting your intention to deliver a memorable speech to an audience of rapt listeners. Don't ever take your audience for granted . . .

You can't design and plan your speech without taking into account the need to stimulate *continually* and bring them along with you. So let's look at the ways you can involve your audience by making them an active part of your speech.

Ask questions

Asking your audience questions and inviting them to respond is one of the best ways to:

- Personalize and customize your speech;
- Find out how they feel and what they know about your subject;
- Show them that they matter to you;
- Accelerate the pace and energy of your presentation.

You know how we all like to do those mini pop-quizzes in the magazines to find out how we rate? Your audience loves the sense of activity and is curious about its shared concerns and common attitudes, even differences of opinion.

One more note: You actually get some useful information from your audience that you can use as catalysts or reference points in your speech!

Group questioning

Design your questions to be as inclusive as possible at the beginning. 'Who in this room has ever . . .?' can cause only some people to raise their hands if the question is too narrow and limited.

Start with a big win by asking a question sure to get a big yes or no or laugh of recognition. After you ask it, tell them to raise their hands, showing what you mean by raising yours. Keep the ball rolling by asking two more. Once they get the feeling, they like doing it, and you've opened a sense of dialogue and shared power as you cede them a piece of your one-way platform.

Follow-up

Pursue it further by getting into the answers a little deeper. Point to one or another of the answerers and ask, 'Why do you think that is?' or, 'When did that start?' By making personal contact with some surrogate members, you make deeper contact with your whole audience. Caution: Choose well by looking for an obviously responsive type. Otherwise it could be threatening, especially to a shy person.

Rhetorical questions

'What would you think the real number is?' 'Did you ever think about how . . .?' 'So what does that mean?'

You needn't actually get an answer. Whenever you ask a rhetorical question, people will feel that you're talking directly to them, wanting to know. They feel stimulated and will automatically *think* an answer. They love to do that because they're not exposed, no one hears what they think, and they also know they're about to get the right answer — from you.

Make them move

If possible, get your audience to stand and stretch as a break in the proceedings after a particularly heavy segment or even as you begin, if they've been sitting there for a while.

Simply say: "Okay, everybody, stretching time. Everyone stand up and put your arms up like this and S T R E T C H ! "

You become an instant friend. It's attention-getting, since people rarely help an audience that way, and you'll get back a much more alert and willing audience.

If you're the type and feel comfortable with it, you can lead them in a few stretches and bends, even some jumps in place, and listen to them laugh and get charged up. It encourages the shy ones and makes for good rapport with your audience.

Whenever I teach something like the effects of eye contact in my seminars, I always ask people to turn to each other and try it out. Giving your audience something to do that bears out a point you're making is another great device for keeing audiences involved, interested, and paying attention.

Demos at their seats

Try to build in demonstrations they can do at their seats, to do something with their hands like drawing or writing. Or get them to stand up and try something as a group to experience it firsthand.

Volunteers from audience

People love to watch someone *else* do something as they sit back and giggle, secretly thrilled that it isn't them but extremely intrigued to see an audience member or friend, one of their own, up there doing something.

You can do benign things like simply asking one or two people to help you move something or hold something (they always get a hand, don't they?). You can build in a demonstration of what you're talking about and ask someone to participate in it with you, if you can't make it a group exercise.

Sum up: Your audience's inattention and disengagement due to their physical and psychological passivity should be handled by including them in the action of your speech. Surprise them by involving them. It's energizing, effective, and memorable.

Now to the content of your speech.

Presenting subject matter

From the familiar to the new

The best way to start explaining a new subject is by describing something familiar and then working up to what's different. The *old* not the *new*, gives an audience the sense of security that they will understand your material. If you start with '. . . something like opening a screw-top jar', they can instantly picture it because they've done that a thousand times. On safe ground conceptually from the start, they'll stay with you as you add the differences one at a time.

'Picture a boat. Now if I add X, it begins to be able to . . .' makes something become interesting as you unfold or add on layers to the rest of your story because they have begun with confidence, able to imagine and identify with it.

Process first — not detail

Everyone can grasp a process when it's pared down to the bare bone. You lose them when you add too many details at the outset.

They're just trying to get the general idea: What it looks like, what it does, and something about how it works. Analyse and give only the *essentials* they need to know; no fancy technical terms or deadly details yet. Otherwise you invite them to shut off the master switch.

Explain and intrigue

Here's a progression of how to edit and unfold information:

- Start slowly with the whole idea.
- Tell them something of what the new idea is about.
- Tell them why they need it.
- Remind them how the old system works and what its failings are.
- Begin to explain about the major differences between the old and the new. (Here's the place to add your visuals.)
- Add just enough to clarify the process further. (Show some more.)

● You might like to open for a few questions here and let the questions become the catalysts for your bringing in more details. This gives people a chance to absorb at their own pace and let you know when they're ready for more.

Visualize and demonstrate

The best clarification in the world is some form of visual reinforcement. Why, how, when, and which ones to use are described in Chapter 5.

Give examples of facts

If you need to describe exact measurements like square feet, yards, inches, or pounds, you should know that everyone has a very inexact vision of them. Most of us don't have an accurate picture of distance and size. To make such references instantly clear and precise to all, measure the distances in advance in the place where you will speak. Then it's quite simple to say. 'That means it's twice as high as this room', or, 'It's from here to the back wall.' You can also bring objects along to show relative size: 'It was only six inches long, like this pencil.'

Topics and transitions

Have you noticed the layout of this book? Each chapter and idea is completely broken down into outline form. From major headings to topic and subheadings to lists, it's designed to show the content's order, to help you *see* where it fits. You've been able to compartmentalize the material and to figure out where you are.

Imagine how hard it would be to visualize this breakdown and organization if you only *heard* it. Your audience can't see your notes! That's why you need to outline for them orally and explicitly so they can 'see' your logic and order.

Also, remember to recap and make transitions to each new subject rather than leaving your audience trying to figure out where they are, on their own.

Humanize and personalize

This seems hard to imagine as you confront the fiscal statement, the sales report, or the new plan for retooling. But — be creative. People identify most with something that smacks of themselves and of life.

- *When you talk of big gains in relation to the financial statement or sales report, add the people who made it happen.* Speak of and verbally applaud the divisions, individuals, the spirit of the company that was an integral part of that success. Personal appreciation gives more motivation to lots of people than figures alone.

- *Talk of feelings of disappointment or anxiety you all share if you have to confront the drop in performance.* Ruminate with them about why it happened, on a personal as well as a professional basis. Allow that they are a part of, actually the key to, what's happening and, 'since we're all human, we need to see how our personal fallibility (disinterest, complacency) can affect the company; what we need to do personally to turn it around.'

- *Focus on a local sports or other hero or some tough human endeavour and what it takes as one confronts a tough situation.* This can take you away from the theoretical, amorphous 'so we must do better', or, 'these figures are very disappointing,' and into the next step — personal motivation and the team approach.

- *The topic is retooling or other technical data?* Again, find the people behind the diagrams. Discuss the creative process as we all go through as we sit before a blank piece of paper trying to come up with something new; how tough and frustrating it is to imagine something that doesn't yet exist and how remarkable it is that we can do that. Discuss the changes in their daily lives such new ideas can bring.

- *Add yourself to the message when you speak.* Use personal examples as a surrogate for them: 'You know, I — like you — sometimes fail at what I'm trying to do and have to confront how to handle that . . .'

If you're the person in power, that dimension is exactly the one that can draw you closer to the troops. Tell them what *you* do.

If you're a stranger, the personal dimension makes a great common denominator with which to identify with your audience. Of course, choose a *common* feeling or experience to personalize, not the one about diving with Jacques Cousteau or falconry . . .

Dramatize

The best way to help people remember a concept is dramatization — Accent, colour, suspense, pulse-quickening techniques that bring your message alive. This moves an alien idea into a place where people will want to follow and remember it. Now this sounds difficult to do with factual business issues. Just think of how you can present your concept as more of a story than a list.

Endings

Endings should be inevitable and satisfying, because they follow the basic structure of life and nature. Not always *happy*, they are nevertheless in order. A natural culmination. They should give the feeling that this is what we set out for and now it's over.

The ending of your speech should feel like deliberate completion — not just stopping because you ran out of things to say. Unlike lots of current rock songs that don't deliberately end but just seem to dwindle away, your ending should be purposeful and memorable. End actively with a flourish, or thoughtfully with a whisper, but always with flair.

Announce the ending

Tell them that you're coming to the end. 'In conclusion', 'To wind up', 'So where have we been' 'Well, we've come to the end . . .' They will listen harder, not in relief (I hope) but because you're now going to wrap up and put in order all they've heard and give them the bottom lines of your message. That's very reassuring.

Last lines

Try to make your last line or two truly eloquent. Meaningful, touching, accurate, and wise. Move it one step beyond your practical message to a deeper understanding of why you're saying this. Reach for an ultimate concept, a basic need, a universal truth.

Always memorize your last few lines so you don't have to look down at your notes. This is the time to deliver straight to them: eye to eye, person to person.

Use a parable, a fable, a quote, a saying, or something from everyone's experience. Quotes from 'my father', 'grandmother', 'favourite teacher' are especially effective, adding basic folk wisdom to a personal note and giving an image of you as a family member or a child basically one of them. Try to leave them with a thought that will continue to provide an echo after you stop.

Pace your leaving

Don't leave too hastily, bolting off the stage or looking around for the exit. Standing still, with eye contact, lets the audience think about your speech or last lines for a moment. It should feel like you're both thinking it over, reluctant to part and break the mood. Then, fold your notes calmly, and walk away.

Now let's turn the spotlight on *you*, the speaker. The star of the moment. What can you, personally, do to make yourself a more interesting and memorable speaker? I can see the beads of perspiration break out as I write, 'The spotlight's on *you*'. I hear that inner voice within you say, 'Now *that's* the real key! That's where we lose them!' I think we got to this topic just in time . . .

PERSONAL STYLE

Being yourself

I started working with the chief executive officer of a major corporation whose staff called me in because of his poor communications skills.

Met in person he was charming — bright, warm, with an easy, bantering manner. I couldn't see what the staff were talking about. Then I asked him to re-deliver to me a speech that he'd given the previous week. From Dr Jekyll to Mr. Hyde!

What I saw was an empty suit of clothes: a dry, serious, monotone-voiced puppet going through the motions of making a speech. When I replayed the videotape we made, his response was, 'Look at him. He's so boring and stiff ! I can't stand him.' What was going on? How did such a 'split personality' develop?

My chief executive officer was trying to act 'chairman-like'. Subconsciously trying to behave as his predecessors had, as corporate chiefs are 'supposed' to look and act. He had no faith that just being *himself* — warm, pleasant, witty — would generate the awe and respect a chairman should get.

I needed to give him permission to relax into himself; to explain what audiences look for and that his innate personal style was not only enough but actually the *best* and most impressive he could be, believable and powerful.

Losing the pressure to 'act like' a powerful executive, he emerged as a genuinely delightful, charismatic speaker — accessible, knowledgeable, decisive, and *uniquely* himself.

Natural is eloquent

Most people stand before others to make a speech thinking that now they have to become something else. 'Just me, just talking, as I usually do' hardly seems the right mode for this occasion. After all, don't you get all dressed up for your performance? Don't you spend lots of hours planning, designing, rehashing, and practising? How can you just come in with your old-slippers type of daily communications skills and think that's enough? Actually the secret is — it is!

Nothing works better than being yourself. You are at your most comfortable because you're on your own solid, natural ground. You sound totally genuine — not put on, phoney, removed, formal, like you're hiding yourself.

The real you *is* enough. What you need is to develop more skills to enhance the real you, and to make you more comfortable, available, and understandable to the public.

How you feel toward your audience

Most people see a great gulf between themselves and their audience when they imagine them, plan for them, and finally stand and present before them. Don't you think 'They ... Them' when you picture your audience? This creates a problem. You're actually *adding* separation between yourself and your audience beyond what the circumstances naturally create.

They are individual listeners

The truth is that when you speak, each person hears you separately. So your style must be attuned to a much more intimate, less formal and aloof approach. With microphones, you don't need to shout and make grand gestures any more. Smaller, more confidential, and much more informal is the way to go, especially with business speeches which can be so technical and detailed or hard-line sales-oriented.

Think of yourself as having a conversation with only one or two members, representatives of the audience, not the whole mass. It's much more persuasive, believable, and easier to listen to. It puts *you* into a

much more relaxed frame of mind and therefore relaxes your audience
and your delivery. It wears better for a longer speech.

They're only people, like you

Seeing your audience in this light can help encourage you to be more
yourself and not quest for some acting image you think will make you
more acceptable. They *want* to be reassured that you're like them, and
that you understand them! Knowing this can get you over the hurdle
of fear and strangeness that any speech usually engenders. But talking
about fear, let's get right into the biggie — stage fright.

Stage fright

What is it?

Stage fright is based on a myth. It's you measuring yourself against
some image of a perfect performance — a '10' — and developing levels
of anxiety based on how far short of that perfect '10' you can, and
think you will, fall. You focus only on what others will think of your
performance, and as you do that, you lose sight of what you're actually
there to do. Fear takes over and you're into high- (or low-) level paralysis.
You begin worrying about what could happen: 'I'll lose my place,' 'I
won't find the right words,' 'I'll be boring,' 'The boss (colleagues, clients)
will think it's dumb (incompetent, ill-conceived, dry, confusing) and
that I am, too.'

Add, 'I never *could* speak in public,' 'My mother (father, teacher)
always said I mumbled,' 'I *hate* making a show of myself,' and you've
got a full-fledged case of stage fright!

Why

It's a shame, but early imprinting has a lot to do with who feels
comfortable on stage and who'd rather die than . . . Those experiences
— and your never-to-be-forgotten adolescence.

Ah yes! Who ever gets over the 'nose: too long; hair: too stringy;
behind: too big; arms: too thin' litany that sang to us every time we
studied that mirror, mirror on the wall? How unacceptable we felt then
haunts us forever, at least in echo, and standing up to expose *that* creature
to public scrutiny still fills us with dread and anxiety.

It particularly wins the battle for your attention and your response as you prepare to speak in public.

What to do?

The cure

● *Accept it*

The best antidote is first to admit your stage fright and stop blaming yourself for 'being such an idiot'. It's such a universal malady, you can take comfort in the fact that most everyone's got it. So — accept it, for now, 'It's there. I feel terrible and scared. Right. That's okay.'

● *No '10'*

Next, start to recognize and then continually remind yourself that *there is no perfect '10'*! There can't be! In order for there to be *one* perfect way to do this, it would have to be duplicable the same way every time. But you, or anyone, would still do it differently the next and every other time.

You'd have to. The day, weather, time, news would be different; what you ate would be different; the audience and their needs would be different; what conflict you just had at home or at work would make you be different; etc., etc. Also, *you* could give a '10' performance and someone *else* could also give another, very different type of '10' performance, and *both* would be very good and very effective. Who's to say which is the 'perfect' one?

So, you can't fail. You can only be more or less effective; more or less comfortable with your material; more or less able to achieve your goal.

● *Focus on your job*

Think about your audience and what you're trying to do for *them*! What you want them to know and why. *You* don't matter as much as your message. Get out of yourself and into the story!

Be open, honest, enthusiastic, committed to your task — and let them see that. *That's* all your audience wants from you in terms of style. When they see *you* comfortable, *they* get comfortable. Your tension broadcasts itself to them and gets in the way of their hearing your message. Let go and get to work! And remember, like anything else, the more you do it, the less uncomfortable it gets.

Getting started

What's involved

- *Your adrenals*
Those marvellous little glands that rise to any stress occasion are your key friends here. They'll charge up, don't you worry! They do that involuntarily, built to save your life when you need it. They'll send you the extra physical energy you need — no problem.
- *Your mind*
That part of you needs to gear up for heavy-duty thinking. it has to reach for the organization and sense of your message; to manufacture words as you go; to listen and criticize as you speak, choosing what to say and what to delay or delete. It feels like it's blank at that moment because of the stress, but reassure yourself, you did bring it along and it's stuffed full of goodies, ready to produce.
- *Your audience*
Their energy and attention *also* has to get up to speed and you're the one who has to do it. You need to get them past the 'stranger in our midst' moment, get them used to your speech tone and rhythm, and make them start tuning into your message. Of course your great opening will take care of that. But they need one special thing from you to get started.
- *Your self-confidence*
Here's the key. You need to sit in your chair as a one-man cheering squad. You need to program your inner voice to say, *before* you get up, 'You can do it. You're terrific. You really know your stuff and are fully prepared. Your material is good. Your message is important. So go for it.'
    Sounds artificial? Rubbish?
    Wrong!
    I've already told you that the mind is like a computer. You program it with negative messages — 'I can't do this. I'm awful at this. The speech is no good' — and it'll do your bidding. It's obedient, like any computer, and has no other choices than what *you* put into it. Your command is its only working system.
    Want to succeed? Program that computer that you *can* and *will* succeed. That when you stand up, you *expect* to be good, effective, competent, if not downright fantastic! That you *are*! That's what

you'll get back in terms of performance. Want to fail? Feed yourself negative images, self-doubts, assumptions of disaster or failure.

It's a belief system, this business of self-confidence. Eliminate the negative voices. Believe you're good and that you *will* be good. Then tell your mind that — and *only* that — message and you *will* be terrific!

Energize yourself

Some people find it helpful to take a number of deep breaths or squeeze their clasped hands or the arms of their chair very tightly before they get up to get themselves physically charged up. This thrusts them into a higher energy level very quickly, and no one can see or notice it. Take your choice. If you're a very physical person, used to heavy exertion, you might like it.

Take your space

- *Walk with assurance*
  Gather your papers, get up, and get moving briskly, with minimum wasted motion, looking purposeful and energetic. The first step or two may feel robot-like, but never mind. The idea is to tell your audience you know what you're doing and can't wait to get there and do it (no matter *what* the truth is).

  If you want to change the mood from the previous speaker or what has been happening, change your pace, quickening or slowing down deliberately.
- *Own your turf*
  How you 'take the stage', how you carve out your turf and take command of it, is very visible and very affecting to your audience.

  Go to your spot on the stage or at the front of the room. Put your notes down. Deliberately. Then take a beat to settle down, take a breath. Not a big heaving sigh. Just an inaudible but galvanizing breath to focus all your energy on one place. Then, pick up your head and look at them. Your audience. Make eye contact with them. Wait a second to get their total attention and silence. Think to yourself: 'Listen, everybody. Settle down. Got something interesting to tell you. Can't wait to do it.' Then, and only then, begin . . .

The lectern or podium

Close your eyes and imagine yourself sitting in any audience. On stage there is a lectern and a speaker walking in with a sheaf of papers (a *large* sheaf of papers). He clears his/her throat and begins. Groan — you're bored already!

The stereotypical image of that device — the lectern — is so branded in our minds as a symbol of lengthy, tedious droners that we have to deal with it. Not only does it carry the negative images of preachers, teachers, and righteous folk who have talked at us, it carries another image as well.

Standing behind a lectern visibly separates you from your audience. It makes you look like you're hiding behind a shield, protecting yourself from them, not as open and vulnerable to them as they are to you.

It makes you look different, chosen, unique — if you're attempting to bond with your audience, that's not the right message. It also makes you look rigid, formal, unfeeling — a difficult place from which to become their leader, helpful teacher and guide.

If you're short, your audience may get an excellent view of your chin or your bald spot as you peer over the top, but not of you.

One more issue: Standing behind a lectern makes you stand still. This is only a boring, immobile image, but it also paralyzes *you* and lowers your own energy level.

By now you've probably guessed that I think standing behind a lectern isn't such a great idea. Why does everyone do it?

1. It's a place to put your notes.
2. It's where the microphone is permanently installed.
3. Everybody does it.

Counterattack:

For 1: Put your notes there but come out from behind and stand to the side of the podium. You can look over at your notes and still be free and available.

For 2: Request, in advance, that they arrange an around the neck microphone or a lapel mike for you with a long cord, so you can move away from that arbitrary prison and, most of all, be free to move your head in any direction.

For 3: Don't be a sheep and follow the flock. Think through what effect that lectern has on your audience and what effect you *want* to have, and then decide for yourself based strictly on the merits, not habit. I'll *haunt* you if you just automatically slide behind the lectern and thereby bring upon you all the negative images I've just described . . .

SPEAKING AND LANGUAGE SKILLS

Given all the other aspects of how you will communicate to your audience, verbal presentation is still the major form by which you will reach them and deliver your message. Which makes us turn now to your choice of language: how you say what you say and what the right words can do for you.

Making language clear

Language builds instant understanding if it is used well and if it uses terms that are acceptable and comfortable for everyone. Once we know a language, we expect its words to be clear. We depend on easy, automatic processing and *expect* to understand. We *don't* expect to get stuck. We get concerned, even angry, when we do.

If you have developed expertise in a given field, you must be very careful about falling into a private shorthand form of talking, where only peers understand you. The serious consequence of this is that you don't have a portable language system any more and canot use it for all occasions, with all kinds of audiences.

It means clients will be left behind as you go on and on about your speciality.

Lay audiences will become alienated and stare off into space.

It even means that among your co-workers you can unwittingly (or maybe even wittingly) develop a kind of oneupmanship that says, 'I'm part of the club. Are you?'

Therefore, step one in making yourself understood is *listen to yourself* ! Question whether your words are supportive for *this* audience and watch which ones you use. If you slip, always explain instantly, with a little laugh about 'Hanging around those computers too much, I'm forgetting how to talk like a person.'

Simplify

Think about the words you choose. Unfamiliar synonyms to explain. Become sensitive to your own speech patterns. Edit your word choices.

Challenge yourself to find ways to explain what you know very well, even instinctively, so others can get it. And be careful not to patronize as you do it. We sometimes feel superior when we know something not everyone knows. When you're out there trying to get others on your wavelength, that's the last thing you want to transmit. Stay humble and enthusiastic about sharing what you know.

Analogies

These are one of the best devices for clarifying a complex or abstract concept. Since they're usually a story or an example drawn from life, they have instant appeal for any audience.

By turning away from a hard-nosed pragmatic approach to your message and finding a basic story, fable, folk legend, quote from classical literature, or example from current events that suits the basic principle involved, you cause people to be persuaded on much more familiar territory. It's reinforcing as well as amusing to listen to. Your audience doesn't have to work too hard to tune right into your wavelength, unlike the unfamiliar material you're asking them to stretch and reach for.

Analogies provide a change of pace and build in a sense of suspense. The audience looks forward to the end when the point of your story comes clear and they can see the connection with what you've been saying. Analogies can underline a basic truth with a seemingly light-hearted moment.

Using an example from daily life puts every member of the audience directly into the story, as well as humanizing you, the teller.

A word of caution: think through your analogy to see how apt it is for making an instant connection between your point and the point of the story. Will everyone get the punch line? Does it really fit?

Use words visually

Use words that make images; that have feelings and shape and colour and description in them; that can provide sensory experiences. 'The bright shiny red exterior of the new unit, complete with chrome trimmings and a *very* quiet purr, instead of the beaten-up old clanking one we've now got in the back corner of the office . . .' makes the unit come alive visually and be real to everyone who's listening.

Learn to use graphically descriptive phrases to make your speech more interesting and compelling. People love to relate to three-dimensional images rather than equations. Your challenge is to see your work product and your subject that way, rather than only as a chart or a graph.

Emphasize

The most common ways are:

- Repetition of a word or phrase
- Pacing — slow down or speed up to make people notice.
- Modulate your voice — hard, soft, more thoughtful or weighty.
- Create a catch phrase or a metaphor that you can use again and again to refer to an act, a fact, or an object.
- Recap — summarize key points you've made in a quick review, thus repeating them and singling them out for special notice.
- Alert your audience by saying, 'This next part is especially important,' or, 'That was especially . . .' and repeat it.

The use of silence

The opposite of talking is knowing when to stop. Speakers often have a problem with that. They're afraid that stopping might look like they forgot or lost what to say next.

It's difficult to realize that as eloquent as well-chosen words are, silence can be equally, and is often more, eloquent. Eloquent not because it gives the audience a chance to stop and think but because it compels them to do so.

When you're hot on the trail of delivering a message, the audience is busy absorbing it, and you're both moving at quite a pace. It is therefore invaluable for them to be given a pause in which to consider what you have just said. Not only for relief from the one-way assault but to be able to think on their own instead of running with you.

I'm not recommending that you sit down and wait. The silences are momentary; that's all the brain needs to reflect and to catch up. But they're very affecting.

When? Whenever you deliver an eloquent or important statement, a challenging statement, a shocking statement. It's a signal that what you just said was meaningful and noteworthy. Your silence says, 'Think about that for a moment. That matters.' It also creates a space between what you just said and what comes next.

Whenever you put a rhetorical question, stop. Give them a moment to answer in their minds. It gets their interest in the answer up.

Don't be afraid to use silence. Welcome it. It's a superb contrast tool.

Well — that's it: Ideas to help you begin to develop personal style and use words well. The rest will come with practice, some of which you might do with a videotape recorder to see yourself as others see you. After you get up off the floor, vowing to lose twenty pounds and have your nose fixed at once, you can develop some good insights about how you come across, what works and what doesn't, and what you'd like to concentrate on.

A POSTSCRIPT

The never-make-a-speech-without-it checklist

Now that you're the ultimate perfect speaker with the ultimate perfect speech, there's only one set of obstacles. Here's what to do, *in advance*, to be sure that you stay in control of the details as well as the content of your speech giving:

Visit the room yourself, with this list in hand. If you can't, at least use these guidelines in your discussion with the hosts to be sure you don't leave anything to chance. and do write a follow-up note.

1. *Microphone and acoustics*
   Request an around-the-neck or lapel mike. Do *not* get stuck with a standing or permanently fixed mike which makes your head movements rigid as you strain to talk into one spot.
2. *Stage*
   If you must be on stage, choose where you'll stand. One side or the other is more informal. Be sure you are on a raised platform in a large room or the audience will have trouble seeing and concentrating on you.
3. *Lectern*
   Once you get free of its tyranny by requesting a movable mike, attached to *you*, not to it, you *can* use it to rest your notes. I prefer to ask for a 4-foot table (readily available in all hotels) to be placed on the stage. I put my notes on it, lean against it, sometimes even

sit on a corner of it. It's a much more flexible, informal piece of furniture, allowing you more leeway in moving around and relating to it and to your audience. A corner of a desk or table in an office meeting room does the same thing. You can also put a small, portable lectern on it, to get your notes closer to you.

4. *Lights*

It's very important that where you stand is *very* well lit. More lit than the surroundings. This helps focus audience attention on you. People hear by watching your mouth and face. Be sure they can do that.

Be sure, if you're at a lectern, that there is a light there to help you see!

Don't put the house lights out! Lights out, to our biological clock says, 'Sleepy time'! *And* — you can't see your audience, your greatest energizer . . .

5. *Shape of room layout*

The most important thing to try for is that your audience doesn't get too far away from you. Not in terms of space between you and the first row, but between you and the *last* row. Therefore, request in advance that your room be set up the wide way. The dais or platform should be put on the long wall. Then the chairs set to face it aren't as deep and far away from the stage.

Don't waste your best eye-contact space, the centre, with an empty aisle. Request two side aisles and a solid middle. Set chairs in a curved shape, curving in to the platform at both sides. Better than straight across lines — they're rigid and the ends have a hard time seeing. You can also angle from the centre to the sides, especially if you're setting up in schoolroom style with tables to write on.

6. *Visual aids requirements*

The drawback of using slides or overhead projectors is how the screen usurps centre stage and becomes so dominant, even without pictures. Therefore, carve out a side of the stage, very well lit, as home base for you. Begin your speech there, then move to the screen or the overhead projection table to continue. Remember: *Don't* turn out the lights. Use rear-screen projection. You need your audience contact much more than the ultimate perfect hard-edged picture.

7. *Take back-ups*

If a light bulk could ever burn out, it'll probably choose your presentation to do it. If a take-up reel needs to be a certain size, *that* projector probably won't have it. So — bring your own: Your own extension lead and remote-control button to be able to control your own slides; your own extra bulbs for slide or overhead projector; your own pointer; an extra copy of video or audio cassette; back-ups of your transparencies in case someone spills the coffee; and so on. Check carefully on their easels. Those little flimsy ones and your big charts or flip charts may not make a good marriage.

Ask for electronic equipment by name, model number, size, and style to be sure you get exactly what you need.

8. *Send a diagram*
Send diagrams for the stage and room arrangement as well as your visual aid requirements. Know what? Your hosts will be relieved and will welcome that.

9. *Be sure about time length*
Find out what the considerations of time for your speech *really* are. Speeches are notorious for starting late, and if yours is crammed full, you may end up having to edit as you speak. Instead, find out what comes after you and what the *real* restraints are. Build in an envelope or two of possible drop-out sections in your speech just to protect yourself; it's best to feel comfortable about when you actually have to stop.

10. *Try it all out*
Arrive early and test the equipment, including sound balance, lights, electronic equipment, who'll hear you carry out the charts, run the projector, etc. Notice the heat or cooling system and if there's taped music playing in the hall outside your door that you can ask to be turned down.

All these details, well handled, make for a smooth, finished performance. Breakdowns in, or inattention to, any of these areas greatly diminishes all your hard work in preparation.

Okay. No more endings. This *is* the end of this chapter. On to the art of answering questions effectively and persuasively.

8
The Art of Being Questioned
The audience or the boss vs. you

Picture yourself responding in the following scenes:

You're at home (aged 10). Your father walks in: 'Why didn't you take out the rubbish like I told you?'

You're in school (aged 8). Your teachers asks: 'What is the answer to that quetion?'

You're at your first job interview. The personnel director puts down your application form: 'Why should you get this job?'

A traffic policeman looks you in the eye: 'How fast do you think you were going?'

Your boss leans across the desk: 'What do *you* think about this?'

A man-on-the-street reporter shoves a mike in your face: 'Are you in favour of . . .?'

How did you feel as you read each one? Could you feel your tension as you confronted having to answer well, correctly, right then and there? Would the answers come easily — or would you fumble? Would you ever consider not answering?

BASIC PRINCIPLES OF ANSWERING QUESTIONS

The questioning process

Of all the acts we perpetrate on each other, the most aggressive, short of touching someone, is questioning them. The process exists in every culture and it's always the same:

- *Questioner*: Asks his questions, his way, at the pace he wishes, in the order he wishes, on the subjects he wishes, where and when he wishes. Total power.
- *You*: Submit and answer. No power.

We're trained to accept this process from our earliest days. People in power have the right to ask and we meekly answer. People become powerful by asking, and we powerless by answering.

In order to understand how to handle being questioned, we need to learn about our conditioned responses when we are questioned.

Conditioning

I've done many demonstrations in the seminars I hold about how we handle questioning. I walk into the audience, filled with high-level executives and bright lawyers. Selecting one of these sharp, sophisticated people, I stand over him/her and begin a barrage of questions: 'Who are you? What do you do? Do you like it? Are you good at it? Are you married? Are you glad?' or, 'You're not married? Why not?' I continue with 'Do you have children? Plan to have any more? When?' or, 'Why not?'

Sounds rude, aggressive, intrusive? Right. But you know what? They all answer! Always! Every question! Every personal, impertinent question — right there in front of their peers! They never ask why, or what do I need to know for, or ever even say, 'Get lost!'

We're conditioned to reply as soon as anyone asks, without even thinking. Searching for the answer, we never think to question the process or the questioner. If a person asks, we automatically endow him with authority and answer. Our anxiety is heightened tenfold if the question is asked publicly, but we do it anyway. How does this whole phenomenon affect the way we answer questions?

How we answer questions

Origins

Remember the spotlight on you in a classroom while the teacher waited for an answer? Everyone cringing in his/her seat thinking, 'Thank God it isn't me!' The biggest challenge facing you was—what? Will your answer be right or wrong? And that's still the number one issue that shapes how we answer.

What else were you thinking about back then? Didn't you worry about someone topping you with the right answer if yours was wrong? Didn't you think about what everyone thought of you? How they judged you? Where you fitted in the group?

Those early school years, that public test, are the source of what we still worry about most as we're questioned, privately or publicly. Although they were years in which we felt most powerless and inadequate in our lives, the concerns of group evaluation and someone's scrutiny remain in our grown-up lives.

What concerns us

Here's what we still worry about as adults whenever we answer questions. You'll find aspects of yourselves and of achievers, affiliators, and influencers in these responses:

- *Right vs. wrong* and the possible humiliation and defeat we'll feel. Our culture likes winners.
- *Group competition*: 'I hope no one else knows it either, or better than I do'. Whether before a group or one-to-one, that sense of competing for status, admiration and approval against our peers remains.
- *Wanting acceptance*: We try to anticipate what kind of answer will be most acceptable to the questioner and the group.
- *What do you really want to know?* We try to read the questioner to discover what kind of answer is expected or wanted, and only give that, rather than what we really think.
- *Privacy*: The caution this concern brings makes us edit and censor automatically as we worry about what you can find out about me if I'm not careful.
- *Consequences*: 'What could the fallout from my answer be?' 'What could you, would you, do with my answer?' Therefore, how much or how little or exactly what should I tell you?
- *Visibility*: Any spotlight shining on us makes most people feel basically uncomfortable and unnerved, especially since questioning is a test, not just a chat.
- *Comparison*: Fitting in with the group, wanting to say something like what others would say, not falling short of the norm — these are deeply rooted needs in us and will alter what we say and how.

- *Performance*: For many of us, our anxiety about our own eloquence, fluency, ability to formulate and articulate what we mean on the spot, chokes us up.

Hardly a picture of comfort and confidence, is it? And it's true for us whether it's a public questioning situation or we're being privately questioned by anyone in authority.

So now we have the foundation for this chapter — our intrinsic, conditioned response to questioning and how it affects what we do and say in such situations.

Our work will be to understand ourselves and the forces that push us well enough to be able to counter that negativity. To figure out how to handle being questioned, a seemingly powerless and anxiety-producing aspect of our working lives. Then, to find out how to feel free enough to let the mind work on what needs to be said, selecting what you want to say, and giving yourself time enough to choose how to say it. We'll also learn how to handle various types of questioners.

THE AUDIENCE VS. YOU: ANSWERING AUDIENCE QUESTIONS

Why answer questions?

Why indeed? Why set yourself up for a public grilling? Is it really useful? For whom?

For you! Inviting questions actually solves many problems of omission and commission in your presentations. Answering questions well helps you stay in control of what people *think* you mean or have said.

Here are some benefits you gain from the question/answer period:

Clarifies

If your basic intention in making a presentation to a group is to explain something you know a lot about, to inform and enlighten, shouldn't you find out whether they understood it?

Although you may think you put everything in clearly and thoroughly when you prepared your speech, letting people ask you questions at the end shows you what they didn't get. It lets you fill in the gaps of what's still confusing or unfinished in their minds. Wouldn't you rather have a chance to explain again and actually accomplish your goal than let them leave unconvinced and misunderstanding you?

A chance to add

You can only talk for so long before you begin to lose your audience. Questions become a great springboard for you to continue to give your speech in a more interesting and dynamic way. Asking questions and your answering them makes the audience feel more connected and involved in what you say. Rhythmically and dynamically a ping-pong match served by various players is more interesting than a one-way speech.

Ensures relevance

You may have talked in abstract or general terms in order to set the scene or give the big picture. Questions from this specific audience tune you into their specific concerns. This makes your subject directly relevant to them. No guessing — they'll ask you what *they* need to know.

Empowers the audience

By giving the audience permission to question you, you tell them it's their turn to hold the stage now. To take back some of the power they gave you when you received their attention.

Shows your power

Only a very secure person, in total control of the facts and the larger ramifications of his/her topic, would subject himself to being questioned indiscriminately, not knowing what the audience will ask. Your obvious comfort and 'Go ahead, ask me anything' attitude are powerful messages.

Uncovers disagreement

True, some of you may not want to do this, especially not publicly. However, not hearing disagreement doesn't mean it isn't there or that it will go away. It's better to unearth the pockets of discontent and find truly constructive, non-damaging ways to handle them rather than to adopt the ostrich approach. The positive end results are that you can usually dispel problems; you can find out what they are so you can work on them. Last but not least, you'll come away with a medal for bravery and strength as well as much more credibility than you went in with.

So step one on the road to feeling comfortable and becoming competent answering audience questions is to get convinced; to know what's good about answering them.

Step two is learning how to prepare for it.

Preparation for Q&A

Going into a Q&A session without a background of what they'll probably ask about, why people ask, and how we usually feel about this exchange is like walking into the lion's den without a chair. Here's how to prepare:

Understand your audience

- *Who are they?*
  The same research you did in preparing for your speech needs to be reviewed as you prepare for the question-and-answer period: Who's there; why they're there; what they expect to hear; what they already know; how your topic fits in with their lives; as well as something of the basic demographics. This tells you about your audience's basic needs, interests, and concerns, and becomes the bedrock of predicting what they'll ask about.
- *What to expect*
  What additional issues and anxieties does your speech bring up for them? Is your presentation threatening to the status quo? Does what you said make them rethink a common belief?

  Analyse where the hostility or rejection could come from: Are there pockets of resistance represented in your audience?

  What about your peers? Who's competitive with you and needs to show off before the group by posing you with a tough question?

  Is this a disparate group who could be asking you questions on different levels about different aspects?

  Still another issue is *will* they ask questions? Anticipating that you might have to live through that agonizing silence after the 'Any questions' invitation will help you either plant a couple to get the ball rolling or prepare a humorous comment that breaks the ice and gets it started (something I'll illustrate in a moment).

The important message here is to *anticipate*: to imagine and think through your question-and-answer period in advance so there are few surprises.

Understand who asks questions

- Some people really are confused and want to know.
- Some people will feel competitive with anyone in the spotlight: they're interested in the by-product, not the product.
- Some people are classic opposers, needing to find fault with anything new, or not their idea.
- Some people have a tenacious, thorough way of thinking and will pursue a point relentlessly.
- Some people came to disagree and make a public statement of their own.

Identifying why they're asking as you hear their questions helps you fit your answer to what the byplay is *really* about.

Understand your adversaries

Next, you need to prepare for disagreement. Know that as impassioned as you are about your topic, there are others who feel just as keenly that you're dead wrong and that their way is *the* way. The key here is to expect this and to see those people not as thorns in your side but from their point of view. Spend a moment thinking *why* they would feel as they do. Imagine believing in something that strongly. Don't you?

You need to understand what your adversary's goals and inner needs are (the old forethought chart again) in order to defuse him/her. (There'll be more on this in 'Handling hostility' in the next section.)

Understand your feelings

To develop good skills for fielding questions extemporaneously, you need to first find out how you truly feel about doing it. Let's look at the most common feelings I've discovered in my private consulting work:

●   *Loss of control*
    Having just been in total control of your subject, the subject will
    now be determined by the questioner. The style of presentation
    will be sent by him/her; the spotlight now shines on the questioner,
    who can then shine a possibly harsh and unflattering light on you.
    You will be forced to cede your sense of power. Or so it seems. . . .
         A major problem in answering questions is feeling put upon
    and powerless. This erodes your ability to think (how can you if
    you think you have no power?). It puts you in the position of *looking
    for* approval instead of giving it.
         Response: The fact is you have enormous power. It's your material.
    You own it. You are still totally in charge of what you'll tell, how
    much you'll tell, how you'll tell it. Even more than that, you have
    the power to ask questions *back* — not just to receive them! You
    can deflect, reroute, add on, analyse, and challenge.
         So, recognize that the first obstacle to answering questions well
    is your feeling that you lost your power and that you think your
    audience now has it. And that's not true!

●   *Nervous*
    You feel anxious about whether or not you can do it well, and
    most of all, whether you'll get trapped into saying something you
    don't mean or would rather not say. We all worry about public
    extemporizing and its consequences (shades of those early school
    years again). We all worry about performance and have great
    expectations of ourselves — wanting perfection.
         Perhaps most of all your nervousness deals with not having time
    enough to think up a good answer, and a carefully edited one,
    without looking like you're stalling or can't think of anything to
    say, and still sounding articulate.
         Response: Remember there is no *perfect* way to do this. This
    question/answer period never existed before. You, your speech,
    your audience, the time and place it's happening, all never came
    together before. Therefore you're writing on a clean slate.
         Think to yourself: 'I will do this *my* way and *that's* the right,
    best, and only way to answer these questions this time. I'm talking
    about *my* material. I'm prepared. They'll ask me about what they've
    just heard, which *I* told them. I *can* handle whatever comes'.

- *Exploited*

Since you have declared open season on yourself, you can begin to feel put upon. You're up there as a target and they can shoot at you. This is a dangerous feeling because you then begin to see the questioners as *taking* something from you rather than *asking* benignly for positive reasons. This can make you testy and hostile.

Response: Although they ask, they do so at your invitation. You're giving a gift. See yourself as Santa Claus — sharing yourself with this one, giving an extra titbit of information to that one. See each momentary relationship as personal and intimate. The action is from you to them. They are only petitioners, *asking* for your gift. *You'll* decide what and how much to give.

- *Exhilarated*

Not all your feelings are negative. If you're a fighter, a competitor, or a performer who likes public performance, answering questions extemporaneously feels exciting, like a contest. That's great, in a way, because it will provide you with the adrenal surge to rise to the occasion and do a good job. The danger here is seeing it as a personal win/lose contest. This makes it very difficult to listen and think. It shuts down your ability to make choices since you've drawn battle lines — and about something other than enlightenment or resolving disputes.

Response: See the process as benign, not competitive. They're not your adversaries. They don't know as much about your subject, and want more, or they know your subject but not from your unique point of view, and need to know more. So you don't need to compete or fight with them. You've already won, by owning the material. Now you're in the position of helping them climb aboard.

ANSWERING TECHNIQUES

Getting started

Create an environment

If you truly mean to invite your audience to ask questions, you have to let them know you really mean for them to do it. A perfunctory 'Any questions?' doesn't inspire your audience to make the effort. People are generally shy and need encouragement in order to expose themselves or even to move. Try this:

'Although I think I told you everything I could within the time allowed, there are probably some things I left out. Maybe something I described was not clear. I really want you to understand my subject, so please ask me whatever else you need or want to know.'

This gets people moving because you gave them a reason to ask and showed them that you genuinely want a chance to clarify. Here's another approach.

'Much of what I said is very complex, technical, and new. Having just given you one glancing blow, I'm sure there are many things still not clear. I would welcome your asking me anything.'

This says, 'I won't be insulted that you didn't get it or think you're dumb for *not* getting it.' Another one:

'Well, you've been such an attentive audience and I've talked non-stop for quite a while. I should calm down now, change the pace, and let it be your turn to ask me questions.'

There's a nice, warm, human touch in this one that says you know how they feel and that you empower them by inviting them to join you in a group endeavour.

Do it yourself

I don't think it's very encouraging or stimulating to an audience to have a moderator or chairperson suddenly appear and ask for questions. It's intrusive and looks like an audience test. Tell him/her you're much more comfortable doing it yourself. He/she can stand there to help pick out who's got questions or to call them by name, if you wish, but *you* do the introduction to the Q&A period yourself. It's an important moment for establishing rapport and developing an encouraging environment for questioning.

What if no one asks?

Gulp! That dreadful moment while you stand there with an expectant smile and no one raises a hand. Makes you feel like your speech was a dud, that they're too bored or confused to ask. How to handle it? Humour!

From my own experience, having used it *many* times myself, I ask my clients to say:

'You know what's happening now? A classic thing all audiences do. It takes about forty-five seconds to a minute' (this makes them feel good; it says they're not unusually stupid or slow). 'You've probably got a question in mind and you're testing it, thinking, "I don't know if that's such a terrific question. Not sure it sounds very clever. Maybe I'll wait till someone else asks one first to see what that's like." So you're all sitting there, waiting for someone else to start, right? *Then* you'll chime right in!'

Result? Big laugh and four hands are raised.

You can also try:

'Okay. I see everyone's taken the old Army advice about never volunteering!'

The key is to confront what's happening, not just stand there smiling blankly or asking again or just waiting. Don't badger or cajole. Laughing *with* it shows your strength.

Why people don't ask

Understanding how people feel and why they're reluctant to ask will help you know what to say to them:

- 'Mine may not be a good question'.
- 'Why stick my neck out in a crowd — especially this crowd with many of my peers and bosses in it?'
- 'I may not be able to articulate my question well.'
- 'I'd like to ask but I feel a little shy about confronting someone, especially an expert'.
- 'My question may not interest too many other people. Better not ask it in public'.

It's also useful to tell them at the beginning to think of questions or write them down as you go along so you can respond at the end. Giving an assignment in advance gives them time to think about a good question and to formulate it well in their own minds.

How to get off if no one asks

If *no one* asks, even after all my suggestions, save face and bow out gracefully. Don't let the momentum of your good speech die:

'Well, I guess I'm a much better speaker than I thought! I must have explained my subject so well that you got it all! Thank you so much for letting me tell you about it', and get off, with a smile and a flourish. (Crying and throwing up later.)

Handling questions

Listen!

Easy to say, hard to do. Because of the melange of all those apprehensive feelings described earlier that you probably have, it's very difficult to squash your anxious inner voices and listen to someone else's. To *truly* listen, not just imagine where they're going and sail off on an answer, you need to:

- Discipline yourself to listen *till the end*; to take in *all* of what the question's about.
- Ask yourself where the question is leading so you'll follow it closely.
- Analyse what he/she really wants to know.
- Notice the tone with which the question is asked: Hostile? Insecure?

This will help you formulate an appropriate answer. (For more on listening skills, see that section in Chapter 9.)

Clarify questions

People often ask questions poorly: two or three points at once or a rambling statement that never becomes a question. Don't just try to answer part of a question, the part you understand or heard last. Make the questioner clarify it. To make your answer truly responsive, *ask!* Maybe something like:

'There's a lot to your question! Let me be sure I got it all. Did you mean . . .?' or, 'I want to respond to what you're asking, so let me be sure I'm on the right track . . .'

Be careful not to sound critical when you clarify, as though it was a lousy question, poorly asked, like: 'Well, exactly what *is* your question?' Instead, take the blame on yourself:

'I was thinking about an answer so hard that I think I missed some of your question. Let me just recap to be sure . . .' Then rephrase it and ask if that's it.

Compliment the asker

Nothing feels better than that old saw: 'That's a really good question' when it's said by the august speaker to little old me in front of the team. No, it's not corny. It's nice to be acknowledged and affirmed for having stuck one's neck out. It also shows others that you, the answerer, are really relishing this whole experience. Furthermore, it encourages others to take part in the game, too.

Treat everyone respectfully

Remember: Audience members have much more in common with each other than they do with you. They subconsciously bond with each other. They notice how you treat each member, feeling him/her a surrogate for the group.

Relax your style

Be warm, curious, direct, open, informal. Remember, answering questions is chatty and conversational. It's not lecture time. Your guard should be down, at least externally, and you should sound like you're sitting down having a cup of coffee with the people you're talking to. It's really a rather intimate exchange. Your mental set should be that, for the moment, you're one of them.

Avoid debates

How often have you seen it or been sucked into it yourself: the derailment of the question-and-answer period into a one-to-one exchange about an ever-narrowing subject? This bores your audience in about two minutes and stops the good flow between you and everyone else. The problem is how to cut a debate off without sounding like you're running away or being rude. Try this:

'You know, this is a great subject, and I know we both have more to say on it. Let's meet after the programme to continue it,' or:

'Listen, you've got me on the horns of a dilemma. I'd like to keep talking about this but there are lots of other eager questioners who want to get the floor. Please see me after the programme.' Still another way:

'That's a really complex technical point. Let me send you X's article (or whatever) on that. Please give me your address after the programme.'

Speak personally and informally, being sure to save face for the idiot who keeps badgering you. This makes you come off as a thoughtful person, sensitive as well as knowledgeable. They *know* he's an idiot . . .

What if you don't know?

Say so! Tell the truth. Nothing else ever really washes. You're a much bigger hero for admitting fallibility than bluffing and transparently letting us know (and we *will* know) that you're too shaky or embarrassed to tell the truth; that you'd rather lie and fool us than give us the straight answer. What this does is to make us suspect everything else you've told us to date. So — how to say it?

'I wish I could rattle off that answer for you, but I can't. I'd need to go back and look at some data' (or, 'I don't really know that but I could probably find out'). 'If you want to know, call me at my office' or, 'I'll send you a note on it', etc.

Sound bad? Stupid? Unprepared? Surely not. It sounds honest and sensible about how much detail *anyone* carries around with them. It shows you don't know the answer but know how to get it, and that you're willing to give it to him/her in a more appropriate manner. it shows you care about being accurate, not glib.

Now let's turn to the bumpy part — when things aren't going well, when you hit snags and difficult people and tough questions, getting that ambushed or 'I'm not in control' feeling.

Handling difficult questions and questioners

Taking back the power

Because of our conditioned 'I am powerless; ask away' mental set, we *allow* too much during question-and-answer sessions. Just keep reminding yourself that you have total power over your answers. Not over the questions, but over the answers.

● *The information is yours*
   Before you speak, think: 'The information is mine. Only I know it this way. No one can forcibly extract it from me. It's my gift to

give, and I alone will decide what to give, how much of it to give, and also how to give it'. This will make you know what a powerful position you're really in.

- *You don't have to tell all*
  You may choose what you say and delete and edit as you go. Since no one can read your mind (not yet, anyway), you can *choose* what to tell.

- *Respond only to what's asked*
  Stay on target. Make your answers short, succinct, and most of all, to the point! Don't tell them *all* you know, just tell them what they asked for. It's not only safer; it's less boring. If they want more, they'll ask a follow-up question, which is a good idea because it makes for a *dialogue*, not a monologue — the proper format for the question-and-answer period. It also gives you more time to think.

Buying time

Probably the most difficult aspect of answering questions is that at the end of the question everyone expects an instant answer. Some of us have great extemporizing abilities and the mind-to-mouth route works really well. Lots of people don't, and further, don't want to blurt out any old answer without a chance to think. This is especially true when the question is a tough one, possibly damaging or difficult to answer.

To solve this, let's first discover a hidden ability most of us don't use very much.

Trust your instincts

Your brain works at lightning speed. We just don't recognize that because we interfere with its natural processes all the time. We *rethink* and *second-guess* and don't dare *trust* our instincts or first impressions. The fact is, you're quite capable of coming up with an immediate answer. The difficulty arises with your expectations. You think that you need to be able to formulate and know your *total* answer in *advance*! Wrong.

The first way to buy time is to trust your instincts. Learn to *start* answering the question. Don't look for your ending yet. You'll hear yourself as you go and can decide along the way. Your mind doesn't only work in advance. It works while you're talking.

Pick the question apart

Asking more about what the questioner really means not only gives you time to think of an answer, it actually highlights *what* to answer.

'Did you mean X or Y?' 'There are two parts to your question. Which shall I answer first?' Even, 'Would you repeat the question?' gives you time to think and figure out what they're asking.

Comment on the question

Commenting before you answer is another way to delay, buy some time, and think:

- You can make a comment about the question itself: 'Good'. 'Tough', 'Interesting', 'Never thought of that before'.
- You can comment on the process. 'I think I hit a sore point you seem to have a barrage of questions!'
- You can comment on how it's asked: 'You were certainly listening!' or, 'You're very concerned about this, aren't you?'

All of these little prologues buy you time, giving you a moment to collect yourself. Further, they give you back your sense of power and balance if the question is a tough one. And they all sound very responsive, not like you're stalling.

Change the rhythm

Don't respond automatically. Stop the action if it's going too fast. It's in your power to handle not only how but *when* to respond. Slow down. 'Let me take a moment to think about that.'

Avoiding the question

The tactic suggested for 'What if you don't know?', above, works equally well here. Any of those responses about answering later will give you time to go back and check; to formulate a carefully worked and thought-out answer, or to check with the powers that be about what the company policy is. Humour works very well here, too:

'I knew someone would ask the *one* thing I don't know the answer to offhand!' It's also very acceptable to say:

'I'm not at liberty to discuss that right now. We're working on it,' or, 'No public comments on *that*. We don't want our competitors to know the answer!'

Turning questions around

Sometimes a question has something in it you'd rather avoid. You need to make a stab at answering it, but then you should take the question off to another realm.

Make it bigger

'Actually, this affects the whole industry, not just our shop . . .' works well. Enlarging the perspective lets you share knowledge about how others are also struggling with the problem. It dilutes problems by making them not so unique or awesome.

Focus it much tighter

Similarly, go down to a much smaller example and get specific instead of trying to stay with an abstract, all-encompassing view.

'Look, I can't speak for all of it and where it's going, yet. I can only speak about the work we've done and what we've found so far.'

Seize the opportunity

'I'm glad you asked that. It gives me an opportunity to straighten that out . . .' or, 'I have heard that,' or, 'You may have read about that. Here's the way it really is.'

Then go into *your* explanation instead of staying on someone else's track. Speak only of the points you want to mention, actively taking the conversation to another plane without sounding defensive.'

Give the context

Often questions are asked based on a false premise or insufficient data.

'In order to answer that, I need to give you some background (or additional information) so we're all on the same wavelength.'

Then fill in the gaps, setting the proper context, etc., and turning the question into a platform. You will sound responsive and informative, yet you'll go where *you* wanted to go.

Cutting people off

Always tricky, the obvious caution is not to look rude or like you're trying to escape. Be *very* careful to apologize as you interrupt: 'I'm really sorry but,' 'This is very difficult,' 'Forgive me for interrupting . . .'

Time or group constraints

'I'm sorry, but others are champing at the bit. I'm going to have to ask you to tighten your question.' Blaming it on an objective outside source saves face for everyone, something you must be keenly aware of.

Ask for their help

'Look, I need your help. I have a real problem. I need to be fair and democratic and not look like a bad guy, but I also have to move on to someone else. Please forgive me.' After such an exchange, ask *everyone*: 'Listen, folks, I know it's hard when you get wound up' (saving face for all), 'but could you *all* try to focus your questions tightly and be really succinct so I'll have time to answer everyone?'

Getting the audience on your side

A tricky play, but necessary when things aren't going well and someone has just attacked or asked a stickler of a question. The idea is to come through as human, vulnerable, trying to do a good job.

Be real

After a tough exchange, the best thing to do is to comment on what just happened. Humour is the very best antidote: 'Well, you didn't know that you came to a boxing match, did you?' or, 'Is there a doctor in the house?'

Don't pretend it didn't happen

The worst and weakest way to handle such an exposure is to avoid it. Even looking at the audience with a wry smile and saying 'No comment' is a powerful move.

Have the last word

That's the reward you get for doing a Q&A session! You *alone* can say one last thing before you move on. Again, the light touch is the way to go. It shows you're unscathed and strong enough to have a broad perspective (unlike your questioner). Something like, 'Well, let's just remember my *original* point so we can go on . . .' and then explain it again.

HANDLING HOSTILITY

Of all the aspects of Q&A sessions, this is the most scary and uncomfortable.

Let's begin by understanding the dynamics of why people get hostile, lose tempers, lash out, and attack in a group situation. This is one of the best ways to reduce your reaction and sets the stage for handling hostility constructively.

Why people get hostile

Passion

We can and do get worked up over issues and some people have less self-control than others. Those who are guided by gut reactions more than logic, whose families were given to more volatile responses, are most prone to this.

Fear and threat

Your subject may raise spectres in others of being asked to do or accept more than someone can deliver or understand. Thinking, 'My life or work will change because of this message. Maybe I can't handle it.' causes some real agitation and attendant loss of control.

Self-protection

Attacking the messenger is an ancient problem. In an effort to focus on 'Whose idea is this, anyway?' and 'Why *should* I change?' belligerence and a need to blame *someone* follow fear and threat.

Defensiveness

People sometimes start out calmly enough to discuss something they disagree with, but then lose their cool when they feel outclassed by logic and hard facts, and become defensive, then aggressive. Hostility covers embarrassment.

Lack of information

Sometimes people build entrenched positions based on bias or one point of view. They can cleave most passionately to this, especially as part of a group. Not having information about the other point of view or the people who have it causes hostility when they're confronted with it. You also draw hostility by simply representing the hated other side.

Sense of impotence

Feeling unable to halt or change something with its resultant sense of loss of control can have the effect of despair for some and real rage in others.

Resentment of opposition figures

Images of someone with more power, influence, money, status, or information can cause resentment and jealousy to the point of hostility and anger.

Isolation

Feeling like a non-believer, alone in a group, can cause some people to strike out against *that* condition, although they sound like they're railing about an issue. We all need a sense of constituency or identification in a group. Being the only one who feels differently sometimes causes overreaction and anger.

Techniques for handling hostility

It's hard to fight our natures and stay calm and rational when someone is insulting or baiting or attacking us in public. Yet, in order to turn such an exchange around to our advantage and come out a clear winner, that process — remaining calm and rational — is the main exercise.

The big goals in confronting hostility and resolving it are, first, to find ways to hear *what* the hostility is about, and second, to add new light, new information, or an alternative point of view to show how *both* sides can resolve the disagreement.

But perhaps the biggest goal is to save face in front of your audience; to show them that you can stay in control of your feelings *and* your facts, and to continue to convince them, even if you're verbally assaulted.

Take a breath

When tempers flare or icy comments slice through the air, our typical next step is to put up our fists and fight back. This is not useful and surely not recommended as your best response in public. And — you actually *have* the time and room to decide on a course of action . . .

Your opponent is already hostile; you're not. So you're at a much lower level of emotion than he/she is. Therefore the first step in handling hostility is to buy some time so you can calm down and think. I suggest you literally 'take a breath'. Not one of those giant heaving sighs, visible in the back row, but a slow internal breath that gives you a sense of slowing down, not speeding up, the blood pressure.

Identify the hostility

Suppose your trousers dropped around your ankles while delivering a speech. What would you do? Try shuffling off the stage with a smile, pretending they're not down around your ankles? Or would you bend down, pick them up, and comment on how the audience is 'getting to know more about you than just your subject matter'?

Choice 1 means you think they're sightless, totally without feelings, or quite accustomed to people losing their trousers. Choice 2 says, 'You and I both know what happened and how it feels. Instead of trying to hide, what can I do now to put us both at ease?'

The biggest mistake people make when trying to handle a hostile questioner is to pretend it's not happening. This makes the audience

more uncomfortable! They can see what just happened. We're all quick
to identify conflict. They're concerned about what you'll do next. Going
blithely on makes you seem either too weak to handle it or too stupid
to have noticed it. Or that you think the *audience* is too stupid to see
it. When someone is hostile or angry, you have to deal with it publicly.

Allow the anger

- *The anatomy of anger*
  We all handle anger in two basic ways: We either fly off the handle
  and vent it, shouting, etc., way out of control. (Let's call him Type
  A.) Or we become *extremely* cool deliberate, obnoxiously slow,
  lethally rational, and insufferably superior. (Let's call her Type B.)
  Taken from anybody's home notebook, this difference results in
  the following typical exchange and response:

  Type A (Flailing arms wildly, screaming): '*X#!X*! You always
  do that and I hate it and . . .'

  Type B (slowly, deliberately, in an icy, low voice): 'Look at you!
  How can I possibly discuss this with you when you're so irrational
  and out of control? Now, when you can calm *down*, I'll be glad
  to talk about it . . .'

  Result? *Aaagh!* The argument escalates as Type A reaches new
  heights of fury and rage! Why? Because Type A *is* out of control
  and knows it! If he *could* calm down and choose another means
  of behaviour, don't you think he would? Irrational rage is an
  involuntary response and secretly embarrassing to the rager. But
  for Type B to point it out, at the same time rubbing it in by becoming
  even more calm, is enough to make Type A blow a gasket!
- *What to do*
  Allow the Type As to be angry, *their* way! No judgement on
  anyone's part. One way isn't better than the other; it just is! It's
  how people are put together.

  To allow the Type A in your audience to be angry and to still
  turn this around rationally, name the anger or hostility. Describe
  it, in a flat, factual, but sympathetic (not patronizing) way:

  'I see you're very concerned (passionate, upset, feel very deeply)
  about this issue,' or, 'I see you're very committed to a point of view
  about this.'

  This provides an instant antidote. The person railing has been
  given a way out. 'Yes, I am,' is his response. You've actually implied,

'It's okay. I understand that you're mad,' by your behaviour. You've taken him out of the realm of feeling defensive about the fact of his anger or hostility and into the beginnings of talking about what he's angry about. And you've saved face for both of you.

So, in order to move out of the smoke and fire, don't put someone's anger down or ask for more self-control. Just say that you see it, you're sympathetic to it, then let them talk it out — their way.

Understand the anger

By absorbing the reasons why people get angry and hostile that I mentioned earlier, you can handle them better. When you identify the *real* source of someone's hostility, you can find a way to connect their anger to a point of view you can talk about.

'I understand how you must feel. My point of view sounds like it will change something you're very committed to. But let me show you how that's not quite true.'

Pinpointing the discussion to the underlying issue helps cut the anger out of the conversation.

Get out of the personal realm

Since hostility often turns to personal attack, don't start out defending yourself. The goal is to get to a factual level, not remain on the personal one.

'I know that your main goal is to get to the bottom of the issue, not necessarily to have a personal grudge match with me. Actually, we don't even know each other! So, as I hear it, you're concerned about . . .' Another way:

'This sounds like one of those "Kill the messenger" moments. I understand that your anger (disagreement) about the subject has included me. Let me rather be the method for clearing up a disagreement.'

Find something in common

'You know, although we seem to be disagreeing, we actually have something in common. We *both* care very much about this issue. I see why you're so worked up. So am I!'

This surprising approach works well not just to dilute your opponent and get you both talking. It plays *very* well for the audience. They see that you're not patronizing your opponent or looking for the upper hand. You seem to actually have room to hear and absorb dissident viewpoints and still hold your ground.

Ask for further clarification

Often, when someone is hostile, they will sound off but not be very coherent about just what's troubling them. Try to get your opponent to focus on the exact objection he/she has. Ask for it. 'To help us come to some understanding,' or, 'To help me respond to exactly what your anger is about, please tell me the essence (or the basic source) of your disagreement.'

Taking the question or issue apart is by itself a cooling-off process, pushing everyone toward logic and reason.

Have faith in the facts

Use demonstrable evidence, practical explanations, and specific examples as your argument. Stay out of global statements and large abstract concepts. The latter sound like you're being unresponsive and will weaken your position in the eyes of the audience.

Settle for disagreement

Be willing, when all avenues are exhausted, to end up still on opposite sides. The key here is to end on a positive note, no matter what. Show your logic; recap your position with some salient argument about why. Then show compassion and understanding for someone else's point of view.

'Well, I think we need to come to some conclusion here. I hear you and what you believe in. I hope you can hear me and my points too; the point that . . . etc. Let's just agree to disagree for now and know that eventually the facts (or history) will bear out the correct position.'

If it suits your personality, you might end it with a bit of humour: 'Well, you think that you're right and I *know* that I'm right . . .' or, 'The audience has heard us both. I think we've exhausted the subject for now. Before we exhaust, and lose, *them*, let's call a moratorium. And when you change your mind, which I hope I've helped you do, please call me.'

To conclude: handling yourself during an audience question-and-answer period is complex because of all our years of conditioning and automatic question answering. It requires the handling of not only the question but also the audience. Yet it's a valuable process and should be done.

It requires some understanding of what audiences want from you, hearing clearly what is being asked, and finding ways and time to think in order to answer. This satisfies the audience and shows your strength and character. Now let's move to another instance in which you need to find ways to answer questions.

THE BOSS VS. YOU

The dynamics of power

In a Q&A session with your boss, your major problem is to find ways to feel that power is shared, to feel that you have some real choices about how you'll behave and what you'll say and do.

When you're called in to a questioning session, the fact that he/she *can* ask you to come, that you *will* come, and that you *must* answer questions makes the balance of power a little different from that in the usual Q&A sessions after a presentation, where you have just demonstrated *your* power and continue it by *inviting* them to ask you for more.

How much room at the top?

First — know your audience. There are certain predictables about any boss.

Bosses

They're all different. The key is to know and study yours well enough to discover how your boss deals with his/her power. What does he/she usually do when confronted with an issue: Lose temper; ask questions; decide alone; give orders; blame others; none of the above? Knowing the unique qualities of *your* boss helps you predict and plan.

Know also that the very nature of their position causes them to have certain traits in common. Being a boss generally brings with it certain predictable and understandable needs for attitudes about power and authority. Knowing these overall basic needs and attributes will also help you understand and prepare for a boss's probable approach to the upcoming session:

- *Leadership*. In order to establish and maintain effective leadership, a boss needs others to know that he/she *is* in charge. This means showing that he/she has legitimate authority and is exercising it to get the job done; making and implementing decisions and seeing to it that these decisions are carried out. No matter how flexible, this 'last word' leadership *must* finally be unchallenged.
- *High profile*. Leaders and bosses need to be visible to the troops. Since they can't ride the white horse at the head of the pack and yell 'Charge!' any more, they must rely in part on visible trappings of power.
- *Comparison*. Since power is relative in any organization, your boss may feel powerless before *his/her* boss. This can cause extra pressure and power-wielding on the staff whenever your boss is in the presence of someone else who wields power over him/her. Also the desire to show *his* boss he isn't too soft on the troops.
- *Pleasure*. Power feels delicious to many of us, particularly to those types who love and want it enough to emerge from the pack and run things. This can sometimes cause muscle-flexing and an abuse of power for its own sake.
- *Respect*. Power brings with it automatic respect. Not always heartfelt and sometimes for the *office* rather than the person, nevertheless the person in charge does get deference from his/her staff and a certain sense of the effect his/her power has over them.
- *Fear*. People wield power unduly when they're afraid they don't have it or are losing it. 'Get it done because I say so' is a typical 'retreat to power' whenever a boss feels unable to deal with a situation or senses the power slipping away.

Most of all, recognize that bosses have egos, vulnerabilities, and needs, just like you. They're just not allowed to show them as much.

Understanding these basic components of what power means to bosses can show you what territory you must cede in order to fulfil their general needs before you can begin to think of how to fulfil your *own* needs and what power you can get a piece of in a one-to-one session.

Now we've set the background against which you will appear. Bosses' predictable needs and behaviour patterns won't change. What *can* be adaptable is your behaviour. Based on what you understand, in advance, so that you aren't surprised or thrown at the meeting, you can develop many options about how you answer questions and how you feel at such a session.

Preparation

Why were you called?

When you're asked to this questioning session by the boss be sure to pinpoint specifically what is being asked about and why you are chosen to be the spokesperson for this (if it isn't personal).

Bosses can call one-to-one questioning meetings to:

- solve a problem before it goes further
- analyse an issue
- discuss or touch base on an ongoing project
- get debriefed on a current 'disaster'
- get to know you better/give kudos.

What do they really want?

Unless you get exact information about what they specifically want, you may prepare too much or too little or not in the right format or focus.

Why?

This may require a little research and thought. Try to analyse why he/she wants this information from you, especially at this time. Is anything going on at the shop right now? New plans? Problems? If it's you personally the boss wants to see, think through what the recent deadlines have been; how's your work been going, what was the last encounter you had and about what.

What documents and materials to bring?

Not only should you prepare notes for what you'll say about A, B, or C if it's a formal session, but you need to bring leave-behinds to bolster your points. Depending on what you need to explain, you should also think through visual exhibits you might want to create and bring so that you can share the information clearly and succinctly.

Okay, so you're ready. Now comes the good part. Actually going in there and doing it.

BASIC TECHNIQUES FOR ANSWERING

First, you need to look like you're ready, willing, and able to answer all questions.

Secondly, you need to answer what he/she asks and to be clearly responsive, not evasive.

Thirdly, you want to be helpful and look for solutions, not defensive, hidden, or obstructive.

Within those parameters there's a lot of leeway. You *do* have many choices. Read again in the previous section how to clarify questions before you answer; how to turn questions around so you get in what you want to say; how to answer only what's asked, sparely and succinctly, and wait for follow-up questions instead of pouring out all you know with the first question.

Power

The power issue is again at the heart of how you answer. Feeling strong and able to withstand what is thrown at you will help you dilute the anxiety over the boss's power. Remember, it's still *your* information, to be delivered *your* way, as much or as little as you decide.

Fear

Answerers often feel fear, and always feel concern for consequence: Fear of what the boss can do and think, and concern for the consequences of how you answer.

Establish rapport

Don't walk in with a hang-dog, 'let's get it over with' look. And don't wait for the boss to start. Greet him/her first. You need to establish contact and show that you aren't thrown by this session, but see it as an encounter with the outcome still to be discovered, by mutual participation.

To show you some specific ways to handle two kinds of one-to-one questioning sessions, let's create a scenario or two and play it out.

Answering informational questions

Scene: The boss calls you in for a performance appraisal. This is a kind of questioning encounter in which the atmosphere is basically evaluating and the exchange of information is a key focus.

Boss: 'Well, Janet. It's that time again. Tell me, how do *you* think you did at your job during this period?'

A common ploy: it may throw you off-guard. It can also smoke out some problems the boss may not know about, and give the boss a chance to hear your opinion of your own work.

If you answer:

'(*Defensively*) Why, I thought I did very well, don't you?'

you haven't told him/her anything except that you're not sure whether you did and you seem to have nothing but the *boss's* affirmation to back you up.

If you use the same words but answer belligerently, you're on the attack, expecting the worst, and nothing has really happened yet! That can make the boss suspicious about why you're so belligerent.

Let me give you a series of suggestions about how to handle the information-getting kind of questioning encounter.

Assume the BEST, not the worst

The old conditioning about how we answer *any* question makes us walk into most such sessions nervous and defensive. Start out feeling *good*, not bad, about the session. This will be an exchange. You'll talk and ask and clarify on *both* sides. It's a chance for you to get things straight — directly, not third hand.

Learn what the meeting's about

Be sure you always find out what the subject of the meeting will be. You can always ask 'in the interest of being prepared for whatever you'll need to know.'

Have back-up material

Don't ask the boss to take your word for anything unless you have data and can back it up. In the case of a performance review, come armed with hard data; comparative figures; completed projects; original self-starter work; letters from satisfied customers; and the like.

Make sure you understand the question

Don't presume too much too soon, a major failing whenever we answer. Both the *form* and the *content* of the question are important.

- *The form of the question*
  This tells you the underlying motivation for the question and helps you know what needs dealing with first. Notice the different mental sets and how the *form* of the question can give you the clue:
  Curious: 'I don't understand exactly what these figures mean . . .' This needs a straightforward informational answer.
  Suspicious: 'Well, exactly *what do* these figures mean . . .?' This needs some background to clarify the whole issue before you answer the question. There's obviously some feeling, perhaps negative, already present. Give context, then details.
  Prejudiced: 'These figures aren't very helpful . . .' Here you need to ask why he/she thinks not, before you start defending. First find out more about why the mind is already closed.
- *The content of the question*
  This tells you exactly *what's* being asked for. Here's where your listening skill is primary, as stated earlier. Listen till the *end* of the question. Make sure you clarify by asking *before* you answer, so you stay on target and don't volunteer too much.

Build a broader answer

Take some initiative. Use the question to build *your case* into the answer. Don't just answer what is asked. Add background, comparisons, implications that embellish the answer (keeping connected to the original question, of course). This can shore up your position, giving it more depth and dimension.

Tell the truth

If you don't know, *say so*! You get extra points for honesty and bad marks for lying or faking.

'I'm sorry, I don't know enough about that, but I can get it for you later today' shows that you *know* when you don't know *and* that you know how to find out. This breeds confidence!

After a statement, ask!

In a performance review, the boss will usually tell you what he/she thinks after that opening question. Stay interested and calm. Listen *very* hard for the areas of difference between what *you* think and what the *boss* thinks. Respond with equanimity (sometimes tough but work on this!) and a constructive outlook:

'I'm listening hard because I like my job and want to know whether or not I'm doing it well and if you're getting what you need from me. Let me ask you to focus further on X. I want very much to know more about how you think I can improve that.' Don't grovel, but show your interest in fixing it *with* the boss's suggestions.

Answering critical questions

The other general category of questions come from an incident in which you made mistakes, or at least *something* went wrong. The biggest problem you have is being able to still the several voices inside that affect how you hear and how you answer.

Let's turn to our three work types and some typical responses they might have to this kind of exchange:

An affiliator subordinate takes it all very personally. Usually fearful of hostility, whatever the issue, affiliators want the boss finally to forgive them.

An achiever boss can't understand the affiliator's response. He/she wants to take a rational, task-oriented view:

'I thought we had a clear set of standards. How did this happen?'

He may actually get angry at *himself* for imperfectly organizing the *task*, but he can't begin to hear the self-absorbed approach of the affiliator.

An influencer boss demands: 'Why didn't you do this?' He/she wants to know that the mistake didn't come from your deliberately *defying* him and his authority. He/she wants to see your willingness to make it right. He wonders about his delegation of authority; aware of the empowering relationship between authority and responsibility, he'll worry about whether he gave you too much or too little.

When answering criticism:

Don't be defensive

The one thing people expect when you're called in for criticism is that you'll look and feel guilty. Beware! That invites them to attack. Continue to explain what you did, why you did it, etc., factually, leaving the door open to admit mistakes or handle further discussion. But don't let the session deteriorate into a personal attack on you and who you are: just on what you did or didn't do.

Don't counter-punch

With your fists either clenched or up in front of your face, don't respond by fighting back. Though you're tempted, do none of these:

'It's not a good system, anyway.'
'Your objection isn't valid . . .'
'It's such a useless task . . .'
'What about when Jack did that?'

Stay with the listening. No comment, yet.

Get specific

Take it in steps. First, be sure what the exact nature of the criticism is:

'Could you please explain what you mean by "unfinished"?'
'How, exactly, had you hoped it would look?'

This shows willingness to listen *and* gives you time to find out what the critique is about, *precisely*.

Ask for suggestions

It's crucial that you show that you want to *improve*, NOT just say that you did nothing wrong. People often have very different views of 'well done'. Your boss's view must prevail. Ask:

'How would you handle it?'
'What format would be better?'
'Could you show me something that would demonstrate more of what you mean?'

Understand the directions

Words like 'maybe more of' or 'not effective enough' or 'too vague' don't help you do a better job next time. Find out exactly what is meant, with demonstration. Sometimes the boss is dissatisfied but can't describe exactly what he/she wants. Help him/her formulate a real position, thus helping to solve the problem together.

Add to or change answer

Sometimes you answer hastily. If you think better of it, it's a sign of accuracy and responsiveness to fix it. 'I'm sorry. In thinking about that last answer I gave you, I forgot X.' Listening to another question can also cause you to add to a previous one. Do it. Again, a strong move to forthrightness and alertness.

Disagree when appropriate

Don't just roll over and play dead. That shows no spirit or conviction about your work. After you get all the information about what the boss perceives as wrong, you can come back with hard data to show that your point of view *also* had validity. Be sure you can show credible evidence, and show how your approach was a viable alternative.

Don't go for a 'win'

In such a confrontation, don't think of it as win-lose. Rather, see it as finding room to accommodate to another point of view, the one held by the person in charge!

If you're wrong

Say it! Don't grovel, but say what you've learned. Show that you now see what the mistake was. But do it constructively.

'In retrospect I can see that was a bad decision. That concerns me very deeply, since I don't like making mistakes — ever. I would surely like not to repeat the process that led me to it. What would you suggest about how to avoid that in the future?'

This will assure the boss that you're open to criticism and willing to learn and fix mistakes, not to deny them and therefore continue to make them.

If it gets personal

Pleasantly, try this:

'Can I ask for a moment here? It feels like we're talking more about my character and less about what I *did* on such-and-such an occasion. You know, I've worked here for a while and proved myself a loyal and conscientious employee. I think you know that. If something went wrong, I'd like to fix it. A mistake in judgement means I have something to learn, but I'm still the same loyal, conscientious person I always was.'

End constructively

The best outcome from such a confrontation is for the boss to know you're mature enough to hear the issues and not also fold personally. Show how well you take direction and how willing you are to try again, his/her way. Make it a team effort. Ask to come in and check as you re-do to be sure you're on the right wavelength. If you can, try:

'I want to tell you that I appreciate your being so honest with me. No one likes to make mistakes, but I'm glad you showed me you have faith in my ability to do this better by calling me in this way. I won't let you down.'

Role play and practice

In closing this chapter, let me again suggest that you practice. Do some role playing by improvising a questioning session, especially with audience questions. Peers can really help you hear because they know the right questions to ask.

Give your friends/family the outline of what the meeting's about, who's coming, what they want, and what they'll probably ask you. This is true whether it's for an audience after a speech or the boss. If you prepare a list of what you think will be asked, you help yourself focus and give your group of players something to work from.

The idea is to find out what it feels like before the big day. To discover some of your weak points both personally and content-wise.

If you have a video camera, you might even want to tape it. You can then judge for *yourself* how you came across, what you said, and if that's how you want to do it.

If you have no camera, you can still audio-tape it. Then listen and criticize.

And, of course, you'll want to ask your friends to give you live feedback so you can discuss how it went with them straight after you do it.

Everything feels better after you've experienced it. Practice not only helps you get used to the upcoming experience; it can stop you from making some errors in attitude and in how you're coming across. It can show you if your presentation and method of explanation work. And it gives you a chance to try out some of these answers and phrases and begin to adapt them to your style.

The bottom line? Remember that giving answers is giving a gift. You own your information and can choose what you'll give and how. Understand your questioners: what they really want, how you affect them. Understand the questioning process and how it has conditioned us to feel powerless and answer without discretion and with fear.

Learn even to enjoy the give-and-take!

Now let's turn to another area of give-and-take: Meetings. How to lead and participate in them effectively.

9
MEETINGS
Leading and participating effectively

Meetings were obviously intended to serve *some* important function in the workplace because there are so many of them! But why do so many people walk away from them mumbling, 'Endless,' 'Boring,' 'Waste of time,' 'Didn't get anywhere,' 'What are we supposed to do now?' and other such critical comments?

In this chapter we'll find out first what meetings are really for; then discover what internal dynamics one can expect in *any* group interaction and what goes wrong with meetings most often. Then, communications skills for leaders and participants, and how to design agendas and meetings and run them successfully.

WHAT GOES WRONG AND WHY

In order to change the perception *and* the techniques with which meetings are run, let's first look at what goes wrong. You've been to meetings. I'm sure you'll find your overt complaints and hidden concerns in what follows:

Factual issues

Passivity

'I feel like I'm just supposed to show up there . . .'

The meeting is the leader's idea and doesn't always feel truly participatory. You arrive to a fixed agenda that you're *supposed* to tune into and become involved in, yet the agenda items don't always concern you. Meeting goers generally don't have any input into the agenda and the proceedings till the end, when they're tired and dying to get out. That's when the leader says, 'Any new items you'd like to bring up?' Groan!

Boring

'They're usually endless and dull, with people talking in circles'.

Because meetings are so product-oriented: 'Let's get down to work and get this over with. X number of items on the agenda. Let's start with No. 1'. People just don't take the time to build in persuasive or involving techniques the way they would when delivering a speech. Sitting through a list of disconnected issues, hearing report after report and perfunctory discussions, group members are rarely stimulated except when they may get to the one or two items that might directly affect *them*.

People don't listen

'I don't think they ever heard what my report was really about'.

Although meetings are meant to be a clearinghouse for ideas, what's brought up at meetings often falls on deaf ears. You often find several people talking at once or interrupting each other. Comments rarely flow in response to what was just said, but more from 'Now it's my turn. Listen to *my* idea'.

Many of us aren't good at listening at the best of times, suffering from both the perfectly human tendency toward self-involvement and the conditioned response to the usual level of speakers. But given all the facets of what's at stake personally at a meeting, it's little wonder that we're really bad at listening there.

Grandstanding

'Two or three people always seem to dominate or try to get control. Feels like you can't get a word in'.

The more powerful or outspoken members may try to take over meetings — talking too much or too often, pre-empting the 'last word' position, and generally putting a damper on effective participation by less aggressive members.

The power of the leader

'How much can you disagree? After all, he's the boss'.

The fact of a person in power, usually your boss, leading the meeting creates still another area of tension. He/she is the person to please; the one you have to keep working for; the one who called the meeting with certain expectations and goals. This creates an 'acting' challenge — to 'act like' you're there and 'with it' wholeheartedly — when you may not feel that way and are actually being very careful about what you do. Even if the meeting caller is not your ultimate boss, for the length of that meeting he/she has the power to direct, to cut you short, and most of all, to remember . . .

Foregone conclusions

'Group discussion is a waste of time since the boss will already know what he wants to do'.

The leader who called the meeting has often already reached a conclusion and knows how he/she wants the decision to come out. Therefore, if the group begins to move in another direction, there is a tug of war or manipulation by the leader. This makes the group feel that it doesn't matter whether there is consensus or not, the end product is a foregone conclusion.

Not useful

'You often walk out not sure exactly what was decided and what to do next'.

One of the greatest problems with meetings is the need for good, definitive closure. Unfortunately, coming to some conclusions about an issue seems to feel like enough to many people. Participants often walk out without a clear action or follow-up plan or a sense of how the new decisions will fit into the total scheme, what the consequences will be, etc.

'Feeling' issues

Fear of exposure

'I'm visible to my peers and the people in my group, as well as to the people in power. What I say (or don't say) is registered for all to see.

I could even be in for some public criticism in relation to a project!'

This is one of the subconscious responses. It is not brought to the surface or admitted, but fear of being exposed is an active part of people's feelings about meetings. Therefore, meeting goers feel wary and guarded, attending much more to their safety than to the business in hand.

Potential conflict

'Will I take a chance and publicly disagree and get into an argument? Will I, should I, stick my neck out?'

Most people are not accustomed to living life by walking uphill, against the prevailing wind. It requires much inner strength and motivation to fight for a cause against the popular consensus or to argue for an unpopular thought, if yours is not a basic 'oppositional' mentality. By nature, we like to avoid conflict. It's personally costly and can expose you to attack by the majority.

Dissenters can also feel isolated or unpopular — not just at a meeting but in the workplace itself. A distaste for the dangers of conflict causes many people to bite their tongues and *not* speak out at meetings.

Anticipating that, for safety's sake, you may have to throttle your desire to speak out and that you'll make yourself play dead at the meeting, makes you enter with anxiety and with another kind of hostility toward the meeting process.

Prior relationships brought to meeting

'I know who'll side with whose position before I even go in. It doesn't matter *what* the facts are'.

There are often factions or pre-aligned groups in the workplace who pull against each other, acting out a power struggle over issues and turf. Also, feelings of personal animosity or competition with people in your shop get heightened as you sit around a table watching each other. Public visibility, vying for position, and the intensity these cause can make meetings unsuccessful and unwelcome.

Concern about consequences

'What will be required of me?' 'If we decide X, how will it affect my job?' 'Can I do what the new plan will ask of me?' 'What can I do to stop something I see being planned that can affect me adversely?'

Meetings often mean change. You can see how these concerns would make going to a meeting an uneasy and unwelcome experience as you think, 'Okay, what are we going to change now?'

So — here's the background for changing how meetings are run. Sounds like a lot of obstacles, doesn't it? Are meetings such a good idea? Worth trying to fix? Who needs them, anyway?

Why meetings?

Here are some reasons why meetings, with their pitfalls, can be the best and often the *only* way to work well together.

- *Getting a sense of the whole*
  So much work is done privately and so many components are delegated in the workplace that it's vital to hear the overall view and see how the pieces, including the ones you're working on, fit together.
- *Comparing notes*
  Knowing that the same knotty problem has also stumped others, or discovering similarities between the workers and the work done elsewhere and in your unit, is most reassuring.
- *Sharing information*
  Learning from what others have learned; hearing ways to solve problems; being able to give something you've learned to the group; picking up data you need — all reasons for, and positive outcomes of, group meetings.
- *Being visible to each other*
  Much of what we do at work we do alone. We need a place to feel in unison. It's important to get the sense of a team pulling together in any group endeavour. Seeing and hearing from each other, experiencing the unity of energies being expended in the same effort, is a powerful team builder. It can also be *the* place for the leader to inspire the troops . . .
- *Comfort of hearing others' opinions openly*
  There is great anxiety around being asked your opinions and ideas privately, one-to-one, by the boss, knowing that he/she will also be asking others. This makes you much less forthcoming as you hedge your answers in fear of being too exposed or too far away

from the opinions of your colleagues. Airing ideas in a group gives everyone some orientation to the norm and helps people decide how far they want to go.

● *Looking for solutions jointly*
'Two heads are better than one' is true for many reasons. You get so committed to the sound of your own inner voice and its ideas that it's shocking to hear how many other ways something can be done. The stimulation your thinking gets when it can play off or incorporate another point of view or even need to justify itself to dissenters is invaluable. The variety and quality of solutions a group can come up with is yet another reason for meetings.

● *Group self-criticism*
In a group, it's safe to join in on the complaining and nitpicking and even laugh about how something's being fouled up, when everyone else is doing it. The leader can also authorize and direct self-criticism about a project at a meeting to make everyone contribute, become aware of the difficulties, and start solving the problems that are brought up.

● *Developing consensus*
The efficiency of unified agreement vs. individual commitments is clear. When you agree as a group and set yourself a course of action, everyone in the group becomes everyone else's conscience as well as spur. Conflicts can be resolved in the open and the final product feels 'right' to the group as a whole.

● *Stimulating ideas*
The atmosphere of many people focusing on one idea brings the creative level up for all. Hearing possible solutions stimulates meeting participants to contribute or take someone else's thought and run with it.

So — meetings *are* an extremely useful, actually invaluable, tool, and absolutely vital in the workplace.

Comparison of what should be and what is

Knowing what business meetings *should* be and what they *could* accomplish, as well as how far short they *usually* fall, can help us design new ways to run and participate in effective meetings.

Read down the list of what meetings should be; then read how they actually work. Compare *your* most recent meeting experience with each list:

Ideal	Actual
Get a sense of the whole	Passive experience
Compare notes	Boring
Share information	People don't listen
Be visible to each other	Not useful
Hear others' opinions	Fear of exposure
Look for solutions jointly	Danger of potential conflict
Group self-criticism	Act out prior relationships
Develop consensus	Grandstanding
Stimulate ideas	Leader overwhelms
	Foregone conclusions
	Concern about consequences

How do your experiences come out? Have *your* meetings added value and quality to your work process? Have *you* perhaps fallen into some of the stereotypical pitfalls? Have you truly maximized the group process? Are you, as leader or as group member, well served?

To avoid the typical pitfalls and ensure effective meetngs and results, let's begin by finding out about how people behave in groups.

Too many meetings don't work because there's not enough, or inappropriate, participation: poor listening; ineffective exchanges of information; polarization; hostility; overbearing leadership; and so on. Therefore I will focus on ways to improve *interpersonal* skills and develop better *communications* skills as a meeting leader or participant. I will *not* deal with the whole subject of group management techniques or with group process, nor will I take an in-depth look at the variations and layers of group dynamics.

BASIC PERSONALITIES AT MEETINGS

You know how when you sit around the table at a meeting, the same people generally speak up, disagree, criticize, or never say a word? Have you ever stopped to think that they actually fall into types; that their behaviour is definable and predictable? That it comes from a whole set of intrinsic behaviour patterns?

Wouldn't it help if you knew the behaviour categories so that you could more readily recognize and understand how people act at a meeting and could handle them better and more productively?

Just like 'You can't know the players without a score card' at a cricket match, there is a kind of 'score card' we can develop to define the basic behaviour types at any meeting. Whenever you can categorize behaviour in recognizable patterns, it helps not only to understand it, but to recognize the hallmarks so that you can move past 'How obnoxious he is', or, 'Why does she always have to find some negative response?' into a knowledgeable countermove.

There are many studies out about how to categorize people in group interactions. The four categories I will describe come from the work of Dr. David Kantor of the Kantor Family Institute in Cambridge, Massachusetts, author of *Inside the Family*.* These categories work in any group situation. They define how we interrelate with each other not only at meetings but also within the family. As you read them, I'm sure you'll recognize every character type and match it to people you know. See if you can also find and define *yourself* as I suggest some skills for handling them.

Players in a group interaction

Mover

This is the one in the group who usually initiates action. He/she defines where you're heading and suggests and develops ideas for how to get there. Movers are usually called 'natural leaders'. They're seen as strong, sure-footed, self-confident. They are very creative, but are often intolerant of alternative ideas, seeing their own ideas as the *only* way. They enjoy power and being in charge but also need and want approval and agreement.

Their value at a meeting is obvious. Giving ideas and the energy to back them up is a most useful and constructive trait. Notice their needs, though, for approval and agreement.

Suggestions: The challenge to the group leader is to harness the mover to pull ahead and be creative, affirming his/her contribution, but to also leave room for others in the group to catch up or to vary the plan he/she initiates. The meeting leader must anticipate the mover and what he/she usually does and set a course within which the mover

* *Inside the Family* (Jossey Bass, 1975).

can function but not dominate the meeting. Be aware that meeting leaders can themselves often be movers and must be aware of their own tendency to pre-empt others' participation . . .

Opposer

This person is a reactor and countermover, in response to the mover's action. Not visible in the initiator role, the opposer moves into gear to push *against* whatever has been put on the table. He/she creates a challenge to the mover by blocking the mover's direction or intended destination. Opposers want others to declare themselves on their side. Then the opposer can become the mover. Like movers, opposers are powerful, too. They can redefine the action established by the mover; to halt or redirect what the mover begins.

Opposers get their attention and consequent sense of importance by the very act of taking a contra stance. They say they don't care about overt approval; they care about the 'facts' and the 'truth'. In this process they can also hurt feelings and make enemies, not only of the people they thwart but of the group itself. Because they are perceived as interrupters not only of one person but of forward progress, groups can often resent opposers.

Suggestions: Although this type sounds like a negative contributor, and the tendency can develop to want to ignore them or put their objections down, opposers actually serve some very useful functions. As those who test ideas and scrutinize data to find flaws, meeting leaders and others can and should use them as a stimulus for further thought and analysis of a mover's idea. By taking the *useful* criticism from their seemingly negative message, opposers can also, if well directed by the leader of the group, redirect and even stimulate more ideas or improvements on the original mover's suggestion.

Ideally, opposers should be motivated to dissent and critize constructively, thus entering into a dialogue with the mover to develop better strategies jointly, rather than simply to oppose.

Meeting leaders should also check up on their own tendency to be opposers. Playing the devil's advocate, finding fault, and criticizing the suggestions of others too often, the leader can lose his/her role as a facilitator who moves the action along.

Follower

This person is a familiar in any group: he/she is the one who 'goes along'. The follower's role is to support someone; in a group meeting, it's the mover or the opposer. Followers 'sign on' to someone else's idea, and as long as they stay in this position, they seldom initiate any ideas of their own. Followers are not necessarily uncreative people. They may simply have greater needs to play it safe, to keep a lower profile, or to wait until they see the general tenor of the group as a whole before they take an overt stand.

They do have interesting kinds of power, though. They can empower others by granting them support and creating a constituency. Everyone wants the follower on his side because we all need supporters and troops to back us when we go out on a limb. Followers can retain their power and independence by shifting sides, or lose their autonomy and weaken their position by prematurely committing support to one side. Sometimes they can maintain joint allegiance by privately professing allegiance to each or by following mover and opposer for separate reasons, double-speaking in an attempt to stay close to all.

Suggestions: For the leader of the group, the message would be to allow the follower to find his own level and not put him on the spot too early with a 'What do you think, John?' Followers are very good implementors once they commit to someone or to an idea. Use that. You'd choke with a room full of only movers and opposers!

Bystander

This is a really interesting character who needs special attention. True, he stays quiet, but he's really quite different from the follower. Whereas the follower can be heard agreeing and 'Me too'ing, the bystander stays out of direct action altogether. He/she makes *no* alliances with any of the other three categories. He watches, witnesses, and keeps opinions to himself. This makes for uneasiness on the part of everyone else because no one knows *what* he's thinking. Bystanders don't express a clear position. Rather, they go for abstractions and cerebral descriptions *about* something rather than emotional commitments *to* something.

Bystanders are most comfortable standing apart, making comments like 'Hmmm,' or, 'I have to to think about that.' In this commentator-like role, they take on an air of objectivity and wisdom (often unwarranted). They therefore have the power to comfort those they watch by making them feel known and valued with a few murmurings or asides. They can also hurt others they ignore by continuing simply to observe silently, in a noncommittal way.

The bystander's position is a very seductive one. Both sides try to get him to declare for them, and since no one knows what he's thinking, there's much attention and energy spent in this pursuit. Unlike the follower, who can be involved and does commit, the bystander wishes to remain apart — enigmatic, there to be wooed.

Suggestions: For the meeting leader, it is useful to know that bystanders don't all do so voluntarily. Some people become bystanders because they're overshadowed or given neither encouragement, confidence, nor training to try any other role. In order to puncture the vacuum they surround themselves with, try giving them a specific role or job, not waiting for them to volunteer or asking them for overt commitment.

Interaction

To understand how these four meeting-behaviour types would interact, let's see how they would deal with a simple social issue: What to do on a Saturday:

Mover (John): 'Hey, let's go to the test match.'
Opposer (David): 'The test match? Hah! Everyone knows it's going to rain Saturday, and besides the parking is impossible.'
Follower (Peter): 'Well, I don't know . . . the test match . . . Hey, that's a good idea!'
Bystander (Robert): 'Yeah. Cricket. The truly English game.'

What could you as a leader or fellow meeting goer — objectively able to see and hear all four approaches — do to find a solution?

First — you could build on the mover's idea and incorporate the opposer's negative concerns by saying:

'The test match is a great idea, John' (*giving the mover credit for his idea*), 'but let's just be sure about the weather' (*drawing in opposer David's idea, too*). 'Robert, why don't you find out about it right now?' (*assigning a task to the noncommital bystander without putting him on the spot about his choice*).

'You know, David mentioned the parking. Probably will be tough. How can we solve that?' (*taking another negative and turning it into a constructive point*).

You could then wait for suggestions from the group, like going early, parking, and having lunch, or turn it back to John, the mover, to come up with another solution.

What about Peter the follower? How can you involve him? Maybe, after the affirmative vote, by saying, 'Peter, you're a good organizer. Why don't you pull this whole thing together and coordinate?'

The bottom line: Since people follow these basic propensities whenever they interact in a group, recognize and help deflect the head-on collisions. That makes meetings and participants productive.

Now let's turn to three basic communication skills we *all* need at meetings, and then focus on individual personal skills for leaders and for participants.

BASIC COMMUNICATION SKILLS FOR MEETINGS

Meetings are a tough challenge because it's normally *very* hard for people to get together, work constructively, and agree on anything, especially in the workplace. We're all such individuals and bring so many agendas to a gathering.

People play many roles at meetings: actual vs. formal leaders, mediators, focused task drivers, idea generators, information testers, etc. For us, in order to get down to basics and give suggestions useful for the widest range, let's just divide meeting behaviour into two general roles. Convener/leader and participant.

- *The leader* needs to recognize the dynamics of the group and guide everyone toward each goal with awareness of the disparate elements at play. He/she needs to know how to go about getting group decisions while also participating him/herself, developing the focus of the meeting, watching the time, and coming up with the results.
- *Participants* also need to be aware of the dynamics of the group, but can sometimes have a more objective view since they're not involved in the overall conduct of the meeting. They can add a calming influence and some perspective, and can often see how two points can fit together. Although their role is to participate, they can often shape the direction of the meeting as much as, if not more than, the leader

Listening

Why do we need lessons in listening? Because in our zeal to tell *our* ideas, to make ourselves known and make a dent in the world, we sometimes fail to consider that someone *else* has ideas, needs, feelings, too, and that we need to take the time to hear them.

This is especially true in a group situation where we are visible to each other *and* to the boss. Our competitive spirit may urge us to dismiss others' contributions or see them as a threat.

The process of non-listening

It works something like this:

You start to talk. I listen to the beginning of what you're saying. Then my mind goes to work to imagine where you're going with this and what you probably mean. I can't wait till you've finished to hear *all* of what you mean because then there'll be no time to think up my countermove. So, in the interests of no 'dead air' time, I start *thinking* — *not* listening — while you're still talking. Then, as soon as you finish, I'm ready. Funny thing is, I often don't even wait till you're finished.

The hallmarks of non-listening are interrupting and cutting off the end of someone's sentence; jumping from one subject to another with no connection to what's just been said; or several people talking at once.

Result? No flow in the discussion. No building up of ideas vertically. Just random blips on a flat horizontal line that don't relate to each other or grow from each other to make a productive whole. Vital information and good ideas get lost. We don't explore issues thoroughly. We don't really know what we agreed to. We expect not to be listened to and understood so we repeat ourselves as we speak.

Not very useful in a meeting process that looks for solutions by a group.

How to fix it? It's not simple because physiologically we're built to think much fster than we can talk. That gives us all that leftover time I told you about in Chapter 2 (only 15 per cent of the brain is needed for understanding words and 85 per cent is left doing nothing), for thinking our own thoughts, criticizing yours, or just going off and thinking about other things entirely.

Techniques to improve listening

Try these, deliberately and actively, and see how much more you will hear and notice.

● *Put yourself aside*
Wipe your slate clean while I talk. I promise your word-well won't
go dry, and when it's your turn to talk, you'll manufacture words
again without having rehearsed them while I'm talking.

● *Get curious*
'What's *his* idea?' Since you already know what *you* think, make
yourself find out and discover a new idea. It's interesting just to
hear how differently we all think and how many solutions there
can be to one problem.

● *Listen openly*
Suspend your judgement. We're so good at criticizing and finding
reasons why *not* to do anything. Wait till you've heard the whole
idea without judgement. Listen wholeheartedly, from the speaker's
point of view, not yours.

● *Listen actively*
Anticipate where the speaker is going.
Weigh what he/she is saying against what you know.
Listen to the supporting evidence.
Keep reviewing and summarizing what is being said.
Sort out evidence and fact from statements unsupported by
evidence.
Categorize: 'This relates to that'.

● *Listen to all of it*
Wait till the very end. As you listen, try to figure out where he/she
is going and what the conclusion will be. But *wait* for it before
you speak.

● *Look at the speaker*
The non-verbal signals we all give off as we speak are often even
more truth-telling than our self-edited words. Notice what else is
going on. Not only is it revealing, it peaks your interest, because
we are drawn to the visual and the active, not just to abstract
listening.

● *Build on*
When it's your turn, hook into what was just said as a point of
departure for your statement:
    'Robert just brought up X. Why don't we . . .' or pick out a few
words you just heard and incorporate them as your opening:
    '"A total overview . . ." You're right, Lynn. As you said, a
total overview is what we need right now.'
    This not only tells everyone you *were* listening, but is a sign
of respect to the previous speaker, making you a friend and

enlisting him/her as a supporter of yours. It also enhances the cumulative idea-building process.

● *Take notes*
If you have lots of trouble listening and doing these steps, you might try taking notes as other people speak. This forces you to focus and make a precis of what is being said, keeping you up with the speaker and taking in the idea.

Helping the group listen

The leader of a meeting who is alert to the signals of non-listening that I mentioned earlier and wants to fix it can actively intercede with a simple:
'Hey, this sounds like no one is listening to each other. Let's everyone make a special effort to listen till the end of a statement before jumping in.' This alerts everyone to what's been happening since we're generally quite unaware that we're not listening.

Another technique could be for the leader to summarize what each person said before moving on to the next step to keep the group's attention:
'So, you want us to rethink that plan because XXX, Linda. Okay. Now, Colin, what did *you* want to say?'

Still another way is to point out when people are obviously not listening because they're being unresponsive:
'Wait a minute, Andrea, Gary was just talking about a problem. Let's stay with that before we go on to the next issue.'

Teaching your group better listening skills is important for their daily work with clients, peers, etc., not just at a meeting.

Supporting

A: 'Hey, here's a good idea.'
B: 'No, we did that already.'
C: 'What about trying this?'
D: 'It'll never work.'
E: 'How about doing it this way?'
F: 'I'll tell you what's wrong with that . . .'

Some of us have trouble finding a positive, supportive thing to say when we hear another's idea. Yet this is one of the best ways to keep the energies flowing and to use the contributions in a group to best advantage. There are several reasons why we don't do this well:

● Because many of us are competitive at work, it's often very difficult for us to be generous to each other.
● It may feel threatening to compliment and support someone else's idea as it could make ours seem less important.
● By nature, most of us tend to be threatened by change, so our first response to anything new is generally negative.
● When we criticize, we actually become an active part of someone else's effort rather than just being a listener.
● Cynicism often is misperceived as an achievement in itself, showing our superior knowledge and experience.

Results? We not only put a damper on new ideas and creativity but if the group norm is to be critical and negative, people become afraid to go out on a limb and even *look* for new solutions. They develop a 'what's the use?' attitude and become more interested in being self-protective than constructive. If this atmosphere prevails, calling meetings to find solutions becomes a waste of time as people expect to be turned down anyway.

So — another interactive skill we need to learn in order to make group endeavours fruitful and stimulating is to support each other's new ideas. This means singling out something good, useful, innovative in someone's suggestion and then using it or incorporating it. It doesn't mean indiscriminate acceptance or a 'That's nice' pat on the head. It means to listen hard, then to select what is useful and mention it.

Techniques for supporting

● *Understand your basic approach*
Achievers may find supporting others difficult since they are so single-minded and tuned into their own goals and standards. Differing approaches and ideas may seem off-target or irrelevant to them.

Influencers may have a hard time supporting, since their object is to make a strong personal impact, not necessarily to move over and let someone else share the limelight.

Affiliators, by their nature, may have a better chance to support, since they want to be liked and accepted, to join in. People are important to them as opposed to the Achiever's interest in *standards* and the Influencer's interest in *impact*. Affiliators' problems are concern over what the group will think, fear that taking up for someone's ideas will bring group disapproval. There's also a tendency to support only those people they 'like', while opposing those they don't like or feel don't like them. (We can probably all find aspects of Achiever, Affiliator, *and* Influencer inside ourselves.)

Here are some examples of support techniques that will help you stimulate the group process and become a more constructive participant.

● *Assume value*
In order to support, we must begin by assuming that there *can* be something of value in *any* idea — even if just to stimulate us to think again, or to point out some basic flaw in what we've all been thinking.

So, to support others, allow their ideas to emerge as important and valuable, too — not easy in the light of our often competitive spirit. Assume *everyone* has *some* useful ideas, some information you don't have, a point of view you can't know, something that could contribute to the group's thinking, and *look* for it.

● *Listen carefully*
Now that you've learned how to listen, do it with a specific purpose: To hear what is useful, innovative, the *beginning* of a good idea, some new information, another point of view or analysis, etc.

Notice that I say 'some', 'the *beginning* of', 'another'. That means the whole idea doesn't have to be fully developed or totally correct. It means to look for a small piece. An addition. A departure. Look for a catalyst to stimulate further thinking, not a finished product. Catalysts are very valuable to a group, worthy of merit and notice.

● *Say it*
Having found it, *say* it.

'Listen, what you just said about X is really good,' or, 'I liked the part about . . . Let's talk about that some more.'

This gives validity to anyone trying to come up with a new idea. It encourages others to try, too. It keeps the creative atmosphere alive. It doesn't waste kernels of good ideas by dumping the whole. It's personal effect is to flatter and affirm, making a friend and an eager participant.

● *Build on*
'You know, building on Jack's idea, we could . . .'

The next step in affirming and supporting is to continue the forward momentum. Add your own ideas. Supporting is only part of the process. Keep the energy moving by connecting that idea with your own. Find ways for co-operation. Hooking into what's being said keeps positive juices flowing and people more willing to accept than reject ideas, yours included.

The results of learning and using good supporting skills are that you add to the team spirit and develop better interpersonal relations as people remember and feel grateful. You also build support for yourself and your ideas.

Now, lest I create an ideal world which finds you all supporting each other to death in meetings with never a contrary word or critical thought, I hasten to teach you how to disagree as well.

Disagreeing

Some of us have trouble disagreeing because we're afraid to hurt feelings or get into an argument. It's vital to the group process, though, because it makes the final solution stronger if it survives some criticism. Being able to differ with each other makes the group stronger because they will become conditioned to rethinking or scrapping an idea. They will also learn to work together with respect for each other's differences and abilities. Being disagreed with constructively makes the individual members stronger because they learn to survive critical comments and still keep working together.

Techniques for disagreeing

- *Respect others' ideas*
  The big trick in disagreeing with someone is to do it in a manner that encourages receptivity rather than defensiveness and resentfulness — a manner that differs with an *idea*, not a person. Be respectful of someone's idea while you disagree with it.
- *Listen and support first*
  Using the previous two skills — really hearing the whole idea and choosing the best parts for positive commendation — makes it easier for the speaker to accept the places where you differ. Always give a gift before you take something away. It doesn't leave the other person with such a loss if you listen and support before you confront.
- *Ask questions*
  'I like X but tell me more about Y.'

In order to get *all* the information out that you might disagree with, start by asking some questions in that area before you criticize or disagree. Get more facts to support your disagreement. You may be able to clear up some misunderstanding *you* had and resolve it for yourself and others before you need to disagree.

- *Be specific and constructive*
Sometimes you and another person disagree but are talking about two different things. Be sure you specify what the issues are that you disagree with before you get into a random negative discussion. Select and focus on specifics.

- *Disagree non-judgementally*
Beware of the adjectives you use. Try:
'Something's troubling me about this', not, 'That's a pretty useless idea.' Be careful *what* you criticize. Just the parts you disagree with, not the total concept or, most of all, the person who generated it. 'How could you even think that . . .?' is not the way. Remember you're talking about a thing, not a person. Keep all the heat out. And watch the tendency towards arrogance. You are neither the final arbiter nor the only one privy to the truth.

- *Offer another solution*
Don't just carp. Be ready to add what you think is best. 'How about changing that last part to include . . .?' Say why you disagree, and then fix it by showing another way or asking the speaker to address that problem and come up with another solution himself. Leaders can suggest: 'I think you've taken it too far but let's stay with the first thought. Everyone think of how we could use it.'

Personal skills for leaders

Leading a meeting

Be clear about your role. You are a traffic manager, a referee, the producer of an event, and most of all, a host. Remember they're there because you invited them. Take care of them — their egos, their physical needs, their attention span, their ability to understand. Facilitate their desire to do a good job. Be a watchdog about the quality of any presentations — their clarity, their interest. Be honest and forthcoming about why you want this meeting. Start discussing an agenda item by asking for their help. Make them know that they're vital to the process and that you can't do it alone.

Staying focused

Keep the group pointing towards solutions or the end product you want from a discussion on an issue. It's easy for a group discussion to deteriorate into nitpicking or a negative push-pull, or to generate other issues that only minimally connect with the one at hand.

Cutting people off

Be strong, because this isn't simple. Consider things like not cutting people off before the idea comes out, helping make people's comments succinct and pointed, and above all sticking to the original time slot agreed on.

One more very important point: Cutting people off requires that you always save face for them before the members of your group. Graceful outs, with some humour, like:

'You're really wound up in this, aren't you, Susan?' before you say you have to move on takes care of Susan's zeal and commitment and lets her off with an excuse. Always give a preface before you peremptorily end someone talking.

Use a flip chart with your agenda and time allotments on it. Blaming your cut-off on that inanimate, objective page made by group decision will usually prevent any problems.

If the subject brought up is irrelevant, say:

'Sounds like another agenda item to me. Will you please save it and bring it up for the next meeting? Please send me a memo on it.'

This is better than saying something harsh or denigrating about irrelevance and makes the gaffe a plus instead.

Increasing participation

'Sorry, folks, but we have only two more minutes on this. Let's hear from . . .' is *not* a good idea.

Putting someone on the spot who hasn't spoken can be dangerous. He/she may have nothing to say or be so intimidated by what has gone before that he can't speak. It's best to *ask* if anyone else has something to say. You know your movers and opposers. Lead them to start, but be careful how you spotlight the non-participants.

For reluctant participants

For followers or bystanders, ask them to comment by saying, 'Let's hear from X, Y, and then Z (the follower) on this,' giving Z plenty of warning to come up with something, yet not asking him/her to be first.

Another way to activate those silent types is to focus people on a specific aspect you want them to talk about:

'Nina, costs are your department. Why don't you help us out with that?'

Try talking to them during a break to get a fix on what they're thinking. Then you could say how valuable an idea that is (strengthening them) and that you'd like them to share it with the group when you reconvene.

Controversial or dangerous subjects

For ticklish subjects where there may be general reluctance to speak out, it helps to break into small groups of three even if your group isn't very big. This is a safer environment for truth telling since the smaller groups come back with a consensus report, avoiding individual exposure.

Just remember that not everyone is equally creative or comfortable. Know your troops. At the meeting itself, ask of them only what you know they can give. Delegate specific assignments for reports, in advance, to those reluctant dragons who *can't* improvise in order to get total participation.

Getting agreement

Voting publicly can be tricky; it broadcasts opinions that people may not want public. They may equivocate or change their vote. There's also the age-old phenomenon of wanting to be part of the group. Watching how many and whose hands go up affects what you say and vote for publicly.

If you want a real reflection of how people feel about an issue, use a secret ballot form of voting. If you've discussed a subject to death and everyone has pretty well made their views clear, the consensus is usually obvious and doesn't need a formal vote; controversial or potentially damaging issues do. Sometimes it helps to *start* the discussion with a secret ballot to find out the group's mental set. We're funny about telling the truth — many forces change what and how much we'll say out loud.

Getting group attention

Meetings can become unruly, especially when they get overheated and several people talk at once. It requires a louder voice than theirs to be heard and get people calmed down. Use it. 'Okay', 'That'll do', 'Hold it' — informal, relaxed, but firm. Don't get heavy-handed and 'bossy'. That's a sign of weakness and feeling out of control. Just set up the rules at the beginning and remind them by saying again why it can't work this way and what your goals are.

To introduce each new item and get attention for it, remember to present it first in terms of the effect on and use to the group. The old self-interest theme . . . But let me say that in the evolution of a group there comes a time where self-interest becomes equated with group interest. It can still break down by section or division, though. There's always a hook that differentiates your and my self-interest.

To start a new subject and get everyone involved, you might poll the group verbally at the beginning of a discussion, going around the table to hear everyone's thoughts on that specific issue (sometimes referred to as the Delphi technique). This can focus the ensuing discussion: find out what the group really thinks so far; surface the main objections or misconceptions. It's a good ice-breaker, forcibly making *everyone* a participant, even if only for a little while.

Handling egos and conflict

Self-control is the key here. Don't blow up at anyone at a meeting. Rather, use your energies to recognize why something negative is happening. Ask yourself: 'What is he really saying?' 'What does she really want or need right now?' If you focus on the inner agenda, too, in order to understand the outward manifestation, you can usually handle any situation. People universally need recognition and stroking of one sort or another, especially before their peers and by their boss. Before or while you deliver any bitter pill, give an antidote.

In one-to-one confrontations between two members, use:

'You know, I don't think this discussion is helpful (constructive, relevant) in getting us to our goal, which you'll remember was to decide X. Let's focus a little more tightly here.'

Personal skills for meeting participants

You want to make useful, commendable contributions and to gain the respect and esteem of your fellow workers by what they see and hear you do at a meeting. But you also very much want to be noticed by the boss and other key members.

You aren't usually visible in your work. This is your chance.

Be prepared

Find out who'll be at the meeting, if at all possible. Try to anticipate their point of view and what they'll probably say. Do all the research suggested in the boss's memo about the meeting, plus anything else you can glean from others. Try to understand the effects to your department or the firm of what's being proposed. Find out about what's happening in the field. Read professional journals, newspaper and magazine articles so you always have a rare bit of extra information to contribute. Getting ahead means getting ahead of the pack in how you work and what you know.

Look confident and interested

No one knows how nervous you are or how out of a discussion you may feel. You can look as if you're listening and concentrating even though your heart's beating fast. Be careful about fidgeting with your things or in your seat. Doodling isn't helpful. Taking notes is better. If you find yourself getting bored or dozing off, get up and get a cup of coffee or go out of the room for a few minutes. Movement and a change help get you back in gear.

Speak up

If you have trouble getting the courage to speak up, go back to Chapter 7. How to Make Memorable Speeches. On page 000 I spoke about stage fright. Read it again. It'll help you speak up at a meeting, something you must do if anyone's ever going to get to know you and your capabilities.

Since you know what the agenda's going to be, get an idea or two formed in your mind. Do a little research. Some people like to discuss things with a friend or two to get a reaction. Don't come in prepared to make a major speech the first time! But do take small steps till you feel comfortable enough to begin to improvise and think at your seat. The more attentively you listen to others at the meeting, the more you'll find things to add that are uniquely your own.

Footnote: Be careful *not* to talk if you have nothing to say or add! It's not how *often* you talk as much as *what* you say that matters and impresses.

Ask questions

Another way to be heard is to ask questions. Not for the sake of it but questions for further clarification or information. This makes you sound interested and sharp (if you ask *good* questions) and allows you still to participate when you don't have a lot to contribute.

Be a team player

Be careful not to see a meeting as a solo performance. Everyone's trying to be heard. Don't monopolize the conversation. If you have disagreed with a solution that finally gets group endorsement, be graceful and forthright, saying:

'Well, you know I wasn't for this, but I will surely support it now that everyone wants it. Since it was your idea, Sue, I'll want to come to you to be sure I understand it well and can help.'

Sit in a powerful place

Sounds a bit predatory, but you should know that placement around the table *does* affect people's response to you *and* also your incentive to participate.

Sit with the powerful movers. If not, sit opposite them. Always try to sit in the middle, where the general sense of action and involvement rubs off and affects you. Sitting at the end or at the back has a look of being outside the action. It can affect you that way, too.

If you're criticized

Don't get defensive! This is a sign of weakness if not downright guilt! Don't do it, especially with your boss. If you're attacked or criticized, the big thing is to get it out of the public arena. Go for further information — both giving and getting.

Try lines like:

'I see what you're saying. There are some other issues you should know about. I don't want to waste the group's time with them. After the meeting, let me share them with you.'

You maintain your dignity and promise a rethink, with an open mind, while giving the boss or colleague more data to change his/her mind — in private.

Ask questions to make your critic be more specific.

'I appreciate your criticism. It would really help me if you explained just what aspect didn't work. I'd like to come and see you after the meeting.'

This shows you as reasonable, willing to learn, and eager to do a good job, as well as strong and unintimidated by criticism.

Now let's consider some functional issues — techniques for developing and managing meetings well.

CREATING AND LEADING EFFECTIVE MEETINGS

Planning

Define objectives

Give or get information	Resolve conflict
Problem solve	Team building
Brainstorm	Task force
Improve work processes	Create
Take action	Motivate
Explain policy change	Inspire

These are some of the main reasons that meetings are called. It's very helpful to get the objectives down to a minimal two- or three-word essence. This makes you clarify the bottom line of what you *really* mean to accomplish and helps sort out what process you need to apply to make that happen.

Challenge your meeting

Question, before you plan your meeting, whether it's truly necessary. Meetings get to be a habit and are called whenever an issue comes

up. Don't wear out their welcome from over-use. Always ask yourself,
'Is this the best way to accomplish my objective? Is there any other way?'

Creating the agenda

The unique aspects of preparing an agenda for a meeting deal with
three issues — the number and positioning of items, time allotted, and
input from others.

Positioning

First — establish your priorities by deciding what the meeting is basically
for. Priorities should be based not only on importance but also on
urgency. Then decide the other items you wish to cover and list them.
   Two issues affect what you do next:

● How many items you can realistically cover well, keeping the group
   involved and the juices flowing. How many levels of intensity can
   you put your group through — from the major to the peripheral
   details? Look hard at what *has* to be done and what can wait.
● How each issue affects the group you're inviting to the meeting.
   This will give you the additional perspective you need in order
   to see: what will get the group's attention; what has greatest relevance
   in their eyes; to what will they respond, and how.
      In order to motivate them to stay with the subjects and give
   their best thinking to each, you need to think about what effect
   an issue will have on your group — negative, dangerous, challenging,
   helpful — and balance your agenda.

Placement on agenda

To create the order of your agenda items, think about whether you
start by getting the small items out of the way and then concentrate
on the biggies, or get to the most important issue right at the start,
when everyone is fresh, and deal with the less important issues
afterwards, or maybe not at this meeting.

● *Small items*
   We need to understand the concept of building to a climax. *If the
   other items on the agenda are truly small and unimportant, and*

if you're well disciplined about organizing what the essentials are, and *if* you can move them out of the way efficiently, keeping to the time allotted like a tenacious bulldog, *then* — and only then — is it okay to put them first so you can spend the rest of the meeting dealing with the major problem. However, the tendency is to get into the second layer on each of the smaller issues and thus use too much time, wearing out the interest span and creative energies of the participants.

It's useful when you have an important brainstorming session to be economical about how you use the time. Look at those little items and see if they need to be brought up to the whole group, or whether you can dispose of them by memos or phone calls.

● *Important issues*
Consider the idea of starting with the main agenda item and putting the little details items last, if you must put them in at all. This is particularly important if it's a meeting called at short notice where everyone hasn't blocked out enough time and may have to leave early.

Another thought is to call a meeting to discuss one item only. This emphasizes its importance and the amount of time you wish everyone to concentrate on it. We often clutter meetings with such disparate material — some vital, some unimportant, some not relevant to the whole group — that the very mix of the agenda invites frustration and inattention.

Time allotment

● *Reality*
This is tough. The sense of time we all have is related to what the number — 5 minutes, 2 minutes — *looks* like it allows rather than a true sense of the amount of time that number actually is worth.

One way to get better at this is to time discussions at meetings, presentations, TV news pieces, commercials, etc., with a stopwatch to discover exactly how much can be said in a *very* short space of time. You can also discover it by reading aloud from this page to see how far you get in ten seconds, thirty seconds, two minutes (it will surprise you). This will give you a better sense of how much time is needed to make X number of points. It will help you set realistic (and shorter) time allotments for the items on your agenda. Try timing actual meeting segments as well.

- *Total time*

  Aside from the considerations of how much time you need to cover the material, think of how people will respond to the total time for the meeting. We get bored faster than fast these days, plus: You've taken people from their daily tasks. They begin to watch the time disappear and think about their tasks piling up. One and a half, maybe two hours maximum is my suggestion unless the meeting is designed as a total immersion brainstorming session, in which case breaks of fifteen to twenty minutes several times a day become necessary.

Input from others

To make people feel represented as you create your agenda, send a memo around, when possible and appropriate, announcing the meeting (start and probable finish time, place, date), telling what your main items will be, and what they need to prepare. Then ask if they have any other items they want to have considered. The benefits are:

- You start making your meeting truly participatory.
- You get others interested in the meeting before it happens and they are better contributors when they get there.
- You have told them what you want to talk about and what to prepare for, so they feel more comfortable, with less surprises.
- You discover other issues or problems in your workplace that you hadn't thought of, when they respond. You can then choose to put such issues on this or succeeding agendas or smoke out more of what they're all about before you decide what to do about them.
- Getting agenda suggestions *before* the meeting rather than at it lets you see where they would fit and how much time to allow. It lets you consider *if* you want to deal with them privately, rather than needing to turn people down publicly at the meeting if you ask for agenda suggestions there.

Designing and implementing the meeting

Physical arrangements

Read the section in Chapter 4 on meeting arrangements again, using the checklist on timing, time of day, the effects of where you meet, and other physical and psychological needs to be considered (like feeding, etc.). Don't ignore the obstacles these issues can create. They can present major stumbling blocks if you don't handle them well, or they can ensure the success of your meeting.

Personnel

Be aware of the effect of the meeting and the demands it will make. Answer the following questions:

- Size of meeting?·
- Who should come and why; what organizational levels? what technical and functional expertise?
- The effect on the staff of the people you invite or don't invite?
- How should they prepare; what to bring? what to read?
- How much advance notice do they need?
- What should you provide for them in advance? At the meeting?
- How much input should you give them in shaping the agenda?

Implementation·

Consider the effects of the following suggestions on your staff or other invitees and the benefits that can be gained from some or all of these procedures:

- Give adequate notice, in writing, of date, time, and place.
- Clarify what is expected; list objectives and agenda so they can begin to think about the issues.
- Describe agenda; items, time allotted, purpose of them (discussion, informational, decision making, progress report).
- Name who will make which presentation.
- List group preparation needs. Tell what to bring to the meeting.
- Provide materials for preparation, if the information is new, or yours.
- List meeting convener (for contact) and members invited.
- Ask for suggestions for additional items, in writing.

Leadership techniques

Meetings may have a wide variety of objectives, such as surfacing differences, delegating work, sharing experiences, or brainstorming. Here are a group of effective techniques for leading any kind of meeting.

Warm-ups

- *Start on time!*
  If you don't you send a sloppy signal with an element in it of forgiveness for irresponsible behaviour. Teaching your group that your meetings start exactly when you say they will, no matter who is or isn't there, makes the group expect that you mean *everything* you say and that you follow through that way. This sharpens others' work habits.

- *Establish group spirit*
  For group input and interaction, you need to create the right mental set and environment in which to make things happen.

  A few minutes of idle chatter turn out not to be idle at all. 'How was the holiday, Jack? I haven't seen you since you got back,' and similar phrases, can result in some effusive, relaxed exchange. This can establish a ripple effect of general joking, personal comments, friendly interaction that reminds your group of their connection to each other and how much of their lives they actually share daily.

- *Get everyone to talk*
  It's a good idea to get everyone involved at the beginning, making them all get used to participating.

  For general connectedness (after holidays; with a disparate group; moving into a new position) you might go around the room and ask each person to give a minute or a minute and a half about what's the most important, interesting, or challenging thing happening in their job at present. No great strain since it's short and impromptu, this opens people up to each other for a moment and offers each one a chance to be important and informative, giving them equal validity and a sense of equal responsibility in sharing and participating. It also orientates the group a little to what's going on and to each other's work, extending those informal opening charts.

  For specific input you might structure this around a task at hand and ask for a similar round-the-table report on where everyone is at the moment.

Openings

Explain goals and agenda

The next step is to develop further group connectedness by focusing on the meeting at hand. Using the original objectives you wrote, describe what the meeting is about in general terms before you discuss the detailed agenda. List your goals for the meeting and what results you want to achieve by writing on the board or a flip chart. Then — go to the agenda.

Make agenda visible

If you have already sent them the agenda and asked for their additional input, your final agenda may be changed. Even if it's the same, it should be made visible to all for discussion. Rather than handing out private printed agendas, prepare one on a board or flip chart complete with your time allotments. This focuses everyone on one common piece of information. It underscores the order and process and keeps the agenda visible to all throughout the meeting. It avoids having people diverted by checking out their own printed agendas, and also makes last-minute changes available and visible to all at once.

Discuss issues, order, and time allotments

Discuss each agenda item. Document the reason it's there and results desired, for example, Solution, Information, Action Plan, etc. This helps focus everyone, getting further suggestions from the group and motivating people toward greater efficiency. It can also smoke out some extra dimensions or details to add to a topic. If yours is a one-task meeting, show an outline of the parameters of your discussion plan. Ask for input about other dimensions.

Ask if they feel the time allotted is adequate. Letting them participate in setting time limits for each discussion fosters self-discipline as each item comes up. Ask for input about the scope of your items. Discuss validity and priority. If you discover the suggestions are sizeable, talk of a second meeting to cover them and set the time then if possible.

If you haven't asked for their suggestions in advance, you can do it here.

Negotiate

Develop a little flexibility. Ask if anyone has to leave early. Negotiate the order or time allotments to accommodate everyone, if possible.

Negotiating the items and time they'll take starts to give people the sense of participating. It shows that you, the meeting convener, are responsive to their input and aware of their needs. Helping design what the work of the meeting will be, they develop a vested interest in seeing that it gets done. This process also gives you an opportunity for a few public strokes, like:

'Glad you brought that up. That's an important aspect to think about,' or,

'That's *your* speciality, Doris. Need some input from *you* especially, on that.'

The body of the meeting

Now that the 'housekeeping' is done and the meeting launched, the discussion and interplay begins. How do you keep the ball rolling to avoid getting bogged down and to be sure everyone ends up on the same wavelength?

Who takes notes and how

I suggest that all your meeting notes (minutes) use these four organizational headings for each subject discussed:

- *What.* A description of the item under discussion; the problem, the ramifications, the goals, suggestions made.
- *How.* The action decided on. What steps will be taken, what they will accomplish.
- *Who.* Who's responsible for what steps. Who reports to whom, what is expected.
- *When.* Due dates, check-up dates, work-in-progress deadlines.

Taking meeting notes organized this way rather than randomly ensures that the substance of the notes will be predictable and well organized. It will also make for a consistent continuum from meeting to meeting.

Assign visual charting

In addition, you should assign one person to take notes on a flip chart in front of the room so they are clearly visible to all and completely documented. These chart notes can then also be converted into notes for circulation.

People agree to lots of things at a meeting, since the due date seems so far away, etc. Watching the record being made causes people to become much more realistic about promises and to consider more carefully what they agree to do. This makes the final consensus much more dependable as people troubleshoot the problems right at the meeting *before* they agree to go on publicly available record.

Circulate the notes

Ask the note taker to send the notes around to everyone for approval and/or corrections, giving everyone the same complete record of what happened.

Make discussions visual

Suggest to your presenters (if any) that they explain their subjects with visuals or at the board or flip chart. Handouts should be back-up, to be given at the end of the meeting for personal study later. At the meeting, keep the format public. (For more about visual aids, see Chapter 5.)

Taking a break

If it's a long meeting, find a logical place to take a break. Not the lengthy fifteen-minute coffee break where everyone leaves the room (unless it's a three-hour session), but an informal break in the proceedings that feeds everyone and gives a bit of respite.

Let me illustrate this with a story:

When I began as a daily talk show host in Boston, guests arrived at about 7:45 in the morning. No one had ever thought to feed them beyond the proverbial cup of coffee. Yet we were asking a *great* deal of them: early rising, giving out to me and an audience in a pressured environment, and affording them very limited time to talk about their favourite subject. Instituting a little tray of food made a *tremendous* difference. It served to loosen people up, made them much more comfortable and available and much less defensive and nervous. it works!

Recap each segment

Don't leave any topic till you've gone over your What, How, Who, When — the notes you've been writing on the board. This makes for a true consensus, allowing for final discussion to clarify any points or argue out the last problems that possibly remain.

Keep to the time allotments

Have a clock visible in your meeting area. Ask everyone to monitor the clock as you remind them (and point out on your agenda on the flip chart) of the time allotment for that item. Give two or three warnings during a discussion, not just one. This gives people a chance to adjust their presentation. Make the group a party to your need to end items and move on.

Though others in the group may do it for you, generally the leader is called upon to handle long-winded people. Try a gentle 'I don't think that's really relevant to this discussion, so in the interest of time, let's schedule that for another meeting', or, 'You know, that aspect isn't really helpful to solving the problem at hand. Let's hold that. If it's an item you want us to consider, bring it up for the next agenda.' *Always* save face for your people publicly.

Closure

Clean-up time

Finish by a total recap with a special focus: 'Are we all clear about what we agreed to?' This is not the time for any more discussion, just factual statements or questions.

Design follow-up procedures

If more action is needed, make a clear, written plan on the board or flip chart about who checks with whom and how that all gets filtered back to you (or someone else) — a refinement of the action plan you decided on in the body of the meeting. Get it written or you write it out to be sure it's it's part of everyone's notes.

Create a positive environment
for troubleshooting

Making people feel that 'I have spoken and therefore it *shall* be done' precludes their ever wanting to open your door and say, 'Hey, this isn't working out.'

Talk to the group about fallibility and about realistic expectations and understanding. Tell them you *want* to know if things aren't working.

Discuss process for next agenda development

Take items not discussed or completed at this meeting and make them the basis for starting the next agenda. Ask for additional items from the group while everyone's together thinking of group projects and problems. This is also a great time to set up the next meeting.

Let group criticize meeting

Ask the whole group to criticize the meeting. In any group, this kind of rethinking and constructive criticism, a *constructive*, practical look at the process, timing, techniques, subjects, and results, opens the atmosphere and can make the group process more efficient. Group self-criticism makes for a feeling of true participation in the meeting process.

To close: Group interaction is hard and requires effort if it is to work well.

- Everyone needs to learn how to listen, support, and disagree constructively, and how to identify and account for predictable behaviour styles, to make meetings be the place where productive discussions, solutions, and consensus happen and team members maximize themselves.
- Having everyone participate when possible in some phase of the planning, the subject matter, the time allowed, helps make the group work together as a unit.
- Presentations should be made interesting, visual, creative, and highly organized, with back-up materials given for further thought after the meeting.

Leaders should lead, not overwhelm.
Participants should bring their best and share it.

Have we come to the very end? Not quite. I still have 'the last word.'

10
The last word

How to close? What lasting words can I leave with you that might convey the essence of what it takes to communicate well in your work? Perhaps this story:

A friend and television colleague of mine was flying across the country and found himself seated next to that most distinguished architect, I.M. Pei. My friend is from Boston where Mr. Pei's famous John Hancock Building dominates the skyline, growing out of a corner of venerable Copley Square. The square is also the home of two landmark nineteenth-century architectural marvels: Trinity Church, a mediaeval-style wonder of multicoloured granite, turrets, and spires, and the Italian Renaissance-styled Boston Public Library, all Romanesque arches, grey stone, and dignity. The John Hancock Building, the newcomer on this scene, is a rhomboid-shaped soaring tower, completely sheathed in reflective glass.

My friend loves architecture, so he seized the opportunity to discuss something with Mr Pei.

'You know,' he said, 'I always wondered why, flanked by those two buildings of magnificent stone and granite, you sheathed the John Hancock Building in glass?'

'Yes. Well, when you look into that glass, what do you see?'

'Why, I — I — see the two magnificent buildings!'

'Exactly.'

Recognizing the value of those landmark buildings, Mr. Pei's intent was to honour them by reflecting them *first*, making *his* architectural statement connect with and include them.

Unless we can 'see ourselves' in your communication, we will have difficulty assimilating it.

To motivate us, your listeners at work, you need to know enough about us to help us 'see ourselves' in what you're talking about.

To capture and hold us, your communication must deal at our level, reflecting our concerns. We absorb your ideas by how well you present them and how hard you try to help us understand them.

Answering questions? We must see ourselves and the essence of our question reflected in your answers.

Leading a meeting? Selling a product? Disagreeing with a client? Reporting to the boss?

In every case, unless we 'see ourselves' reflected in what you're saying and doing, your communication is 'for your eyes only.'

All the techniques I have suggested to you in this book are variations on this theme. They work because they start by including *us*. That's how to talk so people listen.

A personal note

As I sat for long hours writing this book, you were very much with me. I saw you responding to what I was saying, I imagined when you'd be startled, when you might disagree and need to be further convinced, when you'd laugh or maybe look up and reflect on a thought. It's what moved me to write more about something, to cut portions out, to stop and try again.

So — I end reluctantly. There are so many more things I wanted to tell you. So many times I wanted to *show* you, not just tell. But if in our time together I stimulated you to rethink the process by which you communicate at work and to start trying some new ways, my work will have reached its mark and I will rest easy.

Thanks for listening. Now it's your turn.

Index

Acceptance, need for, 23, 25
Achievers, 30, 31-2, 34, 35-6
  emotional needs, 79
Affection, need for, 23, 25, 27
Affiliators, 30, 32, 34, 36
  emotional needs, 79-80
Affirmation, need for, 23
Agenda, 270-2, 275
Amenities, 142-3
Analogies, 203
Anger, handling, 154-6
Answers see Questions,
  answering
Appointments, technique for
  arranging, 108-12
Attention, gaining, 87-9, 93,
  266
Attention span, 120
Audiences
  attendance reasons, 166-8
  forethought about, 69-73
  involvement, 188-91
  members' responses, 161-4
  personalizing speech content,
    192-3
  profiles, 164-6
Awareness, of others, 29-30

Biorhythms, 98-9
Body language see Non-verbal
  communication
Bosses, 65-8, 233-42
Brainstorming, 269, 271
Breakfast meetings, 107-8
Breaks, in meetings, 277
Business encounters see
  Meetings, group

Case-study, Mike and Exec,
  65-8
Change, introducing, 61-2, 63
Chart, forethought, 73-91
Charting, visual, 276-7
Close encounters see Meetings,
  one-to-one
Closing
  meetings, 278
  one-to-one, 156-8
Communication see Non-verbal
  communication; Verbal
  communication
Conflict, and meetings, 248
Content, of presentation, 123-7,
  191-5
Context, setting, 116-17

Criticism
  creative, 150-2
  handling, 268-9

Demonstrations, participatory,
  speech technique, 190
Denial
  of feelings, 21-3
  of motivators, 27
Disagreeing, in meetings, 262-3
Discovery, of self and others,
  29-30
Discussion, 148-50
Dramatization, 193-4

Egos, handling, 266
Emotional needs, 78-84, 93
Emphasizing, speech technique,
  204
Endings, 125-6, 194-5
  see also Closing
Expectations, 84-90, 93

Face-saving, 82-3
Factions, and meetings, 248
Familiar ideas, starting point for
  change, 61-2, 63
Feelings
  confronting, 27
  denial, 21-3, 27
Follow-up procedures, 278
Forethought, 69-94
  checklist, 92-3
  presentations, 170-2

Goals, 75-8, 92, 96, 138, 145
Group interaction, 279

Hand-shaking, 138-9
Holidays, and staff receptivity,
  97

Hostility, 227-8
  handling techniques, 154-6,
    229-33
  to new ideas and learning,
    60-3
Humour, 89
Hunger, 99-100, 106, 164

Images, speech technique, 203-4
Influencers, 30, 32-4, 36
  emotional needs, 80-1

Language
  choice of, 202
  unclear/unfamiliar, 119
Learning, resistance to, 60-3
'Leave-behinds', 129-31
Lectern, 201-2, 205
Lighting, for presentations, 206
Listeners, needs of, 37-47, 55
  see also Audiences
Listening
  discussions, 149
  in meetings, 246, 256-9
Location, choice of, for
  meetings, 102-6
Love, need for, 23
Lunch meetings, 106-7

Measurements, need for
  illustration, 192
Meetings
  constructive, list, 249-51
  creating and leading, 269-79
  leaders, 263-6
  one-to-one, 137-59
  checklist, 158-9
  participants, 245-9, 256
  personal skills, 266-9
  personalities, categories, 251-6
Microphones, placing, 201-205

Money, 26-7
Mood shifts, in speeches, 180-2
Motivators, 122, 147
  self-interest, 39-40, 68-9
Movement (audience),
    receptivity motivator, 190

Names, choice of, 139
No-fault policy, 81, 86
Non-verbal communication,
    57-60, 143-4
Note-taking, at meetings, 276-7
Notes, speaking from, 177,
    178-84

Openers/openings,
  meetings, 275
  one-to-one, 137-8
  speeches, 184-8
Oral presentations, 113-27,
    174-8
  checklist, 126-7
Order, of oral presentation,
    121-7
Organization
  logical, of presentation
    material, 116-18, 119-21
  highlights, 145
Outlines, 177, 178-84
  oral presentation, 121, 123

Participation, in meetings,
    increasing, 264-5
Personal attacks, handling, 242
Personalities, categories
  at meetings, 251-6
  at work, 30-6
Planning and preparation, 65,
    67, 70
  meetings, 95-8

Podium, 201-2, 205
Positive thinking, 199-200
Power sharing, 145-7
Practice session, 242-3
Pre-meetings, 97
Presentations
  design, 113-36
  forethought, 170-2
  oral, 113-27
  structure and content, 172-3
  visual, 127-36, 147-8, 191-2
Public image, 28-30

Questioners, profile, 215, 219
Questioning, speech technique,
    188-9
Questions
  answering, technique, 217-27
  and bosses, 235-42
  conditioned response, 209-12
  from audience
    preparation for, 214-17
    purpose, 126, 212-14

Recapping, 124, 156-7, 278
Receivers see Listeners
Receptivity factors, 161-4
  see also Timing
Recognition, need for, 23, 27
Resistance see Hostility
Role-play, 242-3
Rostrum, 201-2, 205

Scheduling see Timing
Secretaries, appointments
    technique, 109-12
Security, 26
See-think-talk process, 179-80
Segments and recaps, 124-5
Self-awareness, and meetings,
    247

Self-esteem, 82
Self-interest, listening motivator,
    39-40, 68-73
    see also Forethought
Setting
    checklist, 205-7
    speaker's awareness of, 169
    see also presentations
Sharing, power, 145-7
Silence
    awaiting questions, breaking,
    218-20
    speech technique, 204-5
Simplifying, speech technique,
    203
Sit, where to, 141-2
Small talk, 139-41
Smiling, 139
Smokescreens, verbal, 22-3
Socialization, 21-2
Space, personal, 102-3, 140
Speakers
    credentials, 41, 45-7, 122-3,
    166
        Sonya Hamlin, 19-20
    personal style and qualities,
        42-5, 195-7
    roles, list, 171-2
Speaking, one-sided nature,
    37-8
Speeches
    checklist, 205-7
    memorable, 161-207
    pre-speech actions,
        199-202
    written vs oral, 174-8
Stage fright, 197-8
Status, 24-5, 26, 27
Strategies for communication,
    65, 68
    see also Forethought

Subject matter, presentation,
    191-4
Subjects, controversial,
    handling, in meetings, 265
Supporting, in meetings, 259-62
Surprise element, attention
    device, 88-9, 93

Television, 47-56
Thinking, and receptivity,
    organizing material, 114-21
    see also Positive thinking
Timing considerations
    meetings, 96-102, 145
    place in programme, 168-9
Transitions, 124-5
Truth, surprise element, 88-9
Truth-seeking, 152-3
'Turf', 103-6, 140-2

Understanding, and listeners'
    attitudes, 62-3
Usefulness, 25, 27

Verbal communication, 57-9,
    62-3
Videotaping, for self-evaluation,
    205, 243
Visual aids
    design of, 131-4
    presentation checklist, 206-7
Visual presentations, 127-36,
    147-8, 191-2, 277
Volunteers, speech technique,
    190
Voting. 265

Warm-ups
    at meetings, 274
    one-to-one, 138-9
Words see Language; Verbal

communication

Work, as personal investment, 23-4

Work personalities, 30-6

Wrap-up, 125-6

Writing, clarification aid, 74

TALK AND GROW RICH

The apprentice millionaire's handbook

Ron Holland

How often have you tried to remember some elusive fact that hovers just out of reach, only to find that when you've given up and stopped trying, the information simply pops into your head? This is Ron Holland's amazing formula: SSS — silence, stillness and solitude at work.

Here he describes how SSS can be used to discover ways and means to acquire anything we desire, simply by talking to people. He demonstrates:

- How to persuade people to do what you want, but have them think that it was all their idea.

- How to sell anything to anybody, including the most hardened and demanding buyer.

- How to generate so many fool proof ideas that you will need to carry a pen and paper around with you to write them all down.

This book truly is the handbook for all Apprentice Millionaires.

Paperback
ISBN 0-7225-1955-9